THE GOSPEL OF BUDDHA

THE GOSPEL OF BUDDHA

BY

PAUL CARUS

GYAN

ISBN : 978-81-212-1810-8 (HB)

First Published, 1894

Published, 2018

Published by

Gyan Publishing House
5, Ansari Road
Daryaganj, New Delhi-110002==
Phone: 011-47034999, 9811692060
www.gyanbooks.com
E-mail: books@gyanbooks.com

Printed at: G. Print Process, Delhi.

PREFACE.

THIS booklet needs no preface for him who is familiar with the sacred books of Buddhism, which have been made accessible to the Western world by the indefatigable zeal and industry of scholars like Burnouf, Hodgson, Bigandet, Bühler, Foucaux, Senart, Weber, Fausböll, Alexander Csoma, Wassiljew, Rhys Davids, F. Max Müller, Childers, Oldenberg, Schiefner, Eitel, Beal, and Spence Hardy. To those not familiar with the subject it may be stated that the bulk of its contents is derived from the old Buddhist canon. Many passages, and indeed the most important ones, are literally copied from the translations of the original texts. Some are rendered rather freely in order to make them intelligible to the present generation. Others have been rearranged; still others are abbreviated. Besides the three introductory and the three concluding chapters there are only a few purely original additions, which, however, are neither mere literary embellishments nor deviations from Buddhist doctrines. They contain nothing but ideas for which prototypes can be found somewhere among the traditions of Buddhism, and have been added as elucidations of its main principles. For those who want to trace the Buddhism of this book to its fountainhead a table of reference has been added, which indicates as briefly as possible the main sources of the various chapters and points out the parallelisms with Western thought, especially in the Christian Gospels.

Buddhism, like Christianity, is split up into innumerable sects, and these sects not unfrequently cling to their sectarian tenets as being the main and most indispensable features of their religion. The present book follows none of the sectarian doctrines, but takes an ideal position upon which all true Buddhists may stand as upon common ground. Thus the arrangement into harmonious and systematic form of this Gospel of Buddha, as a whole, is the main original feature of the book. Considering the bulk of its various details, however, it must be regarded as a mere compilation, and the aim of the compiler has been to treat his material about in the same way as he thinks that the author of the Fourth Gospel of the New Testament used the accounts of the life of Jesus of Nazareth. He has ventured to present the data of Buddha's life in the light of their religio-philosophical importance; he has cut out most of their apocryphal adornments, especially those in which the Northern traditions abound, yet he did not deem it wise to shrink from preserving the marvellous that appears in the old records, whenever its moral seemed to justify its mention; he only pruned the exuberance of wonder which delights in relating the most incredible things, apparently put on to impress, while in fact they can only tire. Miracles have ceased to be a religious test; yet the belief in the miraculous powers of the Master still bears witness to the holy awe of the first disciples and reflects their religious enthusiasm.*

Lest the fundamental idea of Buddha's doctrines be misunderstood, the reader is warned to take the term "self" in the sense in which Buddha uses it. The "self" of man can be and has been understood in a sense to which Buddha would never have made any objection. Buddha denies the existence of "self" as it was commonly understood in his time; he does not deny man's mentality, his spiritual constitution, the importance of his personality, in a word, his soul. But he does deny the mysterious ego-entity, the âtman, in the sense of a kind of soul-monad which by some schools was supposed to reside behind or within man's bodily and

* As to the royal birth of Buddha see p. 256, *s. v.* Shuddhôdana.

psychical activity as a distinct being, a kind of thing-in-itself, and a metaphysical agent assumed to be the soul.* This philosophical superstition, so common not only in India but all over the world, corresponds to man's habitual egotism in practical life; both are illusions growing out of the same root, which is the vanity fair of worldliness, inducing man to believe that the purpose of his life lies in his self. Buddha proposes to cut off entirely all thought of self, so that it will no longer bear fruit. Thus Buddha's Nirvâna is an ideal state, in which man's soul, after being cleansed from all selfishness and sin, has become a habitation of the truth, teaching him to distrust the allurements of pleasure and to confine all his energies to attending to the duties of life.

Buddha's doctrine is no negativism. An investigation into the nature of man's soul shows that while there is no âtman or ego-entity, the very being of man consists in his karma, and his karma remains untouched by death and continues to live. Thus, by denying the existence of that which appears to be our soul and for the destruction of which in death we tremble, Buddha actually opens (as he expresses it himself) the door of immortality to mankind; and here lies the corner-stone of his ethics and also of the comfort as well as the enthusiasm which his religion imparts. Any one who does not see the positive aspect of Buddhism, will be unable to understand how it could exercise such a powerful influence upon millions and millions of people.

The present volume is not designed to contribute to the solution of historical problems. The compiler has studied his subject as well as he could under given circumstances, but he does not intend here to offer a scientific production. Nor is this book an attempt at popularising the Buddhist religious writings, nor at presenting them in a poetic shape. If this "Gospel of Buddha" helps people to comprehend Buddhism better, and if in its simple style it impresses the reader with the poetic grandeur of Buddha's personal-

*The translation of "âtman" by "soul," which implies that Buddha denied the existence of the soul, is extremely misleading.

ity, these effects must be counted as incidental; its main purpose lies deeper still. The present book has been written to set the reader a-thinking on the religious problems of to-day. It presents a picture of a religious leader of the remote past with the view of making it bear upon the living present and become a factor in the formation of the future.

All the essential moral truths of Christianity are, in our opinion, deeply rooted in the nature of things, and do not, as is often assumed, stand in contradiction to the cosmic order of the world. They have been formulated by the Church in certain symbols, and since these symbols contain contradictions and come in conflict with science, the educated classes are estranged from religion. Now, Buddhism is a religion which knows of no supernatural revelation, and proclaims doctrines that require no other argument than the "come and see." Buddha bases his religion solely upon man's knowledge of the nature of things, upon provable truth. A comparison of Christianity with Buddhism will be a great help to distinguish in both the essential from the accidental, the eternal from the transient, the truth from the allegory in which it has found its symbolic expression. We are anxious to press the necessity of distinguishing between the symbol and its meaning, between dogma and religion, between man-made formulas and eternal truth. This is the spirit in which we offer this book to the public, cherishing the hope that it will help to develop in Christianity not less than in Buddhism the cosmic religion of truth.

It is a remarkable fact that these two greatest religions of the world, Christianity and Buddhism, present so many striking coincidences in their philosophical basis as well as in the ethical applications of their faith, while their modes of systematising them in dogmas are radically different. The strength as well as the weakness of original Buddhism lies in its philosophical character, which enabled a thinker, but not the masses, to understand the dispensation of the moral law that pervades the world. As such the original Buddhism has been called by Buddhists the little vessel of salvation, or Hinayâna; for it is comparable to a small boat on which a man may cross the stream of worldliness so as to reach the shore of Nirvâna. Following the spirit of a missionary propaganda, so natural to religious men who are earnest in their convictions, later Buddhists popularised Buddha's doctrines and made them accessible to the multitudes. It is true that they admitted many mythical and even fantastical notions, but they succeeded nevertheless in bringing its moral truths home to the people who could but incompletely grasp the philosophical meaning of Buddha's religion. They constructed, as they called it, a large vessel of salvation, the Mahâyâna, in which the multitudes would find room and could be safely carried over. Although the Mahâyâna unquestionably has its shortcomings, it must not be condemned offhand, for it serves its purpose. Without regarding it as the final stage of the religious development of the nations among which it prevails, we must concede that it resulted from an adaptation to their condition and has accomplished much to educate them. The Mahâyâna is a step forward in so far as it changes a philosophy into a religion and attempts to preach doctrines that were negatively expressed, in positive propositions.

Far from rejecting the religious zeal which gave rise to the Mahâyâna in Buddhism, we can still less join those who denounce Christianity on account of its dogmatology and mythological ingredients. Christianity is more than a Mahâyâna, and Christian dogmatology too had a mission in the religious evolution of mankind. Christianity is more than a large vessel fitted to carry over the multitudes of those who embark in it; it is a grand bridge, a Mahâsêtu, on which a child can cross the stream of selfhood and worldly vanity with the same safety as the sage. There is no more characteristic saying of Christ's than his words: "Suffer little children to come unto me."

A comparison of the many striking agreements between Christianity and Buddhism may prove fatal to a sectarian conception of Christianity, but will in the end only help to mature our insight into the essential nature of Christianity, and so elevate our religious convictions. It will bring out that nobler Christianity which aspires to be the cosmic religion of universal truth.

Let us hope that this Gospel of Buddha will serve both Buddhists and Christians as a help to penetrate further into the spirit of their faith, so as to see its full width, breadth, and depth.

Above any Hinayâna, Mahâyâna, and Mahâsêtu is the Religion of Truth.

PAUL CARUS.

TABLE OF CONTENTS.

INTRODUCTION.

		PAGE
I.	Rejoice	1
II.	Samsâra and Nirvâna	2
III.	Truth the Saviour	5

PRINCE SIDDHÂRTHA BECOMES BUDDHA.

IV.	Buddha's Birth	7
V.	The Ties of Life	10
VI.	The Three Woes	11
VII.	Buddha's Renunciation	14
VIII.	King Bimbisâra	19
IX.	Buddha's Search	22
X.	Uruvilvâ, the Place of Mortification	27
XI.	Mâra, the Evil One	29
XII.	Enlightenment	30
XIII.	The First Converts	34
XIV.	Brahma's Request	35

FOUNDATION OF THE KINGDOM OF RIGHTEOUSNESS.

XV.	Upaka	37
XVI.	The Sermon at Benares	38
XVII.	The Sangha	43
XVIII.	Yashas, the Youth of Benares	45
XIX.	Sending Out the Disciples	48
XX.	Kâshyapa	49
XXI.	The Sermon at Râjagriha	53
XXII.	The King's Gift	57

PAGE

XXIII. Shâriputra and Maudgalyâyana 58
XXIV. The People Dissatisfied 59
XXV. Anâthapindika 59
XXVI. The Sermon on Charity 63
XXVII. Buddha's Father 64
XXVIII. Yashôdharâ 66
XXIX. Râhula 69
XXX. Jêtavana 70

CONSOLIDATION OF BUDDHA'S RELIGION.

XXXI. Jîvaka, the Physician 75
XXXII. Buddha's Parents Attain Nirvâna 77
XXXIII. Women Admitted to the Sangha 77
XXXIV. The Bhikshus' Conduct Toward Women . . . 78
XXXV. Vishâkhâ 79
XXXVI. The Upavasatha and Prâtimôksha 83
XXXVII. The Schism 85
XXXVIII. The Re-establishment of Concord 88
XXXIX. The Bhikshus Rebuked. 94
XL. Dêvadatta 95
XLI. The Goal 98
XLII. Miracles Forbidden 99
XLIII. The Vanity of Worldliness 101
XLIV. Precepts for the Novices 104
XLV. Rules for the Order 105
XLVI. The Ten Commandments 105
XLVII. The Preacher's Mission 107

BUDDHA, THE TEACHER.

XLVIII. The Dharmapada 111
XLIX. The Two Brahmans. 117
L. Guard the Six Quarters. 122
LI. Simha's Question Concerning Annihilation . . 124
LII. All Existence is Spiritual 130
LIII. Identity and Non-Identity 131
LIV. Bnddha, Not Gautama 140
LV. One Essence, One Law, One Aim 141
LVI. The Lesson Given to Râhula 143
LVII. The Sermon on Abuse 145

PAGE
LVIII. Buddha Replies to the Dêva 146
LIX. Words of Instruction 148
LX. Amitâbha 150
LXI. The Teacher Unknown 156

PARABLES AND STORIES.

LXII. Parables 158
LXIII. The Burning Mansion 158
LXIV. The Man Born Blind 159
LXV. The Lost Son 160
LXVI. The Giddy Fish 161
LXVII. The Cruel Crane Outwitted 162
LXVIII. Four Kinds of Merit. 164
LXIX. The Light of the Word. 165
LXX. Luxurious Living. 166
LXXI. The Communication of Bliss 167
LXXII. The Listless Fool 168
LXXIII. Rescue in the Desert 169
LXXIV. Buddha, the Sower 173
LXXV. The Outcast 174
LXXVI. The Woman at the Well 174
LXXVII. The Peacemaker 175
LXXVIII. The Hungry Dog 176
LXXIX. The Despot 178
LXXX. Vâsavadatta 179
LXXXI. The Marriage-Feast in Jâmbûnada 180
LXXXII. A Party in Search for a Thief 182
LXXXIII. In the Realm of Yamarâja 183
LXXXIV. The Mustard Seed 185
LXXXV. Following the Master Over the Stream . . . 189
LXXXVI. The Sick Bhikshu 190

THE LAST DAYS.

LXXXVII. The Conditions of Welfare 192
LXXXVIII. Upright Conduct 194
LXXXIX. Pâtaliputra 194
XC. Shâriputra's Faith 197
XCL. The Mirror of Truth 199
XCII. Ambapâlî 201

		PAGE
XCIII.	Buddha's Farewell Address	204
XCIV.	Buddha Announces His Death	207
XCV.	Chunda, the Smith	211
XCVI.	Maitrêya	215
XCVII.	Buddha's Death	218

CONCLUSION.

XCVIII.	The Three Personalities of Buddha	225
XCIX.	The Purpose of Being	228
C.	The Praise of All the Buddhas	232

Table of Reference	241
Abbreviations in the Table of Reference	241
Glossary of Names and Terms	243
Pronunciation	260
Index	261

INTRODUCTION.

I. REJOICE.

REJOICE at the glad tidings! Buddha, our Lord, has found the root of all evil. He has shown us the way of salvation. 1

Buddha dispels the illusions of our minds and redeems us from the terrors of death. 2

Buddha, our Lord, brings comfort to the weary and sorrow-laden; he restores peace to those who are broken down under the burden of life. He gives courage to the weak when they would fain give up self-reliance and hope. 3

Ye that suffer from the tribulations of life, ye that have to struggle and endure, ye that yearn for a life of truth, rejoice at the glad tidings! 4

There is balm for the wounded, and there is bread for the hungry. There is water for the thirsty, and there is hope for the despairing. There is light for those in darkness, and there is inexhaustible blessing for the upright. 5

Heal your wounds, ye wounded, and eat your fill, ye hungry. Rest, ye weary, and ye who are thirsty quench your thirst. Look up to the light, ye that sit in darkness; be full of good cheer, ye that are forlorn. 6

Trust in truth, ye that love the truth, for the king-
dom of righteousness is founded upon earth. The
darkness of error is dispelled by the light of truth.
We can see our way and make firm and certain steps. 7
Buddha, our Lord, has revealed the truth. 8
The truth cures our diseases and redeems us from
perdition; the truth strengthens us in life and in death;
the truth alone can conquer the evils of error. 9
Rejoice at the glad tidings! 10

II. SAMSÂRA AND NIRVÂNA.

Look about you and contemplate life! 1
Everything is transient and nothing endures. There
is birth and death, growth and decay; there is combi-
nation and separation. 2
The glory of the world is like a flower: it stands
in full bloom in the morning and fades in the heat of
the day. 3
Wherever you look, there is a rushing and a push-
ing, an eager pursuit of pleasures, a panic flight from
pain and death, a vanity fair, and the flames of burn-
ing desires. The world is full of changes and trans-
formations. All is Samsâra. 4
Is there nothing permanent in the world? Is there
in the universal turmoil no resting-place where our
troubled heart can find peace? Is there nothing ever-
lasting? 5
Is there no cessation of anxiety? Can the burning
desires not be extinguished? When shall the mind be-
come tranquil and composed? 6
Buddha, our Lord, was grieved at the ills of life.
He saw the vanity of worldly happiness and sought

salvation in the one thing that will not fade or perish, but will abide forever and ever. 7

Ye who long for life, know that immortality is hidden in transiency. Ye who wish for a happiness that contains not the seeds of disappointment or of regret, follow the advice of the great Master and lead a life of righteousness. Ye who yearn for riches, come and receive treasures that are eternal. 8

The truth is eternal; it knows neither birth nor death; it has no beginning and no end. Hail the truth, O mortals! Let the truth take possession of your souls. 9

The truth is the immortal part of mind. The possession of truth is wealth, and a life of truth is happiness. 10

Establish the truth in your mind, for the truth is the image of the eternal; it portrays the immutable; it reveals the everlasting; the truth gives unto mortals the boon of immortality. 11

Buddha is the truth; let Buddha dwell in your heart. Extinguish in your soul every desire that antagonises Buddha, and in the end of your spiritual evolution you will become like Buddha. 12

That of your soul which cannot or will not develop into Buddha must perish, for it is mere illusion and unreal; it is the source of your error; it is the cause of your misery. 13

You can make your soul immortal by filling it with truth. Therefore become like unto vessels fit to receive the ambrosia of the Master's words. Cleanse yourselves of sin and sanctify your lives. There is no other way of reaching the truth. 14

Learn to distinguish between Self and Truth. Self is the cause of selfishness and the source of sin; truth cleaves to no self; it is universal and leads to justice and righteousness. 15

Self, that which seems to those who love their self as their being, is not the eternal, the everlasting, the imperishable. Seek not self, but seek the truth. 16

If we liberate our souls from our petty selves, wish no ill to others, and become clear as a crystal diamond reflecting the light of truth, what a radiant picture will appear in us mirroring things as they are, without the admixture of burning desires, without the distortion of erroneous illusion, without the agitation of sinful unrest. 17

He who seeks self must learn to distinguish between the false self and the true self. His ego and all his egotism are the false self. They are unreal illusions and perishable combinations. He only who identifies his self with the truth will attain Nirvâna; and he who has entered Nirvâna has attained Buddhahood; he has acquired the highest bliss; he has become that which is eternal and immortal. 18

All compound things shall be dissolved again, worlds will break to pieces and our individualities will be scattered; but the words of Buddha will remain forever. 19

The extinction of self is salvation; the annihilation of self is the condition of enlightenment; the blotting out of self is Nirvâna. Happy is he who has ceased to live for pleasure and rests in the truth. Verily his composure and tranquillity of mind are the highest bliss. 20

Let us take our refuge in Buddha, for he has found the everlasting in the transient. Let us take our refuge in that which is the immutable in the changes of existence. Let us take our refuge in the truth that is established through the enlightenment of Buddha. 21

III. TRUTH THE SAVIOUR.

The things of the world and its inhabitants are subject to change; they are products of things that existed before; all living creatures are what their past actions made them; for the law of cause and effect is uniform and without exceptions. 1

But in the changing things truth lies hidden. Truth makes things real. Truth is the permanent in change. 2

And truth desires to appear; truth longs to become conscious; truth strives to know itself. 3

There is truth in the stone, for the stone is here; and no power in the world, no God, no man, no demon, can destroy its existence. But the stone has no consciousness. 4

There is truth in the plant and its life can expand; the plant grows and blossoms and bears fruit. Its beauty is marvellous, but it has no consciousness. 5

There is truth in the animal; it moves about and perceives its surroundings; it distinguishes and learns to choose. There is consciousness, but it is not yet the consciousness of Truth. It is a consciousness of self only. 6

The consciousness of self dims the eyes of the mind and hides the truth. It is the origin of error, it is the source of illusion, it is the germ of sin. 7

Self begets selfishness. There is no evil but what flows from self. There is no wrong but what is done by the assertion of self. 8

Self is the beginning of all hatred, of iniquity and slander, of impudence and indecency, of theft and robbery, of oppression and bloodshed. Self is Mâra, the tempter, the evil-doer, the creator of mischief. 9

Self entices with pleasures. Self promises a fairy's paradise. Self is the veil of Mâyâ, the enchanter. But the pleasures of self are unreal, its paradisian labyrinth is the road to hell and its fading beauty kindles the flames of desires that never can be satisfied. 10

Who shall loosen us from the power of self? Who shall save us from misery? Who shall restore us to a life of blessedness? 11

There is misery in the world of Samsâra; there is much misery and pain. But greater than all the misery is the bliss of truth. Truth gives peace to the yearning mind; it conquers error; it quenches the flames of desire and leads to Nirvâna. 12

Blessed is he who has found the peace of Nirvâna. He is at rest in the struggles and tribulations of life; he is above all changes; he is above birth and death; he remains unaffected by the evils of life. 13

Blessed is he who has become an embodiment of truth, for he has accomplished his purpose and is one with himself and truth. He conquers although he may be wounded; he is glorious and happy, although he may suffer; he is strong, although he may break down under the burden of his work; he is immortal, although he may die. The essence of his soul is immortality. 14

Blessed is he who has attained the sacred state of Buddhahood, for he is fit to work out the salvation of his fellow-beings. The truth has made its abode in him. Perfect wisdom illumines his understanding, and righteousness ensouls the purpose of all his actions. 15

The truth is a living power for good, indestructible and invincible! Work the truth out in your mind, and spread it among mankind, for Truth alone is the saviour from sin and misery. The Truth is Buddha, and Buddha is the Truth! Blessed be Buddha! 16

PRINCE SIDDHÂRTHA BECOMES BUDDHA.

IV. BUDDHA'S BIRTH.

THERE was in Kapilavastu a Shâkya king, strong of purpose and reverenced by all men, a descendant of the Ikshvâku, who call themselves Gautama, and his name was Shuddhôdana or Pure-Rice. 1

His wife Mâyâ-dêvî was beautiful as the water-lily and pure in mind as the lotus. As the Queen of Heaven, she lived on earth, untainted by desire, and immaculate. 2

The king, her husband, honored her in her holiness and the spirit of truth descended upon her. 3

When she knew that the hour of motherhood was near, she asked the king to send her home to her parents; and Shuddhôdana, anxious about his wife and the child she would bear him, willingly granted her request. 4

While she passed through the garden of Lumbinî, the hour arrived; her couch was placed under a lofty satin-tree and the child came forth from the womb like the rising sun, bright and perfect. 5

All the worlds were flooded with light. The blind received their sight by longing to see the coming glory of the Lord; the deaf and dumb spoke with one another of the good omens indicating the birth of Buddha. The crooked became straight; the lame walked. All prisoners were freed from their chains and the fires of all the hells were extinguished. 6

No clouds gathered in the skies and the polluted streams became clear, whilst celestial music rang through the air and the angels rejoiced with gladness. With no selfish or partial joy but for the sake of the law they rejoiced, for creation engulfed in the ocean of pain was now to obtain release. 7

The cries of beasts were hushed; all malevolent beings received a loving heart, and peace reigned on earth. Mâra, the evil one, alone was grieved and rejoiced not. 8

The Nâga kings, earnestly desiring to show their reverence for the most excellent law, as they had paid honor to former Buddhas, now went to meet Bôdhisattva. They scattered before him mandâra flowers, rejoicing with heartfelt joy to pay their religious homage. 9

The royal father, pondering the meaning of these signs, was now full of joy and now sore distressed. 10

The queen mother, beholding her child and the commotion which his birth created, felt in her timorous woman's heart the pangs of doubt. 11

At her couch stood an aged woman imploring the heavens to bless the child. 12

Now there was at that time in the grove Asita, a rishi, leading the life of a hermit. He was a Brahman of dignified mien, famed not only for wisdom and scholarship, but also for his skill in the interpretation of signs. And the king invited him to see the royal child. 13

The seer, beholding the prince, wept and sighed deeply. And when the king saw the tears of Asita he became alarmed and asked: "Why has the sight of my son caused thee grief and pain?" 14

But Asita's heart rejoiced, and, knowing the king's mind to be perplexed, he addressed him, saying: 15

"The king, like the moon when full, should feel great joy, for he has begotten a wondrously noble son. 16

"I do not worship Brahma, but I worship this child; and the gods in the temples will descend from their places of honor to adore him. 17

"Banish all anxiety and doubt. The spiritual omens manifested indicate that the child now born will bring deliverance to the whole world. 18

"Recollecting I myself am old, on that account I could not hold my tears; for now my end is coming on. But this son of thine will rule the world. He is born for the sake of all that lives. 19

"His pure teaching will be like the shore that receives the shipwrecked. His power of meditation will be like the cool lake; and all creatures parched with the drought of lust may freely drink thereof. 20

"On the fire of covetousness he will cause the cloud of his mercy to rise, so that the rain of the law may extinguish it. 21

"The heavy gates of despondency he will open, and give deliverance to all creatures ensnared in the self-twined meshes of folly and ignorance. 22

"The king of the law has come forth to rescue from bondage all the poor, the miserable, the helpless." 23

When the royal parents heard Asita's words they rejoiced in their hearts and named their new-born infant Siddhârtha, that is, "he who has accomplished his purpose." 24

And the queen said to her sister, Prajâpatî: "A mother who has borne a future Buddha will never give birth to another child. I shall soon leave this world, my husband the king, and Siddhârtha, my child. When
I am gone, be thou a mother to him." 25

And Prajâpatî wept and promised. 26

When the queen had departed from the living, Prajâpatî took the boy Siddhârtha and reared him. And as the light of the moon little by little increases, so the royal child grew from day to day in mind and in body;
and truthfulness and love resided in his heart. 27

V. THE TIES OF LIFE.

When Siddhârtha had grown to youth, his father desired to see him married, and he sent to all his kinsfolk, commanding them to bring their princesses that
the prince might select one among them as his wife. 1

But the kinsfolk replied and said: "The prince is young and delicate; nor has he learned any of the sciences. He would not be able to maintain our daughter, and should there be war he would be unable to
cope with the enemy." 2

The prince was not boisterous, but pensive in his nature. He loved to stay under the great jambu-tree in the garden of his father, and, observing the ways of
the world, gave himself up to meditation. 3

And the prince said to his father: "Invite our kinsfolk that they may see me and put my strength to the
test." And his father did as his son bade him. 4

When the kinsfolk came, and the people of the city Kapilavastu had assembled to test the prowess and scholarship of the prince, he proved himself manly in all the exercises both of the body and of the mind, and there was no rival among the youths and men of India who could surpass him in any test, bodily or mental. 5

He replied to all the questions of the sages; but when he questioned them, even the wisest among them were silenced. 6

Then Siddhârtha chose himself a wife. He selected Yashôdharâ, his cousin, the gentle daughter of the king of Kôli. And Yashôdharâ was betrothed to the prince. 7

In their wedlock was born a son whom they named Râhula, and King Shuddhôdana, glad that an heir was born to his son, said: 8

"The prince having begotten a son, will love him as I love the prince. This will be a strong tie to bind Siddhârtha's heart to the interests of the world, and the kingdom of the Shâkyas will remain under the sceptre of my descendants." 9

With no selfish aim, but regarding his child and the people at large, Siddhârtha, the prince, attended to his religious duties, bathing his body in the holy Ganges and cleansing his heart in the waters of the law. Even as men desire to give peace to their children, so did he long to give rest to the world. 10

VI. THE THREE WOES.

The palace which the king had given to the prince was resplendent with all the luxuries of India; for the king was anxious to see his son happy. 1

All sorrowful sights, all misery, and all knowledge of misery were kept away from Siddhârtha, and he knew not that there was evil in the world. 2

But as the chained elephant longs for the wilds of the jungles, so the prince was eager to see the world, and he asked his father, the king, for permission to do so. 3

And Shuddhôdana ordered a jewel-fronted chariot with four stately horses to be held ready, and commanded the roads to be adorned where his son would pass. 4

The houses of the city were decorated with curtains and banners, and spectators arranged themselves on either side, eagerly gazing at the heir to the throne. Thus Siddhârtha rode with Channa, his charioteer, through the streets of the city, and into a country watered by rivulets and covered with pleasant trees. 5

There they met an old man by the wayside. The prince, seeing the bent frame, the wrinkled face, and the sorrowful brow, said to the charioteer: "Who is this? His head is white, his eyes are bleared, and his body is withered. He can barely support himself on his staff." 6

The charioteer, much embarrassed, hardly dared to answer the truth. He said: "These are the symptoms of old age. This same man was once a suckling child, and as a youth full of sportive life; but now, as years have passed away, his beauty is gone and the strength of his life is wasted." 7

Siddhârtha was greatly affected by the words of the charioteer, and he sighed because of the pain of old age. "What joy or pleasure can men take," he thought to himself, "when they know they must soon wither and pine away!" 8

And lo! while they were passing on, a sick man appeared on the way-side, gasping for breath, his body disfigured, convulsed and groaning with pain. 9

The prince asked his charioteer: "What kind of man is this?" And the charioteer replied and said: "This man is sick. The four elements of his body are confused and out of order. We are all subject to such conditions: the poor and the rich, the ignorant and the wise, all creatures that have bodies, are liable to the same calamity." 10

And Siddhârtha was still more moved. All pleasures appeared stale to him and he loathed the joys of life. 11

The charioteer sped the horses on to escape the dreary sight when suddenly they were stopped in their fiery course. 12

Four persons passed by carrying a corpse; and the prince, shuddering at the sight of a lifeless body, asked the charioteer: "What is this they carry? There are streamers and flower garlands; but the men that follow are overwhelmed with grief!" 13

The charioteer replied: "That is a dead man: His body is stark; his life is gone; his thoughts are still; his family and the friends who loved him now carry the corpse to the grave." 14

And the prince was full of awe and terror: "Is this the only dead man," he asked, "or does the world contain other instances?" 15

With a heavy heart the charioteer replied: "All over the world it is the same. He who begins life must end it. There is no escape from death." 16

With bated breath and stammering accents the prince exclaimed: "O worldly men! How fatal is your delusion! Inevitably your body will crumble to dust, yet carelessly, unheedingly, you live on." 17

The charioteer observing the deep impression these

sad sights had made on the prince, turned his horses
and drove back to the city. 18

When they passed by the palaces of the nobility, Krishâ Gautamî, a young princess and niece of the king, saw Siddhârtha in his manliness and beauty, and, observing the thoughtfulness of his countenance, said: "Happy the father that begot you, happy the mother that nursed you, happy the wife that calls husband this
lord so glorious." 19

The prince hearing this greeting, said: "Happy are they that have found deliverance. Longing for peace of mind, I shall seek the bliss of Nirvâna." And handing her his precious pearl necklace as a reward for
the instruction she had given him, he returned home. 20

Siddhârtha looked with disdain upon the treasures of his palace. His wife welcomed him and entreated him to tell her the cause of his grief; and he said: "I see everywhere the impression of change; therefore, my heart is heavy. Men grow old, sicken, and die.
That is enough to take away the zest of life." 21

The king, his father, hearing that the heart of the prince had become estranged from pleasure, was greatly overcome with sorrow, and like a sword it pierced his
heart. 22

VII. BUDDHA'S RENUNCIATION.

It was night. The prince found no rest on his soft pillow; he arose and went out into the garden. "Alas!" he cried, "for all the world is full of darkness and ignorance; there is no one who knows how to cure the ills of existence." And he groaned with
pain. 1

Siddhârtha sat down beneath the great jambu-tree

and gave himself to thought, pondering on life and death and the evils of decay. Concentrating his mind he became free from confusion. All low desires vanished from his heart and perfect tranquillity came over him. 2

In this state of ecstasy he saw with his mental eye all the misery and sorrow of the world; he saw the pains of pleasure and the inevitable certainty of death that hovers over every being. Yet men are not awakened to the truth. And a deep compassion seized his heart. 3

While the prince was pondering on the problem of evil, he beheld with his mind's eye under the jambu-tree a lofty figure endowed with majesty, calm and dignified. "Whence dost thou come, and who art thou?" asked the prince. 4

In reply the vision said: "I am a shramana. Troubled at the thought of old age, disease, and death I have left my home to seek the path of salvation. All things hasten to decay; only the truth abideth forever. Everything changes, and there is no permanency; yet the words of Buddhas are immutable. I long for the happiness that does not decay; the treasure that will never perish; the life that knows of no beginning and no end. Therefore, I have destroyed all worldly thought. I have retired into an unfrequented dell to live in solitude; and, begging for food, I devote myself to the one thing that is needed." 5

Siddhârtha asked: "Can peace be gained in this world of unrest? I am struck with the emptiness of pleasure and have become disgusted with lust. All oppresses me, and existence itself seems intolerable." 6

The shramana replied: "Where heat is, there is also a possibility of cold; creatures subject to pain, possess the faculty of pleasure; the origin of evil indicates that good can be developed. For these things are correlatives. Thus where there is much suffering, there will be much bliss, if you but open your eyes to find it. Just as a man who has fallen into a heap of filth ought to seek the great pond of water covered with lotuses, which is near by: even so seek thou for the great deathless lake of Nirvâna to wash off the defilement of sin. If the lake is not sought, it is not the fault of the lake; even so when there is a blessed road leading the man held fast by sin to the salvation of Nirvâna, if the road is not walked upon it is not the fault of the road, but of the person. And when a man who is oppressed with sickness, there being a physician who can heal him, does not avail himself of the physician's help, that is not the fault of the physician: even so when a man oppressed by the malady of evil-doing does not seek the spiritual guide of enlightenment, that is no fault of the sin-destroying guide." 7

The prince listened to the noble words of his visitor and said: "You bring good tidings, for now I know that my purpose will be accomplished. My father advises me to enjoy life and to undertake worldly duties, such as will bring honor to me and my house. He tells me that I am too young still, that my pulse beats too full to lead a religious life. 8

The venerable figure shook his head and replied: "You ought to know that for seeking true religion there is never a time that can be inopportune." 9

A thrill of joy passed through Siddhârtha's heart. "Now is the time to seek religion," he said, "now is the time to sever all ties that would prevent me from attaining perfect enlightenment; now is the time to wander into the wilderness and, leading a mendicant's life, to find the path of deliverance." 10

The celestial messenger heard the resolution of Siddhârtha with approval. 11

"Now, indeed," he added, "is the time to seek religion. Go out Siddhârtha and accomplish your purpose. For thou art Bôdhisattva the Buddha-elect; thou art destined to enlighten the world. 12

"Thou art Tathâgata, the perfect one, for thou wilt fulfil all righteousness and be dharma-râja, the king of truth. Thou art Bhagavant, the Blessed One, for thou art called upon to become the saviour and redeemer of the world. 13

"Do thou fulfil the perfection of truth. Though the thunderbolt descend upon thy head, yield thou never to the allurements that beguile men from the path of truth. As the sun at all seasons pursues his own course, nor ever goes on another, even so if thou forsake not the straight path of righteousness, thou shalt become a Buddha. 14

"Persevere in thy quest and thou shalt find what thou seekest. Pursue thy aim unswervingly and thou shalt reach the prize. Struggle earnestly and thou shalt conquer. The benediction of all deities, of all saints, of all that seek light is upon thee, and heavenly wisdom guides thy steps. Thou shalt be the Buddha, our Master, and our Lord; thou wilt enlighten the world and save mankind from perdition." 15

Having thus spoken, the vision vanished and Siddhârtha's soul was filled with peace. He said to himself: 16

"I have awakened to the truth and I am resolved to accomplish my purpose. I will sever all the ties

that bind me to the world, and I will go out from my
home to seek the way of salvation. 17

"The Buddhas are beings whose words cannot fail:
there is no departure from truth in their speech. 18

"For as the fall of a stone thrown into the air, as
the death of a mortal, as the sunrise at dawn, as the
lion's roaring when he leaves his lair, as the delivery
of a woman with child, as all these things are sure and
certain—even so the word of the Buddhas is sure and
cannot fail. 19

"Verily I shall become a Buddha." 20

The prince returned to the bedroom of his wife to
take a last farewell glance at those whom he dearly
loved above all the treasures of the earth. He longed
to take the boy once more into his arms and kiss him
with a parting kiss. But the child lay in the arms of
its mother and he could not lift the boy without awak-
ing both. 21

There Siddhârtha stood gazing at his beautiful wife
and his beloved son, and his heart grieved. The pain
of parting overcame him powerfully. Although his
mind was determined so that nothing, be it good or
evil, could shake his resolution, the tears came freely
from his eyes, and it was beyond his power to check
or suppress their stream. 22

The prince tore himself away with a manly heart,
suppressing his feelings but not extinguishing his mem-
ory. He mounted his steed Kanthaka, and finding the
gates of the castle wide open, he went out into the
silent night, accompanied only by his faithful charioteer
Channa. 23

Thus Siddhârtha, the prince, renounced worldly
pleasures, gave up his kingdom, severed all ties, and
went into homelessness. 24

Darkness lay upon the earth, but the stars shone brightly in the heavens. 25

VIII. KING BIMBISÂRA.

Siddhârtha had cut his waving hair and had exchanged his royal robe for a mean dress of the color of the ground. Having sent home Channa, the charioteer, together with the noble mare Kanthaka, to king Shuddhôdana to bear him the message that the prince had left the world, Bôdhisattva walked along on the highroad with a beggar's bowl in his hand. 1

Yet the majesty of his mind was ill-concealed under the poverty of his appearance. His erect gait betrayed his royal birth and his eyes beamed with a fervid zeal for truth. The beauty of his youth was transfigured by holiness that surrounded his head like a halo. 2

All the people who saw this unusual sight gazed at him in wonder. Those who were in a haste arrested their steps and looked back; and there was no one who did not pay him homage. 3

Having entered the city of Râjagriha, the prince went from house to house silently waiting till the people offered him food. Wherever the Blessed One came, the people gave him what they had; they bowed before him modestly and were filled with gratitude because he condescended to approach their home. 4

Old and young people were moved and said: "This is a noble muni! His approach is bliss. What a great joy for us!" 5

And king Bimbisâra noticing the commotion in the city inquired for the cause of it, and learning the news sent one of his attendants to observe the stranger. 6

Having heard that the muni must be a Shâkya and of

noble family, and that he had retired to the bank of a flowing river in the woods to eat the food in his bowl, the king was moved in his heart; he donned his royal robe, placed his gold crown on his head and went out in the company of aged and wise counselors to meet
his mysterious guest. 7

The king found the muni of the Shâkya race seated under a tree. Contemplating the composure of his face and the gentleness of his deportment, Bimbisâra
greeted him reverently and said: 8

"O shramana, your hands are fit to grasp the reins of an empire and should not hold a beggar's bowl. I pity your youth. If I did not think you were of royal descent, I should request you to join me in the government of my country and share my royal power. Desire for power is becoming to the noble-minded, and wealth should not be despised. To grow rich and lose religion is not true gain. But he who possesses all three, power, wealth, and religion, enjoying them in discretion and with wisdom, him I call a great mas-
ter." 9

The great Shâkyamuni lifted his eyes and replied: 10

"You are known, O king, as liberal and religious, and your words are prudent. A kind man who makes good use of wealth is rightly said to possess a great treasure; but the miser who hoards up his riches will
have no profit. 11

"Charity is rich in returns; charity is the greatest wealth, for though it scatters, it brings no repen-
tance. 12

"I have severed all ties because I seek deliverance. How is it possible for me to return to the world? He who seeks religious truth, which is the highest treasure of all, must leave behind all that can concern him or draw away his attention, and must be bent upon that one goal alone. He must free his soul from covetousness and lust, and also of the desire for power. 13

"Indulge in lust but a little, and lust like a child will grow. Wield worldly power and you will be burdened with cares. 14

"Better than sovereignty over the earth, better than living in heaven, better than lordship over all the worlds, is the fruit of holiness. 15

"Bôdhisattva has recognised the illusory nature of wealth and will not take poison as food. 16

"Shall the baited fish still covet the hook, or the captive bird be enamoured of the net? 17

"The sick man suffering from fever seeks for a cooling medicine. Shall we advise him to drink that which will increase the fever? Shall we quench a fire by heaping on it fuel? 18

"I pray you, pity me not. Pity rather those who are burdened with the cares of royalty and the sorrows of great riches. They enjoy them tremblingly, for they are constantly threatened with a loss of those boons on the possession of which their hearts are set, and when they die they cannot take along either their gold or the kingly diadem. What is the preference of a dead king over a dead beggar? 19

"Would a rabbit rescued from the serpent's mouth go back to be devoured? Would a man who burned his hand with a torch take it up after he had dropped it to the earth? Would a blind man who has recovered his sight desire to spoil his eyes again? 20

"My heart hankers after no vulgar profit, so I have put away my royal diadem and prefer to be free from the burdens of life. 21

"Therefore do not try to entangle me in new relationship and duties, nor hinder me from completing the work I have begun. 22

"I regret to leave you. But I will go to the sages who can teach me religion and so find the path on which we can escape evil. 23

"May your country enjoy peace and prosperity, and may wisdom be shed upon your rule like the brightness of the meridian sun. May your royal power be strong and may righteousness be the sceptre in your hand." 24

The king, clasping his hands with reverence, bowed down before Shâkyamuni and said: "May you obtain that which you seek, and, having obtained it, come back, I pray you, and receive me as your disciple." 25

Bôdhisattva parted from the king in friendship and good-will, and he purposed in his heart to grant his request. 26

IX. BUDDHA'S SEARCH.

Ârâda and Udraka were renowned as teachers among the Brahmans, and there was no one in those days who surpassed them in learning and philosophical knowledge. 1

Bôdhisattva went to them and sat at their feet. He listened to their doctrines of the âtman or self, which is the ego of the mind and the doer of all doings. He learned their views of the transmigration of souls and of the law of karma; how the souls of bad men had to suffer by being reborn in men of low caste, in animals, or in hell, while those who purified themselves by libations, by sacrifices, and by self-mortification would become kings, or Brahmans, or dêvas, so as to rise higher and higher in the grades of existence.

He studied their incantations and offerings and the methods by which they attained deliverance of the ego from material existence in states of ecstasy. 2

Ârâda said: "What is that self which perceives the actions of the five roots of mind, touch, smell, taste, sight, and hearing? What is that which is active in the two ways of motion, in the hands and in the feet? The problem of the soul appears in the expressions '*I* say,' '*I* know and perceive,' '*I* come,' and '*I* go' or '*I* will stay here.' Thy soul is not thy body; it is not thy eye, not thy ear, not thy nose, not thy tongue; nor is it thy mind. The *I* is he who feels the touch in thy body. The *I* is the smeller in the nose, the taster in the tongue, the seer in the eye, the hearer in the ear, and the thinker in the mind. The *I* moves thy hands and thy feet. The *I* is thy soul. Doubt in the existence of the soul is irreligious, and without discerning this truth there is no way of salvation. Deep speculation will easily involve the mind; it leads to confusion and unbelief; but a purification of the soul leads to the way of escape. True deliverance is reached by removing from the crowd and leading a hermit's life, depending entirely on alms for food. Putting away all desire and clearly recognising the non-existence of matter, we reach a state of perfect emptiness. Here we find the condition of immaterial life. As the munja-grass when freed from its horny case, or as the wild bird escapes from its prison, so the ego liberating itself from all limitations, finds perfect release. This is true deliverance, but those only who will have deep faith will learn." 3

Bôdhisattva found no satisfaction in these teachings. He replied: "People are in bondage, because they have not yet removed the idea of *I*. 4

"The thing and its quality are different in our thought, but not in reality. Heat is different from fire in our thought, but you cannot remove heat from fire in reality. You say that you can remove the qualities and leave the thing, but if you think your theory to the end, you will find that this is not so. 5

"Is not man an organism of many aggregates? Do we not consist of various skandhas, as our sages call them? Man consists of the material form, of sensation, of thought, of dispositions, and, lastly, of understanding. That which men call the ego when they say '*I* am' is not an entity behind the skandhas; it originates by the co-operation of the skandhas. There is mind; there is sensation and thought, and there is truth; and truth is mind when it walks in the path of righteousness. But there is no separate ego-soul outside or behind the thought of man. He who believes that the ego is a distinct being has no correct conception of things. The very search for the âtman is wrong; it is a wrong start and it will lead you in the false direction. 6

"How much confusion of thought comes from our interest in self, and from our vanity when thinking '*I* am so great,' or '*I* have done this wonderful deed?' The thought of your *I* stands between your rational nature and truth; banish it, and then you will see things as they are. He who thinks correctly will rid himself of ignorance and acquire wisdom. The ideas '*I* am' and '*I* shall be' or '*I* shall not be' do not occur to a clear thinker. 7

"Moreover, if your ego remains, how can you attain true deliverance? If the ego is to be reborn in any of the three worlds, be it in hell, upon earth, or be it even in heaven, we shall meet again and again the same inevitable doom of existence. We shall be implicated in egotism and sin. 8

"All combination is subject to separation, and we cannot escape birth, disease, old age, and death. Is this a final escape?" 9

Udraka said: "Do you not see around you the effects of karma? What makes men different in character, station, possessions, and fate? It is their karma, and karma includes merit and demerit. The transmigration of the soul is subject to its karma. We inherit from former existences the evil effects of our evil deeds and the good effects of our good deeds. If that were not so, how could we be different?" 10

The Tathâgata meditated deeply on the problems of transmigration and karma, and found the truth that lies in them. 11

"The doctrine of karma," he said, "is undeniable, for every effect has its cause. What a man soweth he shall reap, and what we reap we must have sown in our previous lives. 12

"I see that the transmission of soul is subject to the law of cause and effect, for the fates of men are of their own making. But I see no transmigration of the *I*. 13

"Is not this individuality of mine a combination, material as well as mental? Is it not made up of qualities that sprang into being by a gradual evolution. The five roots of sense-perception in this organism have come from ancestors who performed these functions. The ideas which I think, came to me partly from others who thought them, and partly they rise from combinations of these ideas in my own mind. Those who used the same sense-organs, and thought the same ideas before I was composed into this individuality of mine are my previous existences; they are my ancestors as much as *I* of yesterday am the father of *I* of to-day, and the karma of my past deeds conditions the fate of my present existence. 14

"Supposing there were an âtman that performs the actions of the senses, then if the door of sight were torn down and the eye plucked out, that âtman would be able to peep through the larger aperture and see the forms of its surroundings better and more clearly than before. It would be able to hear sounds better, if the ears were torn away; smell better, if the nose were cut off; taste better, if the tongue were pulled out; and feel better if the body were destroyed. 15

"I observe the preservation and transmission of soul; I perceive the truth of karma, but see no âtman whom your doctrine makes the doer of your deeds. There is rebirth without the transmigration of self. For this âtman, this self, this ego in the '*I* say' and in the '*I* will' is an illusion. If this self were a reality, how could there be an escape from selfhood? The terror of hell would be infinite, and no release could be granted. The evils of existence would not be due to our ignorance and sin, but would constitute the very nature of our being." 16

And Bôdhisattva went to the priests officiating in the temples. But the gentle mind of the Shâkyamuni was offended at the unnecessary cruelty performed on the altars of the gods. He said: 17

"Ignorance only can make these men prepare festivals and vast meetings for sacrifices. Far better to revere the truth than try to appease the gods by the shedding of blood. 18

"What love can a man possess who believes that the destruction of life will atone for evil deeds? Can a new wrong expiate old wrongs? And can the slaughter of an innocent victim take away the sins of mankind? This is practising religion by the neglect of moral conduct. 19

"Purify your hearts and cease to kill; that is true religion. 20

"Rituals have no efficacy; prayers are vain repetitions; and incantations have no saving power. But to abandon covetousness and lust, to become free from evil passions, and to give up all hatred and ill-will, that is the right sacrifice and the true worship." 21

X. URUVILVÂ, THE PLACE OF MORTIFICATION.

Bôdhisattva went in search of a better system and came to a settlement of five bhikshus in the jungle of Uruvilvâ; and when the Blessed One saw the life of those five men, virtuously keeping in check their senses, subduing their passions, and practising austere self-discipline, he admired their earnestness and joined their company. 1

With holy zeal and a strong heart, Shâkyamuni gave himself up to mortification and thoughtful meditation. While the five bhikshus were severe, Shâkyamuni was severer still, and they revered him as their master. 2

So Bôdhisattva continued for six years patiently torturing himself and suppressing the wants of nature. He trained his body and exercised his mind in the modes of the most rigorous ascetic life. At last he ate each day one hemp-grain only, seeking to cross the ocean of birth and death and to arrive at the shore of deliverance. 3

Bôdhisattva was shrunken and attenuated, and his body was like a withered branch ; but the fame of his holiness spread in the surrounding countries, and people came from great distances to see him and receive his blessing. 4

However, the Holy One was not satisfied. Seeking true wisdom he did not find it, and he came to the conclusion that mortification would not extinguish desire and afford enlightenment in ecstatic contemplation. 5

Seated beneath a jambu-tree, he considered the state of his mind and the fruits of his mortification. My body has become weaker and weaker, he thought, and my fasts have not advanced me in my search for salvation. This is not the right path. I should rather try to strengthen my body by drink and food and thus enable my mind to seek composure. 6

He went to bathe in the river, but when he strove to leave the water he could not rise on account of his weakness. Then espying the branch of a tree and taking hold of it, he raised himself and left the river. 7

While the Blessed One was walking to return to his abode, he staggered and fell to the ground, and the five bhikshus thought he was dead. 8

There was a chief herdsman living near the grove whose eldest daughter was called Nandâ ; and Nandâ happened to pass by the spot where the Blessed One had swooned, and bowing down before him she offered him rice-milk and he accepted the gift. 9

Having eaten, all his limbs were refreshed, his mind became clear again, and he was strong to receive the highest enlightenment. 10

After this occurrence, Bôdhisattva partook again of food. His disciples having witnessed the scene of

Nandâ and observing the change in his mode of living, were filled with suspicion. They were convinced that Siddhârtha's religious zeal was flagging and that he whom they had hitherto revered as their Master had become oblivious of his high purpose. 11

Bôdhisattva when he saw the bhikshus turning away from him, felt sorry for their lack of confidence, and he was aware of the loneliness in which he lived. 12

Suppressing his grief he wandered on alone and his disciples said, "Siddhârtha leaves us to seek a more pleasant abode." 13

XI. MÂRA THE EVIL ONE.

The Holy One directed his steps to that blessed Bôdhi-tree beneath whose shade he should accomplish his search. 1

As he walked, the earth shook and a brilliant light transfigured the world. 2

When he sat down the heavens resounded with joy and all living beings were filled with good cheer. 3

Mâra alone, lord of the five desires, bringer of death and enemy of truth, was grieved and rejoiced not. With his three daughters, the tempters, and with his host of evil demons, he went to the place where the great shramana sat. But Shâkyamuni minded him not. 4

Mâra uttered fear-inspiring threats and raised a whirl-storm so that the skies were darkened and the ocean roared and trembled. But the Blessed One under the Bôdhi-tree remained calm and feared not. The Enlightened One knew that no harm could befall him. 5

The three daughters of Mâra tempted Bôdhisattva, but he paid no attention to them, and when Mâra saw that he could kindle no desire in the heart of the victorious shramana, he ordered all the evil spirits at his command to attack him and overawe the great muni. 6

But the Blessed One watched them as one would watch the harmless games of children. All the fierce hatred of the evil spirits was of no avail. The flames of hell became wholesome breezes of perfume, and the angry thunderbolts were changed into lotus-flowers. 7

When Mâra saw this, he fled away with his army from the Bôdhi-tree. Whilst from above a rain of heavenly flowers fell, and invisible voices of good spirits were heard: 8

"Behold the great muni! his mind unmoved by hatred; the host of the wicked one has not overawed him. He is pure and wise, loving, and full of mercy. 9

"As the rays of the sun drown the darkness of the world, so he who perseveres in his search will find the truth and the truth will enlighten him." 10

XII. ENLIGHTENMENT.

Bôdhisattva having put to flight Mâra, gave himself up to meditation. All the miseries of the world, the evils produced by evil deeds and the sufferings arising therefrom passed before his mental eye, and he thought: 1

"Surely if living creatures saw the results of all their evil deeds, they would turn away from them in disgust. But selfhood blinds them, and they cling to their obnoxious desires. 2

"They crave for pleasure and they cause pain; when death destroys their individuality, they find no peace; their thirst for existence abides and their selfhood reappears in new births. 3

"Thus they continue to move in the coil and can find no escape from the hell of their own making. And how empty are their pleasures, how vain are their endeavors! Hollow like the plantain-tree and without contents like the bubble. 4

"The world is full of sin and sorrow, because it is full of error. Men go astray because they think that delusion is better than truth. Rather than truth they follow error, which is pleasant to look at in the beginning but causes anxiety, tribulation, and misery." 5

And Bôdhisattva began to expound the dharma. The dharma is the truth. The dharma is the sacred law. The dharma is religion. The dharma alone can deliver us from error, sin, and sorrow. 6

Pondering on the origin of birth and death, the Enlightened One recognised that ignorance was the root of all evil; and these are the links in the development of life, called the twelve nidânas: 7

"In the beginning there is existence blind and without knowledge; and in this sea of ignorance there are appetences formative and organising. From appetences, formative and organising, rises awareness or feelings. Feelings beget organisms that live as individual beings. These organisms develop the six fields, that is, the five senses and the mind. The six fields come in contact with things. Contact begets sensation. Sensation creates the thirst of individualised being. The thirst of being creates a cleaving to things. The cleaving produces the growth and continuation of selfhood. Selfhood continues in renewed births. The renewed births of selfhood are the cause of suffering, old age, sickness, and death. They produce lamentation, anxiety, and despair. 8

"The cause of all sorrow lies at the very beginning;

it is hidden in the ignorance from which life grows. Remove ignorance and you will destroy the wrong appetences that rise from ignorance; destroy these appetences and you will wipe out the wrong perception that rises from them. Destroy wrong perception and there is an end of errors in individualised beings. Destroy errors in individualised beings and the illusions of the six fields will disappear. Destroy illusions and the contact with things will cease to beget misconception. Destroy misconception and you do away with thirst. Destroy thirst and you will be free of all morbid cleaving. Remove the cleaving and you destroy the selfishness of selfhood. If the selfishness of selfhood is destroyed you will be above birth, old age, disease, and death, and you escape all suffering." 9

The Enlightened One saw the four noble truths which point out the path that leads to Nirvâna or the extinction of self: 10

"The first noble truth is the existence of sorrow. Birth is sorrowful, growth is sorrowful, illness is sorrowful, and death is sorrowful. Sad it is to be joined with that which we do not like. Sadder still is the separation from that which we love, and painful is the craving for that which cannot be obtained. 11

"The second noble truth is the cause of suffering. The cause of suffering is lust. The surrounding world affects sensation and begets a craving thirst, which clamors for immediate satisfaction. The illusion of self originates and manifests itself in a cleaving to things. The desire to live for the enjoyment of self entangles us in the net of sorrow. Pleasures are the bait and the result is pain. 12

"The third noble truth is the cessation of sorrow. He who conquers self will be free from lust. He no longer craves, and the flame of desire finds no material to feed upon. Thus it will be extinguished. 13

"The fourth noble truth is the eightfold path that leads to the cessation of sorrow. There is salvation for him whose self disappears before Truth, whose will is bent upon what he ought to do, whose sole desire is the performance of his duty. He who is wise will enter this path and make an end of sorrow. 14

"The eightfold path is (1) right comprehension; (2) right resolutions; (3) right speech; (4) right acts; (5) right way of earning a livelihood; (6) right efforts; (7) right thoughts; and (8) the right state of a peaceful mind." 15

This is the dharma. This is the truth. This is religion. And the Enlightened One uttered this stanza:

"Long have I wandered! Long!
Bound by the chain of desire
Through many births,
Seeking thus long in vain,
Whence comes this restlessness in man?
Whence his egotism, his anguish?
And hard to bear is samsâra
When pain and death encompass us.
Found! it is found!
The cause of selfhood.
No longer shalt thou build a house for me.
Broken are the beams of sin;
The ridge-pole of care is shattered,
Into Nirvâna my mind has passed,
The end of cravings has been reached at last." 16

There is self and there is truth. Where self is, truth is not. Where truth is, self is not. Self is the fleeting error of samsâra; it is individual separateness and that egotism which begets envy and hatred. Self is the yearning for pleasure and the lust after vanity. Truth is the correct comprehension of things; it is the permanent and everlasting, the real in all existence, the bliss of righteousness. 17

The existence of self is an illusion, and there is no wrong in this world, no vice, no sin, except what flows from the assertion of self. 18

The attainment of truth is possible only when self is recognised as an illusion. Righteousness can be practised only when we have freed our mind from the passions of egotism. Perfect peace can dwell only where all vanity has disappeared. 19

Blessed is he who has understood the dharma. Blessed is he who does no harm to his fellow-beings. Blessed is he who overcomes sin and is free from passion. To the highest bliss has he attained who has conquered all selfishness and vanity. He has become Buddha, the Perfect One, the Blessed One, the Holy One. 20

XIII. THE FIRST CONVERTS.

The Blessed One tarried in solitude seven times seven days, enjoying the bliss of emancipation. 1

At that time Tapussa and Bhallika, two merchants, came travelling on the road near by, and when they saw the great shramana, majestic and full of peace, they approached him respectfully and offered him rice-cakes and honey. 2

This was the first food that the Enlightened One ate since he attained Buddhahood. 3

And Buddha addressed them and pointed out to them the way of salvation. The two merchants conceiving in their minds the holiness of the conqueror of Mâra, bowed down in reverence and said: "We take our refuge, Lord, in the Blessed One and in the Dharma." 4

Tapussa and Bhallika were the first that became lay disciples of Buddha. 5

XIV. BRAHMA'S REQUEST.

The Blessed One having attained Buddhahood pronounced this solemn utterance: 1

"Blissful is freedom from malice. Blissful is absence of lust and the loss of all pride that comes from the thought '*I* am.' 2

"I have recognised the deepest truth, which is sublime and peace-giving, but difficult to understand. For most men move in a sphere of worldly interests and find their delight in worldly desires. 3

"The worldling will not understand the doctrine, for to him there is happiness in selfhood only, and the bliss that lies in a complete surrender to truth is unintelligible to him. 4

"He will call resignation what to the Enlightened One is the purest joy. He will see annihilation where the perfected one finds immortality. He will regard as death what the conqueror of self knows to be life everlasting. 5

"The truth remains hidden from him who is in the bondage of hate and desire. Nirvâna remains incomprehensible and mysterious to the vulgar mind that worldly interests surround as with clouds. 6

"Should I preach the doctrine and mankind not comprehend it, it would bring me only fatigue and trouble." 7

Then Brahmâ Sahampati descended from the heaven and, having worshipped the Blessed One, said: 8

"Alas! the world must perish, should the Holy One, the Tathâgata, decide not to teach the dharma. 9

"Be merciful to those that struggle; have compassion upon the sufferers; pity the creatures who are hopelessly entangled in the snares of sorrow. 10

"There are some beings that are almost pure from the dust of worldliness. If they hear not the doctrine preached, they will be lost. But if they hear it, they will believe and be saved." 11

The Blessed One, full of compassion, looked with the eye of a Buddha upon all sentient creatures, and he saw among them beings whose minds were but scarcely covered by the dust of worldliness, who were of good disposition and easy to instruct. He saw some who were conscious of the dangers of lust and sin. 12

And the Blessed One said: "Wide open be the door of immortality to all who have ears to hear. May they receive the dharma with faith." 13

Then, Brahmâ Sahampati understood that the Blessed One had granted the request and would preach the doctrine. 14

FOUNDATION OF THE KINGDOM OF RIGHTEOUSNESS.

XV. UPAKA.

NOW the Blessed One thought: "To whom shall I preach the doctrine first? My old teachers are dead. They would have received the good news with joy. But my five disciples are still alive. I shall go to them, and to them shall I first proclaim the gospel of deliverance." 1

At that time the five bhikshus dwelt in the Deer Park at Benares, and the Blessed One not thinking of their unkindness in having left him at a time when he was most in need of their sympathy and help, but mindful only of the services which they had ministered unto him, and pitying them for the austerities which they practised in vain, rose and journeyed to their abode. 2

Upaka, a young Brahman and a Jain, a former acquaintance of Siddhârtha, saw the Blessed One while he journeyed to Benares, and, amazed at the majesty and sublime joyfulness of his appearance said: "Your countenance, friend, is serene; your eyes are bright and indicate purity and blessedness." 3

The holy Buddha replied: "I have obtained deliverance by the extinction of self. My body is chastened, my mind is free from desire, and the deepest truth has taken abode in my heart. I have obtained Nirvâna, and this is the reason that my countenance is serene and my eyes are bright. I now desire to found the kingdom of truth upon earth, to give light to those who are enshrouded in darkness and to open the gate of immortality to men." 4

Upaka replied: "You profess then, friend, to be Jina, the conqueror of the world, the absolute one and the holy one." 5

The Blessed One said: "Jinas are all those who have conquered self and the passions of self, those alone are victors who control their minds and abstain from sin. Therefore, Upaka, I am the Jina." 6

Upaka shook his head. "Venerable Gautama," he said, "your way lies yonder," and taking another road, he went away. 7

XVI. THE SERMON AT BENARES.

The five bhikshus saw their old teacher approach and agreed among themselves not to salute him, nor to address him as a master, but by his name only. "For," so they said, "he has broken his vow and has abandoned holiness. He is no bhikshu but Gautama, and Gautama has become a man who lives in abundance and indulges in the pleasures of worldliness." 1

But when the Blessed One approached in a dignified manner, they involuntarily rose from their seats and greeted him in spite of their resolution. Still they called him by his name and addressed him as "friend." 2

When they had thus received the Blessed One, he said: "Do not call the Tathâgata by his name nor address him 'friend,' for he is Buddha, the Holy One. Buddha looks equally with a kind heart on all living beings and they therefore call him 'Father.' To disrespect a father is wrong; to despise him, is sin. 3

"The Tathâgata," Buddha continued, "does not seek salvation in austerities, but for that reason you must not think that he indulges in worldly pleasures, nor does he live in abundance. The Tathâgata has found the middle path. 4

"Neither abstinence from fish or flesh, nor going naked, nor shaving the head, nor wearing matted hair, nor dressing in a rough garment, nor covering oneself with dirt, nor sacrificing to Agni, will cleanse a man who is not free from delusions. 5

"Reading the Vêdas, making offerings to priests, or sacrifices to the gods, self-mortification by heat or cold, and many such penances performed for the sake of immortality, these do not cleanse the man who is not free from delusions. 6

"Anger, drunkenness, obstinacy, bigotry, deception, envy, self-praise, disparaging others, superciliousness, and evil intentions constitute uncleanness; not verily the eating of flesh. 7

"Let me teach you, O bhikshus, the middle path, which keeps aloof from both extremes. By suffering, the emaciated devotee produces confusion and sickly thoughts in his mind. Mortification is not conducive even to worldly knowledge; how much less to a triumph over the senses! 8

"He who fills his lamp with water will not dispel the darkness, and he who tries to light a fire with rotten wood will fail. 9

"Mortifications are painful, vain, and profitless. And how can any one be free from self by leading a wretched life if he does not succeed in quenching the fires of lust. 10

"All mortification is vain so long as self remains, so long as self continues to lust after either worldly or heavenly pleasures. But he in whom self has become extinct is free from lust; he will desire neither worldly nor heavenly pleasures, and the satisfaction of his natural wants will not defile him. Let him eat and drink according to the needs of the body. 11

"Water surrounds the lotus-flower, but does not wet its petals. 12

"On the other hand, sensuality of all kind is enervating. The sensual man is a slave of his passions, and pleasure-seeking is degrading and vulgar. 13

"But to satisfy the necessities of life is not evil. To keep the body in good health is a duty, for otherwise we shall not be able to trim the lamp of wisdom, and keep our mind strong and clear. 14

"This is the middle path, O bhikshus, that keeps aloof from both extremes." 15

And the Blessed One spoke kindly to his disciples, pitying them for their errors, and pointing out the uselessness of their endeavors, and the ice of ill-will that chilled their hearts melted away under the gentle warmth of the Master's persuasion. 16

Now the Blessed One set the wheel of the most excellent law a-rolling, and he began to preach to the five bhikshus, opening to them the gate of immortality, and showing them the bliss of Nirvâna. 17

And when the Blessed One began his sermon, a rapture thrilled through all the universes. 18

The dêvas left their heavenly abodes to listen to the sweetness of the truth; the saints that had parted from life crowded around the great teacher to receive the glad tidings; even the animals of the earth felt the bliss that rested upon the words of the Tathâgata: and all the creatures of the host of sentient beings, gods, men, and beasts, hearing the message of deliverance, received and understood it in their own language. 19

Buddha said: 20

"The spokes of the wheel are the rules of pure conduct; justice is the uniformity of their length; wisdom is the tire; modesty and thoughtfulness are the hub in which the immovable axle of truth is fixed. 21

"He who recognises the existence of suffering, its cause, its remedy, and its cessation has fathomed the four noble truths. He will walk in the right path. 22

"Right views will be the torch to light his way. Right aims will be his guide. Right words will be his dwelling-place on the road. His gait will be straight, for it is right behavior. His refreshments will be the right way of earning his livelihood. Right efforts will be his steps: right thoughts his breath; and peace will follow in his footprints." 23

And the Blessed One explained the instability of the ego. 24

"Whatsoever is originated will be dissolved again. All worry about the self is vain; the ego is like a mirage, and all the tribulations that touch it will pass away. They will vanish like a nightmare when the sleeper awakes. 25

"He who has awakened is freed from fear; he has become Buddha; he knows the vanity of all his cares, his ambitions, and also of his pains. 26

"There was a man who, having taken a bath, stepped upon a wet rope, and he thought it was a snake. Horror overcame him, and he shook from fear, anticipating in his mind all the agonies caused by its venomous bite. What a relief does this man experience when he sees that it is no snake. The cause of his fright lies in his error, his ignorance, his illusion. If the true nature of the rope is recognised, his tranquillity of mind will come back to him; he will feel relieved; he will be joyful and happy. 27

"This is the state of mind of one who has recognised that there is no self, that the cause of all his troubles, cares, and vanities is a mirage, a shadow, a dream. 28

"Happy is he who has overcome all selfishness; happy is he who has attained peace; happy is he who has found the truth. 29

"The truth is noble and sweet; the truth can deliver you from evil. There is no saviour in the world except the truth. 30

"Have confidence in the truth, although you may not be able to comprehend it, although you may suppose its sweetness to be bitter, although you may shrink from it at first. Trust in the truth. 31

"The truth is best as it is. No one can alter it; neither can any one improve it. Have faith in the truth and live it. 32

"Errors lead astray; illusions beget miseries. They intoxicate like strong drinks; but they fade away soon and leave you sick and disgusted. 33

"Self is a fever; self is a transient vision, a dream; but truth is wholesome, truth is sublime, truth is everlasting. There is no immortality except in truth. For truth alone abideth forever." 34

And when the doctrine was propounded, the venerable Kaundinya, the oldest one among the five bhikshus, discerned the truth with his mental eye, and he

said: "Truly, O Buddha, our Lord, thou hast found
the truth." 35

And the dêvas and saints and all the good spirits
of the departed generations that had listened to the
sermon of the Tathâgata, joyfully received the doctrine
and shouted: "Truly, the Blessed One has founded
the kingdom of righteousness. The Blessed One has
moved the earth; he has set the wheel of Truth roll-
ing, which by no one in the universe, be he god or
man, can ever be turned back. The kingdom of Truth
will be preached upon earth; it will spread; and
righteousness, good-will, and peace will reign among
mankind." 36

XVII. THE SANGHA.

Having pointed out to the five bhikshus the truth,
Buddha said: 1

"A man that stands alone, having decided to obey
the truth may be weak and slip back into his old ways.
Therefore stand ye together, assist one another, and
strengthen one another's efforts. 2

"Be like unto brothers; one in love, one in holi-
ness, and one in your zeal for the truth. 3

"Spread the truth and preach the doctrine in all
quarters of the world, so that in the end all living crea-
tures will be citizens of the kingdom of righteous-
ness. 4

"This is the holy brotherhood; this is the church
of Buddha; this is the Sangha that establishes a com-
munion among all those who have taken their refuge
in Buddha." 5

And Kaundinya was the first disciple of Buddha
who had thoroughly grasped the doctrine of the Holy

One, and the Tathâgata looking into his heart said: "Truly Kaundinya has understood the truth." Hence the venerable Kaundinya received the name "Âjnyâta-Kaundinya," that is, "Kaundinya who has understood the doctrine." 6

Then the venerable Kaundinya spoke to Buddha and said: "Lord, let us receive the ordination from the Blessed One." 7

And Buddha said: "Come, O bhikshus! Well taught is the doctrine. Lead a holy life for the extinction of suffering." 8

Then Kaundinya and the other bhikshus uttered three times these solemn vows: 9

"To Buddha will I look in faith: He, the Perfect One, is holy and supreme. Buddha conveys to us instruction, wisdom, and salvation, He is the Blessed One, who knows the laws of being, He is the Lord of the world, who yoketh men like oxen, the Teacher of gods and men, the Exalted Buddha. To Buddha will I look in faith. 10

"To the doctrine will I look in faith: well-preached is the doctrine by the Exalted One. The doctrine has been revealed so as to become visible; the doctrine is above time and space. The doctrine is not based upon hearsay, it means 'come and see'; the doctrine leads to welfare; the doctrine is recognised by the wise in their own hearts. To the doctrine will I look in faith. 11

"To the community will I look in faith; the community of Buddha's disciples instructs us how to lead a life of righteousness; the community of Buddha's disciples teaches us how to exercise honesty and justice; the community of Buddha's disciples shows us how to practise the truth. They form a brotherhood of kindness and charity. Their saints are worthy of reverence. The community of Buddha's disciples is founded as a holy alliance in which men bind themselves together to teach the behests of rectitude and to do good. To the community will I look in faith." 12

XVIII. YASHAS, THE YOUTH OF BENARES.

At that time there was in Benarès a noble youth, Yashas by name, the son of a wealthy merchant. Troubled in his mind about the sorrows of the world, he secretly rose up in the night and stole away to the Blessed One. 1

The Blessed One saw Yashas, the noble youth, coming from afar. And Yashas approached and exclaimed: "Alas, what distress! What tribulations!" 2

The Blessed One said to Yashas: "Here is no distress; here are no tribulations. Come to me and I will teach you the truth, and the truth will dispel your sorrows." 3

And when Yashas, the noble youth, heard that there were neither distress, nor tribulations, nor sorrows, his heart was comforted. He went into the place where the Blessed One was, and sat down near him. 4

Then the Blessed One preached about charity and morality. He explained the vanity of desires, their sinfulness, and their evils, and pointed out the path of deliverance. 5

Instead of disgust at the world, Yashas felt the cooling stream of holy wisdom, and, having obtained the pure and spotless eye of truth, he looked at his person, richly adorned with pearls and precious stones, and his heart was filled with shame. 6

The Tathâgata, knowing his inward thoughts, said: 7

"Though a person be ornamented with jewels, the heart may have conquered the senses. The outward form does not constitute religion or affect the mind. Thus the body of a shramana may wear an ascetic's garb while his mind is immersed in worldliness. 8

"A man that dwells in lonely woods and yet covets worldly vanities, is a worldling, while the man in worldly garments may let his heart soar high to heavenly thoughts. 9

"There is no distinction between the layman and the hermit, if but both have banished the thought of self." 10

Seeing that Yashas was ready to enter upon the path, the Blessed One said to him: "Follow me!" And Yashas joined the brotherhood, and having put on the yellow robe, received the ordination. 11

While the Blessed One and Yashas were discussing the doctrine, Yashas's father passed by in search of his son; and in passing he asked the Blessed One: "Pray, Lord, have you seen Yashas, my son?" 12

Buddha said to Yashas's father: "Come in, sir, you will find your son; and Yashas's father became full of joy and he entered. He sat down near his son, but his eyes were holden and he knew him not; and the Lord began to preach. And Yashas's father, understanding the doctrine of the Blessed One, said: 13

"Glorious is the truth, O Lord! The Buddha, the Holy One, our Master, sets up what has been overturned; he reveals what has been hidden; he points out the way to the wanderer that has gone astray; he lights a lamp in the darkness so that all who have eyes to see can discern the things that surround them. I take refuge in the Buddha, our Lord: I take refuge in the doctrine revealed by him: I take refuge in the brotherhood which he has founded. May the Blessed One receive me from this day forth while my life lasts as a disciple who has taken refuge in him." 14

Yashas's father was the first lay-member who joined the Sangha. 15

When the wealthy merchant had taken refuge in Buddha, his eyes were opened and he saw his son sitting at his side in yellow robes. "My son, Yashas," he said, "your mother is absorbed in lamentation and grief. Return home and restore your mother to life." 16

Then Yashas looked at the Blessed One, and the Blessed One said: "Should Yashas return to the world and enjoy the pleasures of a worldly life as he did before?" 17

And Yashas's father replied: "If Yashas, my son, finds it a gain to stay with you, let him stay. He has become delivered from the bondage of worldliness." 18

When the Blessed One had cheered their hearts with words of truth and righteousness, Yashas's father said: "May the Blessed One, O Lord, consent to take his meal with me together with Yashas as his attendant?" 19

The Blessed One, having donned his robes, took his alms-bowl and went with Yashas to the house of the rich merchant. When they had arrived there, the mother and also the former wife of Yashas saluted the Blessed One and sat down near him. 20

Then the Blessed One preached, and the women having understood his doctrine, exclaimed: "Glorious is the truth, O Lord! The Buddha, the Holy One, our Master, sets up what has been overturned; he reveals what has been hidden; he points out the way to the wanderer who has gone astray; he lights a lamp in the darkness, so that all who have eyes to see can discern the things that surround them. We take refuge in the Buddha, our Lord. We take refuge in the doctrine revealed by him. We take refuge in the brotherhood which has been founded by him. May the Blessed One receive us from this day forth while our life lasts as disciples who have taken refuge in him." 21

The mother and the wife of Yashas, the noble youth of Benares, were the first women who became lay-disciples and took their refuge in Buddha. 22

Now there were four friends of Yashas belonging to the wealthy families of Benares. Their names were Vimala, Subâhu, Punyajit, and Gavâmpati. 23

When Yashas's friends heard that Yashas had cut off his hair and put on yellow robes to give up the world and go forth into homelessness, they thought: "Surely that cannot be a common doctrine, that must be a noble renunciation of the world, if Yashas, whom we know to be good and wise, has shaved his hair and put on yellow robes to give up the world and go forth into homelessness." 24

And they went to Yashas, and Yashas addressed the Blessed One, saying: "May the Blessed One administer exhortation and instruction to these four friends of mine." And the Blessed One preached to them and Yashas's friends accepted the doctrine and took refuge in the Buddha, the Dharma, and the Sangha. 25

XIX. SENDING OUT THE DISCIPLES.

And the gospel of the Blessed One increased from day to day, and many people came to hear him and to accept the ordination to lead thenceforth a holy life for the sake of the extinction of suffering. 1

And the Blessed One seeing that it was impossible

to attend to all who wanted to hear the truth and receive the ordination, sent out from the number of his disciples such as were to preach the dharma and said unto them : 2

"Go ye now, O bhikshus, for the benefit of the many, for the welfare of mankind, out of compassion for the world. Preach the doctrine which is glorious in the beginning, glorious in the middle, and glorious in the end, in the spirit as well as in the letter. There are beings whose eyes are scarcely covered with dust, but if the doctrine is not preached to them they cannot attain salvation. Proclaim to them a life of holiness. They will understand the doctrine and accept it. 3

"The Dharma and the Vinaya proclaimed by the Tathâgata shine forth when they are displayed, and not when they are concealed. But let not this doctrine, so full of truth, so excellent, fall into the hands of those unworthy of it, where it would be despised and contemned, treated shamefully, ridiculed and censured. 4

"I now grant you, O bhikshus, this permission. Confer henceforth in the different countries the ordination to those who are eager to receive it, when you find them worthy." 5

And it became an established custom that the bhikshus went out preaching while the weather was good, but in the rainy season they came together again and joined their master, to listen to the exhortations of the Tathâgata. 6

XX. KÂSHYAPA.

At that time there lived in Uruvilvâ the Jatilas, believers of Krishna, worshipping the fire ; and Kâshyapa was their chief. 1

Kâshyapa was renowned throughout all India, and his name was honored as one of the wisest men on earth and an authority on religion. 2

And the Blessed One went to Kâshyapa of Uruvilvâ, the Jatila, and said: "Let me stay a night in the room where you keep your sacred fire." 3

Kâshyapa seeing the Blessed One in his majesty and beauty thought to himself: "This is a great muni and a noble teacher. Should he stay over night in the room where the sacred fire is kept, the serpent will bite him and he will die." And he said: "I do not object to your staying over night in the room where the sacred fire is kept, but the serpent fiend will kill you and I should be sorry to see you perish." 4

But Buddha insisted and Kâshyapa admitted him to the room where the sacred fire was kept. 5

And the Blessed One sat down, keeping his body erect, and surrounding himself with watchfulness. 6

In the night the dragon came to Buddha, belching forth in rage his fiery poison, and filling the air with burning vapor, but could do him no harm, and the fire consumed itself while the world-honored remained composed. And the venomous fiend became very wroth so that he died in his anger. 7

When Kâshyapa saw the light shining forth from the room he said: "Alas, what misery! Truly the countenance of Gautama the great Shâkyamuni is beautiful but the serpent will destroy him." 8

In the morning the Blessed One showed the dead body of the fiend to Kâshyapa, saying: "His fire has been conquered by my fire." 9

And Kâshyapa thought to himself. "Shâkyamuni is a great shramana and possesses high powers, but he is not holy like me." 10

There was in those days a festival, and Kâshyapa thought: "The people will come hither from all parts of the country and will see the great Shâkyamuni. When he speaks to them, they will believe in him and abandon me." And he grew envious. 11

When the day of the festival arrived, the Blessed One retired and did not come to Kâshyapa. And Kâshyapa went to Buddha and said: "Why did the great Shâkyamuni not come?" 12

The Tathâgata replied: "Did you not think, O Kâshyapa, that it would be better if I stayed away from the festival?" 13

And Kâshyapa was astonished and thought: "Great is Shâkyamuni, but he is not holy like me." 14

And the Blessed One addressed Kâshyapa and said: "You see the truth, but you do not accept it because of the envy that dwells in your heart. Is envy holiness? Envy is the last remnant of self that has remained in your mind. You are not holy, Kâshyapa; you have not as yet entered the path." 15

And Kâshyapa gave up his resistance. His envy disappeared, and, bowing down before the Blessed One, he said: "Lord, our Master, let me receive the ordination from the Blessed One." 16

And the Blessed One said: "You, Kâshyapa, are chief of the Jatilas. Go, then, first and inform them of your intention, and let them do what you think fit." 17

Then Kâshyapa went to the Jatilas and said: "I am anxious to lead a religious life under the direction of the great Shâkyamuni, who is Buddha, our Lord. You may do as you think best." 18

And the Jatilas replied: "We have conceived a

profound affection for the great Shâkyamuni, and if you will join his brotherhood, we will do likewise." 19

The Jatilas of Uruvilvâ now flung their paraphernalia of fire-worship into the river and went to the Blessed One. 20

Nadî Kâshyapa and Gayâ Kâshyapa, brothers of the great Uruvilvâ Kâshyapa, powerful men and chieftains among the people, were dwelling below on the stream, and when they saw the instrumentalities used in fire-worship floating in the river, they said: "Something has happened to our brother." And they came with their folk to Uruvilvâ. Hearing what had happened, they, too, went to Buddha. 21

The Blessed One, seeing the Jatilas of Nadî and Gayâ, who had practised severe austerities and worshipped fire, come to him, preached a sermon on fire, and said: "Everything, O Jatilas, is burning. The eye is burning, thoughts are burning, all the senses are burning. They are burning with the fire of lust. There is anger, there is ignorance, there is hatred, and as long as the fire finds inflammable things upon which it can feed, so long will it burn, and there will be birth and death, decay, grief, lamentation, suffering, despair, and sorrow. Considering this, a disciple of truth will see the four truths and walk in the noble, eightfold path. He will become wary of his eye, wary of his thoughts, wary of all his senses. He will divest himself of passion and become free. He will be delivered from selfishness and attain the blessed state of Nirvâna." 22

And the Jatilas rejoiced and took refuge in the Buddha, the Dharma, and the Sangha. 23

XXI. THE SERMON AT RÂJAGRIHA.

And the Blessed One having dwelt some time in Uruvilvâ went forth to Râjagriha, accompanied by a great number of bhikshus, many of whom had been Jatilas before; and the great Kâshyapa, formerly chief of the Jatilas, was with him. 1

When the Magadha king, Sainya Bimbisâra, heard of the arrival of Gautama Shâkyamuni, of whom the people said, "He is the Holy One, the blessed Buddha, guiding men as a driver curbs a bullock, the teacher of high and low," he went out surrounded with his counsellors and generals and came to the place where the Blessed One was. 2

There they saw the Blessed One in the company of Kâshyapa, the great religious teacher of the Jatilas, and they were astonished and thought: "Has the great Shâkyamuni placed himself under the spiritual direction of Kâshyapa, or has Kâshyapa become a disciple of Gautama?" 3

And the Tathâgata, reading the thoughts of the people, said to Kâshyapa: "What knowledge have you gained, O Kâshyapa, and what has induced you to renounce the sacred fire and give up your austere penances?" 4

Kâshyapa said: "The profit I derived from adoring the fire was continuance in the wheel of individuality with all its sorrows and vanities. This service I have cast away, and instead of continuing penances and sacrifices I have gone in quest of the highest Nirvâna." 5

Buddha, perceiving that the whole assembly was

ready as a vessel to receive the doctrine, spoke to Bimbisâra the king: 6

"He who knows the nature of his self and understands how his senses act, finds no room for the *I*, and thus he will attain peace unending. The world holds the thought of *I*, and from this arises false apprehension. 7

"Some say that the *I* endures after death, some say it perishes. Both are wrong and their error is most grievous. 8

"For if they say the *I* is perishable, the fruit they strive for will perish too, and at some time there will be no hereafter. This salvation from sinful selfishness is without merit. 9

"When some, on the other hand, say the *I* will not perish, then in the midst of all life and death there is but one identity unborn and undying. If such is their *I*, then it is perfect and cannot be perfected by deeds. The lasting, imperishable *I* could never be changed. The self would be lord and master, and there would be no use in perfecting the perfect; moral aims and salvation would be unnecessary. 10

"But now we see the marks of joy and sorrow. Where is any constancy? If it is not an *I* that does our deeds, then there is no *I*; there is no actor behind the doing, no perceiver behind the knowing, no lord behind the living! 11

"Now attend and listen: The senses meet the object and from their contact sensation is born. Thence results recollection. Thus, as the sun's power through a burning-glass causes fire to appear, so through the knowledge born of sense and object, that lord, whom you call self, is born. The shoot springs from the seed; the seed is not the shoot; both are not one and the same, yet not different! Such is the birth of animated life. 12

"Ye that are slaves of the *I*, that toil in the service of self from morn to night, that live in constant fear of birth, old age, sickness, and death, receive the good tidings that your cruel master exists not. 13

"Self is an error, an illusion, a dream. Open your eyes and awake. See things as they are and you will be comforted. 14

"He who is awake will no longer be afraid of nightmares. He who has recognised the nature of the rope that seemed to be a serpent ceases to tremble. 15

"He who has found there is no *I* will let go all the lusts and desires of egotism. 16

"The cleaving to things, covetousness, and sensuality, inherited from former existences, are the causes of misery and of the vanity in the world. 17

"Surrender the grasping disposition of your selfishness and you will attain to that sinless calm state of mind which conveys perfect peace, goodness, and wisdom. 18

"As a mother, even at the risk of her own life, protects her son, her only son: so let him that has recognised the truth, cultivate good-will without measure among all beings. 19

"Let him cultivate good-will without measure toward the whole world, above, below, around, unstinted, unmixed with any feeling of making distinctions or of showing preferences. 20

"Let a man remain steadfast in this state of mind while he is awake, whether he is standing, walking, sitting, or lying down. 21

"This state of heart is best in the world. It is Nirvâna! 22

"To abandon all wrong-doing; to lead a virtuous life, and to cleanse one's heart. This is the religion of all Buddhas." 23

When the enlightened one had finished his sermon, the Magadha king said to the Blessed One: 24

"In former days, Lord, when I was a prince, I cherished five wishes. I wished, O, that I might be inaugurated as a king. This was my first wish, and it has been fulfilled. Further, I wished: Might the Holy Buddha, the Perfect One, appear on earth while I rule and may he come into my kingdom. This was my second wish and it is fulfilled now. Further, I wished: Might I pay my respects to him. This was my third wish and it is fulfilled now. The fourth wish was: Might the Blessed One preach the doctrine to me, and this is fulfilled now. The greatest wish, however, was the fifth wish: Might I understand the doctrine of the Blessed One! And this wish is fulfilled too. 25

"Glorious Lord! Most glorious is the truth preached by the Tathâgata! Our Lord, the Buddha sets up what has been overturned; he reveals what has been hidden; he points out the way to the wanderer who has gone astray; he lights a lamp in the darkness so that those who have eyes to see might see. 26

"I take my refuge in the Buddha! I take my refuge in the Dharma. I take my refuge in the Sangha." 27

The Tathâgata by the exercise of his virtue and by wisdom showed his unlimited spiritual power. He subdued and harmonised all minds. He made them see and accept the truth, and throughout the kingdom the seeds of virtue were sown. 28

XXII. THE KING'S GIFT.

The king, having taken his refuge in Buddha, invited the Tathâgata to his palace, saying: "Might the Blessed One consent to take his meal with me to-morrow together with the fraternity of bhikshus?" 1

The next morning Sainya Bimbisâra, the king, announced to the Blessed One that it was time for dinner: "You are my most welcome guest, O Lord of the world, come; the dinner is ready." 2

And the Blessed One having donned his robes, took his alms-bowl and entered, together with a great number of bhikshus, the city of Râjagriha. 3

Shakra, the king of the Dêvas, assuming the appearance of a young Brahman walked in front, singing these lines: 4

"He who teaches self-control with those who have learned self-control; the redeemer with those whom he has redeemed; the Blessed One with those to whom he has given peace, has entered Râjagriha! Hail, Buddha, our Lord! Honored be his name and blessings to all who take refuge in him." 5

When the Blessed One had finished his meal, and cleansed his bowl and his hands, the king sat down near him and thought: 6

"Where may I find a place for the Blessed One to live in, not too far from the town and not too near, suitable for going and coming, easily accessible for all people who want to see him, a place that is by day not too crowded and by night not exposed to noise, wholesome and well fitted for a retired life? 7

"There is my pleasure-garden, the bamboo forest

Vênuvana, fulfilling all these conditions. I shall offer it to the fraternity of bhikshus with the Buddha at their head." 8

And the king dedicated his pleasure-garden to the fraternity and said: "May the Blessed One accept the gift." 9

Then the Blessed One having silently shown his consent, gladdened and edified the Magadha king by religious discourse, rose from his seat and went away. 10

XXIII. SHÂRIPUTRA AND MAUDGALYÂYANA.

At that time Shâriputra and Maudgalyâyana, two Brahmans and chiefs of the followers of Sanjaya, led a religious life. They had given their words to each other: "He who first attains Nirvâna shall tell the other one." 1

And Shâriputra seeing the venerable Ashvajit begging for alms, modestly keeping his eyes to the ground and dignified in deportment, exclaimed: "Truly this shramana has entered the right path, I will address him and ask, In whose name, friend, have you retired from the world? Who is your teacher, and what doctrine do you profess?" 2

And Ashvajit replied: "I am a follower of the great Shâkyamuni. He is the Buddha, the Blessed One, and in his name have I retired from the world. The Blessed One is my teacher and his doctrine do I profess." 3

And Shâriputra went to Maudgalyâyana and told him, and they said: "We will go to the Blessed One, that he, the Blessed One, may be our teacher." And they went with all their followers to the Tathâgata and took their refuge in Buddha. 4

And the Holy One said: "Shâriputra is like the first-born son of a world-ruling monarch who assists the king as his chief follower to set the wheel of the law a-rolling." 5

XXIV. THE PEOPLE DISSATISFIED.

And the people were annoyed. Seeing that many distinguished young men of the kingdom of Magadha led a religious life under the direction of the Blessed One, they became angry and murmured: "Gautama Shâkyamuni induces fathers to leave their wives and causes families to become extinct." 1

When they saw the bhikshus, they reviled them, saying: "The great Shâkyamuni has come to Râjagriha subduing the minds of men. Who will be the next to be led by him?" 2

The bhikshus told it to the Blessed One, and the Blessed One said: "This murmuring, O bhikshus, will not last long. It will last seven days. If they revile you, O bhikshus, answer them with these words: 3

"'It is by preaching the truth that Tathâgatas lead men. Who will murmur at the wise? Who will blame the virtuous? Self-control, righteousness, and a clean heart are the injunctions of our Master.'" 4

XXV. ANÂTHAPINDIKA.

At this time there was Anâthapindika, a man of unmeasured wealth, visiting Râjagriha. Being of a charitable character, he was called "The supporter of the orphans and the friend of the poor." 1

Hearing that Buddha had come into the world and

was stopping in the bamboo grove near the city, he set out in the very night to meet the Blessed One. 2

And the Blessed One saw at once the sterling quality of Anâthapindika's heart and greeted him with words of religious comfort. And they sat down together, and Anâthapindika listened to the sweetness of the truth preached by the Blessed One. And Buddha said: 3

"The restless, busy nature of the world, this, I declare, is at the root of pain. Attain that composure of mind which is resting in the peace of immortality. Self is but a heap of composite qualities, and its world is empty like a fantasy. 4

"Who is it that shapes our lives? Is it Îshvara, a personal creator? If Îshvara be the maker, all living things should have silently to submit to their maker's power. They would be like vessels formed by the potter's hand; and if it were so, how would it be possible to practise virtue? If the world had been made by Îshvara there should be no such thing as sorrow, or calamity, or sin; for both pure and impure deeds must come from him. If not, there would be another cause beside him, and he would not be the self-existent one. Thus, you see, the thought of Îshvara is overthrown. 5

"Again it is said that the Absolute has created us. But that which is absolute cannot be a cause. All things around us come from a cause as the plant comes from the seed; but how can the Absolute be the cause of all things alike? If it pervades them, then, certainly, it does not make them. 6

"Again it is said that Self is the maker. But if self is the maker, why did he not make things pleasing? The causes of sorrow and joy are real and objective. How can they have been made by self? 7

"Again, if you adopt the argument, there is no maker, our fate is such as it is, and there is no causation, what use would there be in shaping our lives and adjusting means to an end? 8

"Therefore, we argue that all things that exist are not without cause. However, neither Îshvara, nor the absolute, nor the self, nor causeless chance, is the maker, but our deeds produce results both good and evil. 9

"The whole world is under the law of causation, and the causes that act are not un-mental, for the gold of which the cup is made is gold throughout. 10

"Let us, then, surrender the heresies of worshipping Îshvara and praying to him; let us not lose ourselves in vain speculations of profitless subtleties; let us surrender self and all selfishness, and as all things are fixed by causation, let us practise good so that good may result from our actions." 11

And Anâthapindika said: "I see that thou art Buddha, the Blessed One and the Holy One, and I wish to open to you my whole soul. Having listened to my words advise me what I shall do. 12

"My life is full of work, and having acquired great wealth, I am surrounded with cares. Yet do I enjoy my work, and I apply myself to it with all diligence. Many people are in my employ and depend upon the success of my enterprises. 13

"Now, I have heard your disciples praise the bliss of the hermit and denounce the unrest of the world. 'The Holy One,' they say, 'has given up his kingdom and his inheritance, and has found the path of righteousness, thus setting an example to all the world how to attain Nirvâna.' 14

"My soul yearns to do what is right and to be a blessing unto my fellow-beings. Let me then ask you, Must I give up my wealth, my home, and my business enterprises, and, like you, go into homelessness in order to attain the bliss of a religious life?" 15

And Buddha replied: "The bliss of a religious life is attainable by every one who walks in the noble eightfold path. He that cleaves to wealth, had better cast it away than allow his heart to be poisoned by it; but he who does not cleave to wealth, and possessing riches, uses them rightly, will be a blessing unto his fellow-beings. 16

"I say unto thee, remain in thy station of life and apply thyself with diligence to thy enterprises. It is not life and wealth and power that enslave men, but the cleaving to life and wealth and power. 17

"The bhikshu who retires from the world in order to lead a life of leisure will have no gain. For a life of indolence is an abomination, and lack of energy is to be despised. 18

"The dharma of the Tathâgata does not require a man to go into homelessness or to resign the world, unless he feels called upon to do so; but the dharma of the Tathâgata requires every man to free himself from the illusion of self, to cleanse his heart, to give up his thirst for pleasure, and lead a life of righteousness. 19

"And whatever men do, whether they remain in the world as artisans, merchants, and officers of the king, or retire from the world and devote themselves to a life of religious meditation, let them put their whole heart into their task; let them be diligent and energetic, and, if they are like the lotus, which, although it grows in the water, yet remains untouched by the water, if they struggle in life without cherishing envy or hatred, if they live in the world not a life of self but a life of truth, then surely joy, peace, and bliss will dwell in their minds." 20

XXVI. THE SERMON ON CHARITY.

Anâthapindika rejoiced at the words of the Blessed One and said: "I dwell at Shrâvastî, the capital of Kôsala, a land rich in produce and enjoying peace. Prasênajit is the king of the country, and his name is renowned among our own people and our neighbors. Now I wish to found there a vihâra which shall be a place of religious devotion for your brotherhood, and I pray you to kindly accept it." 1

Buddha saw into the heart of the supporter of orphans; and knowing that unselfish charity was the moving cause of his offer, in acceptance of the gift, the Blessed One said: 2

"The charitable man is loved by all; his friendship is prized highly; in death his heart is at rest and full of joy, for he suffers not from repentance; he receives the opening flower of his reward and the fruit that ripens from it. 3

"Hard it is to understand: By giving away our food, we get more strength, by bestowing clothing on others, we gain more beauty; by founding abodes of purity and truth, we acquire great treasures. 4

"There is a proper time and a proper mode in charity; just as the vigorous warrior goes to battle, so is the man who is able to give. He is like an able warrior, a champion strong and wise in action. 5

"Loving and compassionate he gives with reverence and banishes all hatred, envy, and anger. 6

"The charitable man has found the path of salvation. He is like the man who plants a sapling securing thereby the shade, the flowers, and the fruit in future years. Even so is the result of charity, even so is the joy of him who helps those that are in need of assistance; even so is the great Nirvâna. 7

"We reach the immortal path only by continuous acts of kindliness and we perfect our souls by compassion and charity." 8

Anâthapindika invited Shâriputra to accompany him on his return to Kôsala and help him in selecting a pleasant site for the vihâra.

XXVII. BUDDHA'S FATHER.

At the time when Buddha was residing at Râjagriha, Shuddhôdana, his father, sent word to him saying: "I wish to see my son before I die. Others have had the benefit of his doctrine, but not his father nor his relatives." 1

And the messenger said: "O world-honored Tathâgata, your father looks for your coming as the lily longs for the rising of the sun." 2

The Blessed One consented to the request of his father and set out on his journey to Kapilavastu. Soon the tidings spread in the native country of Buddha: "Prince Siddhârtha, who wandered forth from home into homelessness to obtain enlightenment, having attained his purpose, is coming back." 3

Shuddhôdana went out with his relatives and ministers to meet the prince. When the king saw Siddhârtha, his son, from afar, he was struck with his beauty and dignity, and he rejoiced in his heart, but his mouth found no words to utter. 4

This indeed was his son; these were the features of Siddhârtha. How near was the great shramana to his heart, and yet what a distance lay between them. That noble muni was no longer Siddhârtha his son; he was Buddha, the Blessed One, the Holy One, Lord of truth, and teacher of mankind. 5

Shuddhôdana the king, considering the religious dignity of his son, descended from his chariot and having saluted his son first, said: "It is now seven years since I saw you. How I have longed for this moment!" 6

Buddha took a seat opposite his father, and the king eagerly gazed at his son. He longed to call him by his name but he dared not. "Siddhârtha," he exclaimed silently in his soul, "Siddhârtha, come back to your old father and be his son again!" But seeing the determination of his son, he suppressed his sentiments, and desolation overcame him. 7

Thus the king sat face to face with his son, rejoicing in his sadness and sad in his rejoicing. Well might he be proud of his son, but his pride broke down at the idea that his great son would never be his heir. 8

"I would offer thee my kingdom," said the king, "but if I did, thou wouldst account it but as ashes." 9

And Buddha said: "I know that the king's heart is full of love and that for his son's sake he feels deep grief. But let the ties of love that bind you to the son whom you lost embrace with equal kindness all your fellow-beings, and you will receive in his place a greater one than Siddhârtha; you will receive Buddha, the teacher of truth, the preacher of righteousness, and the peace of Nirvâna will enter into your heart." 10

Shuddhôdana trembled with joy when he heard the melodious words of his son, the Buddha, and clasping his hands exclaimed with tears in his eyes: "Wonderful is this change! The overwhelming sorrow has passed away. At first my sorrowing heart was heavy, but now I reap the fruit of your great renunciation. It was right that, moved by your mighty sympathy, you should reject the pleasures of royal power and achieve your noble purpose in religious devotion. Having found the path you can now preach the law of immortality to all the world that yearns for deliverance." 11

The king returned to the palace while Buddha remained in the grove before the city. 12

XXVIII. YASHÔDHARÂ.

On the next morning Buddha took his bowl and set out to beg his food. 1

And the news spread: "The prince Siddhârtha is going from house to house to receive alms in the city where he used to ride in a chariot attended by his retinue. His robe is like a red clod and he holds in his hand an earthen bowl." 2

On hearing the strange rumor, the king went forth in great haste and exclaimed: "Why do you disgrace me thus? Do you not know that I can easily supply you and your bhikshus with food?" 3

And Buddha replied: "It is the custom of my race." 4

But the king said: "How can this be? You are descended from kings, and not one of them ever begged for food." 5

"O great king," rejoined Buddha, "you and your race may claim the descent from kings; my descent is from the Buddhas of old. They, begging their food, lived on alms." 6

The king made no reply, and the Blessed One continued: "It is customary, O king, when one has found a hidden treasure, for him to make an offering of the most precious jewel to his father. Suffer me, therefore, to open this treasure of mine which is the dharma, and accept from me this gem:" 7

And the Blessed One recited the following stanza:

"Rise from dream and loiter not,
Listen to the Law.
Practise righteousness and lo,
Eternal bliss is thine." 8

Then the king conducted the prince into the palace, and the ministers and all the members of the royal family greeted him with great reverence, but Yashôdharâ, the mother of Râhula, did not make her appearance. The king sent for Yashôdharâ, but she replied: "Surely, if I am deserving of any regard, Siddhârtha will come and see me." 9

The Blessed One, having greeted all his relatives and friends, asked: "Where is Yashôdharâ?" And on being informed that she had refused to come, he rose straightway and went to her apartments. 10

"I am free," the Blessed One said to his disciples Shâriputra and Maudgalyâyana, whom he had bidden to accompany him to the princess's chamber; "the princess, however, is not as yet free. Not having seen me for a long time, she is exceedingly sorrowful. Unless her grief be allowed its course her heart will cleave. Should she touch the Tathâgata, the Holy One, you must not prevent her." 11

Yashôdharâ sat in her room, dressed in mean garments, and her hair cut. When the prince Siddhârtha entered, she was, from the abundance of her affection, like an overflowing vessel, unable to contain herself. 12

Forgetting that the man whom she loved was Buddha, the Lord of the world, the preacher of truth, she held him by his feet and wept bitterly. 13

Remembering, however, that Shuddhôdana was present, she felt ashamed and rose up seating herself reverently at a little distance. 14

The king apologised for the princess, saying: "This arises from her deep affection, and is more than a temporary emotion. During the seven years that she has lost her husband, when she heard that Siddhârtha had shaved his head, she did likewise; when she heard that he had left off the use of perfumes and ornaments, she also refused their use. Like her husband she has eaten at appointed times from an earthen bowl only. Like him she has renounced high seats with splendid coverings, and when other princes asked her in marriage, she replied that she was still his. Therefore, grant her forgiveness." 15

And the Blessed One spoke kindly to Yashôdharâ, telling of her great merits inherited from former existences. She, indeed, in his former lives had been of great assistance to him. Her purity, her gentleness, her devotion had been invaluable to Bôdhisattva when he aspired to the highest aim of mankind to attain enlightenment. And so holy had she been that she desired to become the wife of a Buddha. This, then, is her karma, and it is the result of great merits. Her grief has been unspeakable, but the consciousness of the glory that surrounds her spiritual inheritance increased by her noble attitude during her life will be a balm that will miraculously transform all sorrows into heavenly joy. 16

XXIX. RÂHULA.

Many people in Kapilavastu believed in the Tathâgata, taking refuge in his doctrine, and among the young men who joined the Sangha were Ânanda, Siddhârtha's half-brother, the son of Prajâpatî; Dêvadatta, his cousin and brother-in-law; Upâli the barber; and Anuruddha the philosopher. 1

Ânanda was a man after the heart of the Blessed One; he was his most beloved disciple, profound in comprehension and gentle in spirit. And Ânanda remained always near the Blessed Master of truth, until death parted them. 2

On the seventh day after the arrival in Kapilavastu, Yashôdharâ dressed Râhula, now seven years old, in all the splendor of a prince and said to him: 3

"This holy man, whose appearance is so glorious that he looks like the great Brahma, is your father. He possesses four great mines of wealth which I have not yet seen. Go to him and entreat him to put you in their possession, for the son ought to inherit the property of the father." 4

Râhula replied: "I know of no father but the king. Who is my father?" 5

The princess took the boy in her arms and from the window she pointed out to him Buddha, who happened to be near the palace, partaking of food. 6

Râhula then went to Buddha, and looking up in his face said without fear and with much affection: "My father!" 7

And standing near by him, he added: "O shramana, even your shadow is a place of bliss!" 8

When the Tathâgata had finished his repast, he gave blessings and went away from the palace, but Râhula followed and asked his father for his inheritance. 9

No one prevented the boy, nor did the Blessed One himself. 10

Then the Blessed One turned to Shâriputra, saying: "My son asks for his inheritance. I cannot give him perishable treasures that will bring cares and sorrows, but I can give him the inheritance of a holy life, which is a treasure that will not perish." 11

Addressing Râhula with earnestness, the Blessed One said: "Gold and silver and jewels are not in my possession. But if you are willing to receive spiritual treasures, and are strong enough to carry them and to keep them, I shall give you the four truths which will teach you the eightfold path of righteousness. Do you desire to be admitted to the brotherhood of those who devote their life to the culture of the mind seeking for the highest bliss attainable?" 12

And Râhula replied with firmness: "I do." 13

When the king heard that Râhula had joined the brotherhood of bhikshus he was grieved. He had lost Siddhârtha and Ânanda, his sons, and Dêvadatta, his nephew. Now his grandson had been taken from him, he went to the Blessed One and spoke to him. And the Blessed One promised that henceforth he would not ordain any minor without the consent of his parents or guardians. 14

XXX. JÊTAVANA.

Anâthapindika, the friend of the destitute and the supporter of orphans, having returned home, saw the garden of the heir-apparent, Jêta, with its green groves and limpid rivulets, and thought: "This is the place which will be most suitable as a vihâra for the fraternity of the Blessed One." And he went to the prince and asked for leave to buy the ground. 1

The prince was not inclined to sell the garden for he valued it highly. He at first refused but said at last. "If you can cover it with gold, then, and for no other price, shall you have it." 2

Anâthapindika rejoiced and began to spread his gold; but Jêta said: "Spare yourself trouble for I will not sell." But Anâthapindika insisted. Thus they differed and contended until they resorted to the magistrate. 3

Meanwhile the people began to talk of the unwonted proceeding and the prince hearing more of the details, and knowing that Anâthapindika was not only very wealthy, but also straightforward and sincere, inquired into his plans. On hearing the name of Buddha, the prince became anxious to share in the foundation and he accepted only one-half of the gold, saying: "Yours is the land but mine are the trees. I will give the trees as my share of the offering to Buddha." 4

Then Anâthapindika took the land and Jêta the trees, and they settled them in trust of Shâriputra. 5

Having made the foundation, they began to build the hall which rose loftily in due proportions according to the directions which Buddha had laid down; and it was beautifully decorated with appropriate carvings. 6

This vihâra was called Jêtavana, and the friend of the orphans invited the Lord to come to Shrâvastî and receive the donation. And the Blessed One left Kapilavastu and came to Shrâvastî. 7

While the Blessed One entered Jêtavana, Anâthapindika scattered flowers and burned incense, and as a sign of the gift he poured water from a golden dragon pitcher, saying, "This Jêtavana vihâra I give for the use of the brotherhood throughout the world." 8

The Blessed One received the gift and replied: "May all evil influences be overcome; may the offering promote the kingdom of righteousness and be a permanent blessing to mankind in general and especially also to the giver." 9

Then the king Prasênajit, hearing that the Lord had come, went in his royal equipage to the Jêtavana vihâra and saluted the Blessed One with clasped hands, saying: 10

"Blessed is my unworthy and obscure kingdom that it has met with so great a fortune. For how can calamities and dangers befall it in the presence of the Lord of the world, the Dharma Râja, the King of Truth. 11

"Now that I have seen your sacred features, let me partake of the refreshing waters of your teachings. 12

"Worldly profit is fleeting and perishable, but religious profit is eternal and inexhaustible. A worldly man, though a king, is full of trouble, but even a common man who is holy has peace of mind." 13

Knowing the tendency of the king's heart, weighed down by avarice and love of pleasure, Buddha seized the opportunity and said: 14

"Even those who, by their evil karma, have been born in low degree, when they see a virtuous man, feel reverence for him. How much more must an independent king, who by his previous conditions of life has acquired much merit, when he encounters Buddha, conceive reverence. 15

"And now as I briefly expound the law, let the

Mahârâja listen and weigh my words, and hold fast
that which I deliver! 16

"Our good or evil deeds follow us continually like
shadows. 17

"That which is most needed is a loving heart! 18

"Regard your people as we do an only son. Do
not oppress them, do not destroy them; keep in due
check every member of your body, forsake unrighteous
doctrine and walk in the straight path; do not exalt
yourself by trampling down others. But comfort and
befriend the suffering. 19

"Neither ponder much on kingly dignity, nor listen
to the smooth words of flatterers. 20

"There is no profit in vexing oneself by austerities,
but meditate on Buddha and weigh his righteous
law. 21

"We are enclosed on all sides by the rocks of birth,
old age, disease, and death, and only by considering
and practising the true law can we escape from this
sorrow-piled mountain. 22

"What profit, then, in practising iniquity? 23

"All who are wise spurn the pleasures of the body.
They loathe lust and seek to promote their spiritual
existence. 24

"When a tree is burning with fierce flames, how
can the birds congregate therein? Truth cannot dwell
where passion lives. Without a knowledge of this the
learned man, though he may be praised as a sage, is
ignorant. 25

'To him who has this knowledge true wisdom
dawns. To acquire this wisdom is the one aim needed.
To neglect it implies the failure of life. 26

"The teachings of all schools should centre here,
for without it there is no reason. 27

"This truth is not for the hermit alone; it concerns every human being, priest and layman alike. There is no distinction between the monk who has taken the vows, and the man of the world living with his family. There are hermits who fall into perdition, and there are humble householders who mount to the rank of rishis. 28

"The tide of lust is a danger common to all; it carries away the world. He who is involved in its eddies finds no escape. But wisdom is the handy boat, reflexion is the rudder. The slogan of religion calls you to the rescue of your soul from the assaults of Mâra, the enemy. 29

"Since it is impossible to escape the result of our deeds, let us practise good works. 30

"Let us inspect our thoughts that we do no evil, for as we sow so shall we reap. 31

"There are ways from light into darkness and from darkness into light. There are ways, also, from the gloom into deeper darkness, and from the dawn into brighter light. The wise man will use the light he has to receive more light. He will constantly advance to the knowledge of the truth. 32

"Exhibit true superiority by virtuous conduct and the exercise of reason; meditate deeply on the vanity of earthly things, and understand the fickleness of life. 33

"Elevate the mind, and seek sincere faith with firm purpose; transgress not the rules of kingly conduct, and let your happiness depend, not upon external things, but upon your own mind. Thus you will lay up a good name for distant ages and will secure the favor of the Tathâgata." 34

The king listened with reverence and remembered all the words of Buddha in his heart. 35

CONSOLIDATION OF BUDDHA'S RELIGION.

XXXI. JÎVAKA, THE PHYSICIAN.

LONG before the Blessed One had attained enlightenment, self-mortification had been the custom among those who earnestly sought for salvation. Their final aim appeared to them the deliverance of the soul from all bodily necessities, and finally from the body itself. Thus they avoided everything that might be a luxury in food, shelter, and clothing, and lived like the beasts in the woods. Some went naked, while others wore the rags cast away upon cemeteries or dung-heaps. 1

When the Blessed One retired from the world, he recognised at once the error of the naked ascetics, and considering the indecency of their habit, clad himself in cast-off rags. 2

Having attained enlightenment and rejected all unnecessary self-mortifications, the Blessed One and his bhikshus continued for a long time to wear the cast-off rags of cemeteries and dung-hills. 3

Then it happened that the bhikshus were visited with diseases of all kinds, and the Blessed One allowed them and explicitly ordered the use of medicines, and among them he even enjoined, whenever needed, the use of unguents. 4

One of the brethren suffered from a sore on his foot, and the Blessed One enjoined the bhikshus to wear foot-coverings. 5

Now it happened that a disease befell the body of the Blessed One himself, and Ânanda went to Jîvaka, physician to Bimbisâra, the king. 6

And Jîvaka, a faithful believer in the Holy One, ministered unto the Blessed One with medicines and baths until the body of the Blessed One was completely restored. 7

At that time, Pradyôta, king of Ujjayinî, was suffering from jaundice, and Jîvaka, the physician to Bimbisâra râja, was consulted. When king Pradyôta had been restored to health, he sent to Jîvaka a suit of the most excellent cloth. And Jîvaka said to himself: "This suit is made of the best cloth, and nobody is worthy to receive it but the Blessed One, the perfect and holy Buddha, or the Magadha king, Sainya Bimbisâra." 8

Then Jîvaka took that suit and went to the place where the Blessed One was; having approached him, and having respectfully saluted the Blessed One, he sat down near him and said: "Lord, I ask a boon of the Blessed One." 9

Buddha replied: "The Tathâgatas, Jîvaka, do not grant boons before they know what they are." 10

Jîvaka said: "Lord it is a proper and unobjectionable demand." 11

"Speak, Jîvaka," said the Blessed One. 12

"Lord of the world, the Blessed One wears only robes made of rags taken from a dust heap or a cemetery, and so does the fraternity of bhikshus. Now, Lord, this suit has been sent to me by king Pradyôta, which is the best and most excellent, and the first and the most precious, and the noblest that can be found. Lord of the world, may the Blessed One accept from me this suit, and may he allow the fraternity of bhikshus to wear lay robes." 13

The Blessed One accepted the suit, and after having delivered a religious discourse, he addressed the bhikshus thus: 14

"He who likes may wear cast-off rags, but he who likes may accept lay robes. Whether you are pleased with the one or with the other, I shall approve it." 15

When the people at Râjagriha heard, "The Blessed One has allowed the bhikshus to wear lay robes," those who were willing to bestow gifts became glad. And in one day many thousands of robes were presented at Râjagriha to the bhikshus. 16

XXXII. BUDDHA'S PARENTS ATTAIN NIRVÂNA.

When Shuddôdana had grown old, he fell sick and sent for his son to come and see him once more before he died; and the Blessed One came and stayed at the sick-bed, and Shuddôdana having attained the perfect enlightenment died in the arms of the Blessed One. 1

And it is said that the Blessed One, for the sake of preaching to his mother Mâyâ-dêvî, ascended to heaven and dwelled with the dêvas. Having concluded his pious mission, he returned to the earth and went about again, converting those who listened to his teachings.2

XXXIII. WOMEN ADMITTED TO THE SANGHA.

Yashôdharâ had three times requested of Buddha that she might be admitted to the Sangha, but her wish was not granted. Now Prajâpatî, the foster-mother of the Blessed One, in the company of Yashôdharâ, and many other women, went to the Tathâgata entreating him earnestly to let them take the vows and be ordained as disciples of Buddha. 1

And the Blessed One, seeing their zeal for the truth, could no longer resist, and he accepted them as his disciples. 2

Prajâpatî was the first woman that became a disciple of Buddha and received the ordination as a bhikshunî. 3

XXXIV. THE BHIKSHUS' CONDUCT TOWARD WOMEN.

The bhikshus came to the Blessed One and asked him: 1

"O Tathâgata, our Lord and Master, what conduct toward women do you prescribe to the shramanas who have left the world?" 2

And the Blessed One said: 3

"Guard against looking on a woman. 4

"If you see a woman, let it be as though you saw her not, and have no conversation with her. 5

"If, after all, you must speak with her, let it be with a pure heart, and think to yourself, 'I as a shramana will live in this sinful world as the spotless leaf of the lotus, unsoiled by the mud in which it grows.' 6

"If the woman be old, regard her as your mother, if young, as your sister, if very young, as your child. 7

"The shramana who looks at a woman as a woman, or touches her as a woman has broken his vow and is no longer a disciple of the Shâkyamuni. 8

"The power of lust is great with men, and is to be

feared withal; take then the bow of earnest perseverance, and the sharp arrow-points of wisdom. 9

"Cover your head with the helmet of right thought, and fight with fixed resolve against the five desires. 10

"Lust beclouds a man's heart, when it is confused with woman's beauty, and the mind is dazed. 11

"Better far with red-hot irons bore out both your eyes, than encourage in yourselves sensual thoughts, or look upon a woman's form with lustful desires. 12

"Better fall into the fierce tiger's mouth, or under the sharp knife of the executioner, than to dwell with a woman and excite in yourself lustful thoughts. 13

"A woman of the world is anxious to exhibit her form and shape, whether walking, standing, sitting, or sleeping. Even when represented as a picture, she desires to captivate with the charms of her beauty, and thus to rob men of their steadfast heart! 14

"How then ought you to guard yourselves? 15

"By regarding her tears and her smiles as enemies, her stooping form, her hanging arms, and all her disentangled hair as toils designed to entrap man's heart. 16

"Therefore, I say, restrain the heart, give it no unbridled license." 17

XXXV. VISHÂKHÂ.

Vishâkhâ, a wealthy woman in Shrâvastî who had many children and grandchildren, had given to the order the Pûrvârâma or Eastern Garden, and was the first to become a matron of the lay sisters. 1

When the Blessed One stayed at Shrâvastî, Vishâkhâ went up to the place where the Blessed One was, and tendered Him an invitation to take his meal at her house, which the Blessed One accepted. 2

And a heavy rain fell during the night and the next morning; and the bhikshus doffed their robes to keep them dry and let the rain fall upon their bodies. 3

When on the next day the Blessed One had finished his meal, she took her seat at his side and spoke thus: "Eight are the boons, Lord, which I beg of the Blessed One." 4

Said the Blessed One: "The Tathâgatas, O Vishâkhâ, grant no boons unless they know what they are." 5

Vishâkhâ replied: "Proper, Lord, and unobjectionable are the boons I ask." 6

Having received permission to ask the boons, Vishâkhâ said: "I desire, Lord, through all my life long to bestow robes for the rainy season on the Sangha, and food for incoming bhikshus, and food for outgoing bhikshus, and food for the sick, and food for those who wait upon the sick, and medicine for the sick, and a constant supply of rice-milk and bathing robes for the bhikshunîs, the sisters." 7

Said Buddha: "But what circumstance is it, O Vishâkhâ, that you have in view in asking these eight boons of the Tathâgata?" 8

And Vishakha replied: 9

"I gave command, Lord, to my maid-servant, saying, 'Go thou and announce to the fraternity that the meal is ready.' And my maid went, but when she came to the vihâra, she observed that the bhikshus had doffed their robes, while it was raining, and she thought: 'These are not bhikshus, but naked ascetics letting the rain fall on them.' So she returned to me and reported accordingly, and I had to send her a second time. Impure, Lord, is nakedness, and revolting. It was this circumstance, Lord, that I had in view in desiring to provide the Sangha my life long with special garments for use in the rainy season. 10

"As to my second wish, Lord, an incoming bhikshu, not being able to take the direct roads, and not knowing the places where food can be procured, comes on his way wearied out by seeking for alms. It was this circumstance, Lord, that I had in view in desiring to provide the Sangha my life long with food for incoming bhikshus. 11

"Thirdly, Lord, an outgoing bhikshu, while seeking about for alms, may be left behind, or may arrive too late at the place whither he desires to go, and will set out on the road in weariness. 12

"Fourthly, Lord, if a sick bhikshu does not obtain suitable food, his sickness may increase upon him, and he may die. 13

"Fifthly, Lord, a bhikshu who is waiting upon the sick will lose his opportunity of going out to seek food for himself. 14

"Sixthly, Lord, if a sick bhikshu does not obtain suitable medicines, his sickness may increase upon him, and he may die. 15

"Seventhly, Lord, I have heard that the Blessed One has praised rice-milk, because it gives readiness of mind, dispels hunger and thirst; it is wholesome for the healthy as nourishment, and for the sick as a medicine. Therefore I desire to provide the Sangha my life long with a constant supply of rice-milk. 16

"Finally, Lord, the bhikshunîs are in the habit of bathing in the river Achiravatî with the courtesans, at the same landing-place, and naked. And the courtesans, Lord, ridicule the bhikshunîs, saying, 'What is the good, ladies, of your maintaining chastity when you are young? When you are old, maintain chastity then; thus will you be obtainers of both ends.' Impure, Lord, is nakedness for a woman, disgusting, and revolting. 17

"These are the circumstances, Lord, that I had in view." 18

The Blessed One said: "But what was the advantage you had in view for yourself, O Vishâkhâ, in asking these eight boons of the Tathâgatha?" 19

Vishâkhâ replied: 20

"Bhikshus who have spent the rainy seasons in various places will come, Lord, to Shrâvastî to visit the Blessed One. And on coming to the Blessed One they will ask, saying: 'Such and such a bhikshu, Lord, has died. What, now, is his destiny?' Then will the Blessed One explain that he has attained the fruits of conversion; that he has entered Nirvâna or attained arhantship, as the case may be. 21

"And I, going up to them, shall ask, 'Was that brother, Sirs, one of those who had formerly been at Shrâvastî?' If they reply to me, 'He has formerly been at Shrâvastî,' then shall I arrive at the conclusion, 'For a certainty did that brother enjoy either the robes for the rainy season, or the food for the incoming bhikshus, or the food for the outgoing bhikshus, or the food for the sick, or the food for those that wait upon the sick, or the medicine for the sick, or the constant supply of rice-milk.' 22

"Then will gladness spring up within me; thus gladdened, joy will come to me; and so rejoicing all my frame will be at peace. Being thus at peace I shall experience a blissful feeling of content; and in that bliss my heart will be at rest. That will be to me an exercise of my moral sense, an exercise of my moral powers, an exercise of the seven kinds of wisdom!

This, Lord, was the advantage I had in view for myself in asking those eight boons of the Blessed One." 23

The Blessed One said: "It is well, it is well, Vishâkhâ. Thou hast done well in asking these eight boons of the Tathâgata with such advantages in view. Charity bestowed upon those who are worthy of it is like good seeds sown on a good soil that yields an abundance of fruits. But alms given to those who are yet under the tyrannical yoke of the passions are like a seed deposited in a bad soil. The passions of the receiver of the alms choke, as it were, the growth of merits." 24

And the Blessed One gave thanks to Vishâkhâ in these verses: 25

"Whatsoever donation a woman upright in life, a disciple of the Happy One, may bestow in gladness of heart and without stint, her gift is heavenly, destructive of sorrow, and productive of bliss. 26

"A blissful life does she attain, entering upon the path that is free from corruption and impurity; 27

"Aiming at good, happy does she become; and she rejoices in her charitable actions." 28

XXXVI. THE UPAVASATHA AND PRÂTIMÔKSHA.

Sainya Bimbisâra, the Magadha king, retired from the world and led a religious life. And he observed that there were Brahmanical sects in Râjagriha keeping sacred certain days, and the people went to their meeting-houses and listened to their sermons. 1

Concerning the need of keeping regular days for retirement from worldly labors and religious instruction, the king went to the Blessed One and said: "The Parivrâjaka, who belong to the Tîrthika school, prosper and gain adherents because they keep the eighth day and also the fourteenth or fifteenth day of each half-month. Would it not be advisable for the reverend brethren of the Sangha also to assemble on days duly appointed for that purpose?" 2

And the Blessed One commanded the bhikshus to assemble on the eighth day and also on the fourteenth or fifteenth day of each half-month, and to devote these days to religious exercises. 3

This is the Upavasatha or Sabbath of the disciples of Buddha. 4

Now, the bhikshus, in obedience to the rule laid down by the Blessed One, assembled in the vihâra on the day appointed, and the people went to hear the dharma, but they were greatly disappointed, for the bhikshus remained silent and delivered no discourse. 5

When the Blessed One heard of it, he ordered the bhikshus to recite the Prâtimôksha, which is the ceremony of disburdenment; and he commanded them to make confession of their trespasses so as to receive the absolution of the order. 6

For a fault, if there be one, should be confessed by the bhikshu who remembers it and desires to be cleansed. For a fault when confessed shall be light to him. 7

And the Blessed One said: "The Prâtimôksha must be recited in this way: 8

"Let a competent and venerable bhikshu make the following proclamation to the Sangha: 'May the Sangha hear me! To-day is Upavasatha, the eighth, or the fourteenth or fifteenth day of the half-month. If the Sangha is ready, let the Sangha hold the Upavasatha service and recite the Prâtimôksha. I will recite the Prâtimôksha.' 9

"And the bhikshus shall reply: 'We hear it well and fix well the mind on it, all of us.' 10

"Then the officiating bhikshu shall continue: 'He who has committed an offence, may confess it; if there be no offence, you shall remain silent; from your being silent I shall understand that the reverend brethren are free from offences. 11

"'As a single person who has been asked a question answers it, so also, if before an assembly like this a question is solemnly proclaimed three times, an answer is expected: if a bhikshu, after a threefold proclamation, does not confess an existing offence which he remembers, he commits an intentional falsehood. 12

"'Now, reverend brethren, an intentional falsehood has been declared an impediment by the Blessed One. Therefore, by a bhikshu who has committed an offence, and remembers it, and desires to become pure, an existing offence should be confessed; for if it has been confessed, it is treated duly.'" 13

XXXVII. THE SCHISM.

While the Blessed One dwelt at Kaushâmbî, a certain bhikshu was accused of having committed an offence, and, as he refused to acknowledge it, the fraternity pronounced against him a sentence of expulsion. 1

Now that bhikshu was erudite. He knew the dharma, had studied the rules of the order, and was wise, learned, intelligent, modest, conscientious, and ready to submit himself to discipline. And he went to his companions and friends among the bhikshus, saying: "This is no offence, friends, this is no reason for a sentence of expulsion. I am not guilty. The verdict is unconstitutional and invalid. Therefore I consider myself still as a member of the order. May the venerable brethren assist me in maintaining my right." 2

Those who sided with the expelled brother went to the bhikshus who had pronounced the sentence, saying: "This is no offence"; while the bhikshus who had pronounced the sentence replied: "This is an offence." 3

Thus altercations and quarrels arose, and the Sangha was divided into two parties, reviling and slandering one another. 4

And all these happenings were reported to the Blessed One. 5

Then the Blessed One went to the place where the bhikshus were that had pronounced the sentence of expulsion, and said to them: "Do not think, O bhikshus, that you are to pronounce expulsion against a bhikshu, whatever be the facts of the case, simply by saying: 'It occurs to us that it is so, and therefore we are pleased to proceed thus against our brother.' Let those bhikshus who frivolously pronounce a sentence against a brother who knows the dharma and the rules of the order, who is learned, wise, and intelligent, modest, conscientious, and ready to submit himself to discipline, stand in awe of causing divisions. They must not pronounce a sentence of expulsion against a brother merely because he refuses to see his offence." 6

Then the Blessed One rose and went to the brethren who sided with the expelled brother and said to them: "Do not think, O bhikshus, that if you have given offence you need not atone for it, thinking: 'We are without offence.' When a bhikshu has committed an offence, which he considers no offence, while the fraternity consider him as guilty, he should think:

'These brethren know the dharma and the rules of the order; they are learned, wise, intelligent, modest, conscientious, and ready to submit themselves to discipline; it is impossible that they should on my account act with selfishness or in malice or in delusion or in fear.' Let him stand in awe of causing divisions, and rather acknowledge his offence on the authority of his brethren." 7

Both parties continued to hold Upavasatha and perform official acts independently of one another; and when their deportment was related to the Blessed One, he ruled that the holding of Upavasatha and the performance of official acts were lawful, unobjectionable, and valid for both parties. For he said: "the bhikshus who side with the expelled brother form a different communion from those who pronounced the sentence. There are venerable brethren in both parties. As they do not agree, let them hold Upavasatha and perform official acts separately." 8

And the Blessed One reprimanded the litigious bhikshus saying to them: 9

"Vulgar people make much noise; but who can be blamed when divisions arise in the Sangha? Hatred is not appeased in those who think: 'He has reviled me, he has wronged me, he has injured me.' 10

"For not by hatred is hatred appeased. Hatred is appeased by not-hatred. This is an eternal law. 11

"There are some who do not know the need of self-restraint; if they are quarrelsome we may excuse their behavior. But those who know better, should learn to live in concord. 12

"If a man finds a wise friend who lives righteously and is constant in his character, he may live with him, overcoming all dangers, happy and mindful. 13

"But if he finds not a friend who lives righteously and is constant in his character, let him rather walk alone like a king who leaves his empire and the cares of his empire behind him to lead a life of retirement like a lonely elephant in the forest. 14

"With fools there is no companionship. Rather than to live with men who are selfish, vain, litigious, and obstinate let a man walk alone." 15

And the Blessed One thought to himself: "It is no easy task to instruct these headstrong and infatuate fools." And he rose from his seat and went away. 16

XXXVIII. THE RE-ESTABLISHMENT OF CONCORD.

The dispute between the parties not being settled, the Blessed One left Kaushâmbî, and wandering from place to place he at last came to Shrâvastî. 1

And in the absence of the Blessed One the quarrels grew worse, so that the lay devotees of Kaushâmbî became annoyed and they said: "These litigious monks are a great nuisance and will bring upon us misfortunes. Worried by their altercations the Blessed One is gone, and has selected another abode for his residence. Let us, therefore, neither salute the bhikshus nor support them. They are not worthy of wearing yellow robes, and must either propitiate the Blessed One, or return to the world." 2

And the bhikshus of Kaushâmbî, when no longer honored and no longer supported by the lay devotees, began to repent and said: "Let us go to the Blessed One and have him settle the question of our disagreement." 3

And both parties went to Shrâvastî to the Blessed One. And the venerable Shâriputra, having heard of their arrival, addressed the Blessed One and said: "These litigious, disputatious, and quarrelsome bhikshus of Kaushâmbî, the authors of dissensions, have come to Shrâvastî. How am I to behave, O Lord, toward those bhikshus." 4

"Do not scold them, Shâriputra," said the Blessed One, "for harsh words are pleasant to no one. Assign separate dwelling-places to each party and treat them with impartial justice. Listen with patience to both parties. He alone who weighs both sides is called a muni. When both parties have presented their case, let the Sangha come to an agreement and declare the establishment of concord." 5

And Prajâpatî the matron asked the Blessed One for advice, and the Blessed One said: "Let both parties enjoy the gifts of lay members, be they robes or food, as they may need, and let no one receive any noticeable preference over the other." 6

And the venerable Upâli, having approached the Blessed One asked concerning the re-establishment of peace in the Sangha: "Would it be right, O Lord," said he, "that the Sangha, to avoid further disputations, should declare the restoration of concord without inquiring into the matter of the quarrel?" 7

And the Blessed One said: 8

"If the Sangha declares the re-establishment of concord without having inquired into the matter, the declaration is neither right nor lawful. 9

"There are two ways of re-establishing concord; one is in the letter, and the other one is in the spirit and in the letter. 10

"If the Sangha declares the re-establishment of

concord without having inquired into the matter, the peace is concluded in the letter only. But if the Sangha after having inquired into the matter and gone to the bottom of it decides to declare the re-establishment of concord, the peace is concluded in the spirit and also in the letter. 11

"The concord re-established in the spirit and in the letter is alone right and lawful." 12

And the Blessed One addressed the bhikshus and told them the story of Prince Dîrghâyu. He said: 13

"In former times, there lived at Benares a powerful king whose name was Brahmadatta of Kâshî; and he went to war against Dîrghêti, the king of Kôsala, for he thought, 'The kingdom of Kôsala is small and Dîrghêti will not be able to resist my armies.' 14

"And Dîrghêti, seeing that resistance was impossible against the great host of the king of Kâshî, fled, leaving his little kingdom in the hands of Brahmadatta, and having wandered from place to place, he came at last to Benares, and lived there with his consort in a potter's dwelling outside the town. 15

"And the queen bore him a son and they called him Dîrghâyu. 16

"When Dîrghâyu had grown up, the king thought to himself: 'King Brahmadatta has done us great harm, and he is fearing our revenge; he will seek to kill us. Should he find us he will slay us all three.' And he sent his son away, and Dîrghâyu having received a good education from his father, applied himself diligently to learn all arts, becoming very skilful and wise. 17

"At that time the barber of king Dîrghêti dwelt at Benares, and he saw the king, his former master, and being of an avaricious nature betrayed him to king Brahmadatta. 18

"When Brahmadatta, the king of Kâshî heard that the fugitive king of Kôsala lived with his wife, unknown and in disguise, a quiet life in a potter's dwelling, he ordered him and his queen to be bound and executed; and the sheriff to whom the order was given seized king Dîrghêti and led him to the place of execution. 19

"While the captive king was led through the streets of Benares he saw his son who had returned to visit his parents, and, careful not to betray the presence of his son, yet anxious to communicate to him his last advice, he cried: 'O Dîrghâyu, my son! Do not look long, do not look short, for not by hatred is hatred appeased; hatred is appeased by not-hatred only.' 20

"The king of Kôsala was executed together with his wife, but Dîrghâyu their son bought strong wine and made the guards drunk. When the night arrived he laid the bodies of his parents upon a funeral pyre and burned them with all honors and religious rites. 21

"When king Brahmadatta heard of it, he became afraid, for he thought, 'Dîrghâyu, the son of king Dîrghêti, will take revenge for the death of his parents, and if he espies a favorable occasion, he will assassinate me.' 22

"Young Dîrghâyu went to the forest and wept to his heart's content. Then he wiped his tears and returned to Benares. Hearing that assistants were wanted in the royal elephants' stable, he offered his services and was engaged by the master of the elephants. 23

"And it happened that the king heard a sweet voice ringing through the night and singing to the lute a beautiful song that gladdened his heart. And having inquired among his attendants who the singer might be, was told that the master of the elephants had in his service a young man of great accomplishments, and beloved by all his comrades. They said, 'He was wont to sing to the lute, and he must have been the singer that gladdened the heart of the king.' 24

"And the king ordered the young man before him and, being much pleased with Dîrghâyu, gave him employment in the royal castle. Observing how wisely the youth acted, how modest he was and yet punctilious in the performance of his work, the king very soon gave him a position of trust. 25

"Now it came to pass that the king went a hunting and became separated from his retinue, young Dîrghâyu alone remaining with him. And the king worn out from the hunt laid his head into the lap of young Dîrghâyu and slept. 26

"And Dîrghâyu thought: 'This king Brahmadatta has done us great injury; he robbed us of our kingdom and slew my father and my mother. He is now in my power.' Thinking thus he unsheathed his sword. 27

"Then Dîrghâyu thought of the last words of his father: 'Do not look long, do not look short. For not by hatred is hatred appeased. Hatred is appeased by not-hatred alone.' Thinking thus, he put his sword back into the sheath. 28

"The king became restless in his sleep and he awoke, and when the youth asked 'Why do you look frightened, O king?' he replied: 'My sleep is always restless because I often dream that young Dîrghâyu comes upon me with his sword. While I lay here with my head in your lap I dreamed the dreadful dream again; and I awoke full of terror and alarm.' 29

"Then the youth laying his left hand upon the defenceless king's head and with his right hand drawing his sword said: 'I am Dîrghâyu, the son of king Dîrghêti, whom you have robbed of his kingdom and slain together with his wife, my mother. The time of revenge has come.' 30

"The king seeing himself at the mercy of young Dîrghâyu raised his hands and said: 'Grant me my life, my dear Dîrghâyu, grant me my life, my dear Dîrghâyu!' 31

"And Dîrghâyu said without bitterness or ill-will. 'How can I grant you your life, O king, since my life is endangered by you. It is you, O king, who must grant me my life.' 32

"And the king said: 'Well, my dear Dîrghâyu, then grant me my life, and I will grant you your life.' 33

"Thus, king Brahmadatta of Kâshî and young Dîrghâyu granted each other life and took each other's hands and swore an oath not to do any harm to each other. 34

"And king Brahmadatta of Kâshî said to young Dîrghâyu: 'Why did your father say to you in the hour of his death: "Do not look long, do not look short, for hatred is not appeased by hatred. Hatred is appeased by not-hatred alone,"—what did your father mean by that?' 35

"The youth replied: 'When my father, O king, in the hour of his death said: "Not long," he meant let not your hatred last long. And when my father said, "Not short," he meant, Do not be hasty to fall out with your friends. And when he said, "For not by hatred is hatred appeased; hatred is appeased by not-hatred," he meant this: You have killed my father and mother, O king. If I should deprive you of life, then your partisans would deprive me of life; my partisans again would deprive those of life. Thus by hatred, hatred

would not be appeased. But now, O king, you have
granted me my life, and I have granted you your life;
thus by not-hatred hatred has been appeased.' 36

"Then king Brahmadatta of Kâshî thought: 'How
wise is young Dirghâyu that he understands in its full
extent the meaning of what his father spoke so con-
cisely.' 37

"And the king gave him back his father's troops and
vehicles, his realm, his treasuries, and store-houses,
and gave him his daughter in marriage." 38

When the Blessed One had told this story to the
bhikshus, he dismissed them. 39

And the bhikshus met in conference and investi-
gated the question of their dissensions, and having
come to the bottom of the matter, the concord of the
Sangha was re-established. 40

XXXIX. THE BHIKSHUS REBUKED.

And it happened that the Blessed One walked up
and down in the open air unshod. 1

When the elders saw that the Blessed One walked
unshod, they put away their shoes and did likewise.
But the novices did not mind the example of their elders
and kept their feet covered. 2

Some of the brethren noticed the irreverent beha-
vior of the novices and told the Blessed One; and the
Blessed One rebuked the novices and said: "If the
brethren, even now, while I am yet living, show so
little respect and courtesy to one another, what will
they do when I have passed away? 3

"And the Blessed One was filled with anxiety for
the welfare of the truth; and he continued: 4

"Even the laymen, O bhikshus, who move in the world, pursuing some handicraft that they may procure them a living, will be respectful, affectionate, and hospitable to their teachers. Do you, therefore, O bhikshus, so let your light shine forth, that you, having left the world and devoted your entire life to religion and to religious discipline, may observe the rules of decency, be respectful, affectionate, and hospitable to your teachers and superiors, or those who rank as your teachers and superiors. Your demeanor, O bhikshus, will not conduce to the conversion of the unconverted, and to the increase of the number of the faithful. It will serve, O bhikshus, to repel the unconverted and estrange them." 5

XL. DÊVADATTA.

When Dêvadatta, the son of the Suprabuddha, and a brother of Yashôdharâ, became a disciple, he cherished the hope of attaining the same distinctions and honors as Gautama Siddhârtha. His ambitions being disappointed, he conceived in his heart a jealous hatred, and, attempting to excel the Perfect One in virtue, he found fault with his regulations and reproved them as too lenient. 1

Dêvadatta went to Râjagriha and gained the ear of Ajâtashatru, the son of king Bimbisâra. And Ajâtashatru built a new vihâra for Dêvadatta, and founded a sect whose disciples were pledged to severe rules and self-mortification. 2

Soon afterwards the Blessed One himself came to Râjagriha and stayed at the Vênuvana vihâra. 3

Dêvadatta called on the Blessed One, requesting him to sanction his rules of greater stringency, in which

a greater holiness might be procured. "The body," he said, "consists of its thirty-two parts and has no divine attributes. It is conceived in sin and born in corruption. Its attributes are liability to pain and the dissolution of what is impermanent. It is the receptacle of karma which is the curse of our former existences; it is the dwelling-place of sin and diseases and its organs constantly discharge disgusting secretions. Its end is death and its goal the charnel house. Such being the condition of the body it behooves us to treat it as a carcass full of abomination and to clothe it in such rags only as have been gathered in cemeteries or upon
dung-hills." 4

The Blessed One said: "Truly, the body is full of impurity and its end is the charnel house, for it is impermanent and destined to be dissolved into its elements. But being the receptacle of karma, it lies in your power to make it a vessel of truth and not of sin. It is not good to indulge in the pleasures of the body, but neither is it good to neglect our bodily needs and to heap filth upon impurities. The lamp that is not cleansed and not filled with oil will be extinguished, and a body that is unkempt, unwashed, and weakened by penance will not be a fit receptacle for the light of truth. Your rules will not lead the disciples on the middle path which I have taught. Certainly, no one can be prevented from keeping more stringent rules, if he sees fit to do so, but they should not be imposed
upon any one, for they are unnecessary." 5

Thus the Tathâgata refused Dêvadatta's proposition; and Dêvadatta left Buddha and went into the vihâra speaking evil of the Lord's path of salvation as
too lenient and altogether insufficient. 6

When the Blessed One heard of Dêvadatta's intrigues, he said: "Amongst men there is no one who is not blamed. People blame him who sits silent and him who speaks, they also blame the man who preaches the middle path." 7

Dêvadatta instigated Ajâtashatru to plot against his father Bimbisâra, the king, to make himself king in the latter's place; and Bimbisâra died leaving the kingdom of Magadha to his son Ajâtashatru. 8

The new king listened to the evil advice of Dêvadatta, and he gave orders to take the life of the Tathâgata. However, the murderers sent out to kill the Lord could not perform their wicked deed, and became converted as soon as they saw him and listened to his preaching. The rock hurled down from a precipice upon the great Master split in twain, and both pieces passed by without doing him harm. The wild elephant let loose to destroy the Lord, became gentle in his presence; and Ajâtashatru, suffering greatly from the pangs of his conscience, went to the Blessed One and sought peace in his distress. 9

The Blessed One received Ajâtashatru kindly and taught him the way of salvation; but Dêvadatta still tried to become the founder of a religious school of his own. 10

Dêvadatta did not succeed in his plans and having been abandoned by many of his disciples, he fell sick, and he repented. He entreated those who had remained with him to carry his litter to Buddha, saying: "Take me, children, take me to him; though I have done evil to him, I am his brother-in-law. For the sake of our relationship Buddha will save me." And they obeyed, although reluctantly. 11

And Dêvadatta in his impatience to see the Blessed One rose from his litter while his carriers were wash-

ing their hands. But his feet burned under him; he
sank to the ground; and having repeated the praise
of Buddha died. 12

XLI. THE GOAL.

And the Blessed One thus addressed the bhik-
shus: 1

"It is through not understanding and grasping the
four noble truths, O bhikshus, that we have had to run
so long and to wander in this weary path of transmi-
gration, both you and I. 2

"The soul migrates through all forms, from the
stone, through plants and all kinds of animal bodies,
through men of various characters, until it reaches per-
fect enlightenment in the Buddha. 3

"All creatures are what they are through the karma
of their deeds done in former and in present exist-
ences. 4

"The rational nature of man is the spark of en-
lightenment, which, however, once procured will re-
main a lasting possession. But new births are required
to insure a transmigration to the summit of existence,
where the unmeasurable light is gained which is the
source of all righteousness. 5

"Having attained this higher birth, I have found
the truth and taught you the noble path that leads to
the glad city of peace. 6

"I have shown you the way to the lake of Ambro-
sia, which washes away all sin. 7

"I have given you the refreshing drink called the
perception of truth, and he who drinks it becomes free
from excitement, passion, and wrong-doing. 8

"The very gods envy the bliss of him who has escaped from the floods of passion and climbed the shores of Nirvâna. His heart is cleansed from all defilement and free from all illusion. 9

"He is like unto the lotus which grows in the water yet not a drop of water adheres to its petals. 10

"The man who walks in the noble path lives in the world, and yet his heart is not defiled by worldly desires. 11

"As a mother, even at the risk of her own life, protects her son, her only son, so he cultivates good-will without measure among all beings. 12

"Let a man remain steadfastly in this state of mind, whether he is standing or walking, awake or asleep, suffering from sickness, or enjoying good health, living or dying: for this state of heart is the best in the world. 13

"He who does not see the four noble truths has still a long path to traverse by repeated births through the desert of ignorance with its mirages of illusion and through the morasses of sin. 14

"But now they are grasped, the cause of further migrations and aberrations is removed. The goal is reached. The craving of selfishness is destroyed, and the truth is attained. 15

"This is true deliverance; this is salvation; this is heaven and the bliss of a life immortal." 16

XLII. MIRACLES FORBIDDEN.

Jyotishka, the son of Subhadra, was a householder living in Râjagriha. Having received a precious bowl of sandal-wood decorated with jewels, he erected a long pole before his house and put the bowl on its top with this legend: "Should a shramana take this bowl down without using a ladder or a stick with a hook, but by magic power, he shall receive whatever he desires." 1

And the people came to the Blessed One, full of wonder and their mouths overflowing with praise, saying: "Great is the Tathâgata. His disciples perform miracles. Kâshyapa, the disciple of Buddha, saw the bowl on Jyotishka's pole, and, stretching out his hand, he took it down, carrying it away in triumph to the vihâra." 2

When the Blessed One heard what had happened, he went to Kâshyapa, and, breaking the bowl to pieces, forbade his disciples to perform miracles of any kind. 3

Soon after this it happened that in one of the rainy seasons many bhikshus were staying in the Vriji territory during a famine. And one of the bhikshus proposed to his brethren that they should praise one another to the householders of the village, saying: "This bhikshu is a saint; he has seen celestial visions; and that bhikshu possesses supernatural gifts; he can work miracles." And the villagers said: "It is lucky, very lucky for us, that such saints are spending the rainy season with us." And they gave willingly and abundantly, and the bhikshus prospered and did not suffer from the famine. 4

When the Blessed One heard it, he told Ânanda to call the bhikshus together, and he asked them: "Tell me, O bhikshus, when does a bhikshu cease to be a bhikshu?" 5

And Shâriputra replied: 6

"An ordained disciple must not commit any unchaste act. The disciple who commits an unchaste act is no longer a disciple of the Shâkyamuni. 7

"Again, an ordained disciple must not take except what has been given him. The disciple who takes, be it so little as a penny's worth, is no longer a disciple of the Shâkyamuni. 8

"And lastly, an ordained disciple must not knowingly and malignantly deprive any harmless creature of life, not even an earth-worm or an ant. The disciple who knowingly and malignantly deprives any harmless creature of its life is no longer a disciple of the Shâkyamuni. 9

"These are the three great prohibitions." 10

And the Blessed One addressed the bhikshus and said: 11

"There is another great prohibition which I proclaim to you: 12

"An ordained disciple must not boast of any superhuman perfection. The disciple who with evil intent and from covetousness boasts of a superhuman perfection, be it celestial visions or miracles, is no longer a disciple of the Shâkyamuni. 13

"I forbid you, O bhikshus, to employ any spells or supplications, for they are useless, since the law of karma governs all things. He who attempts to perform miracles has not understood the doctrine of the Tathâgata." 14

XLIII. THE VANITY OF WORLDLINESS.

There was a poet by the name of Che who had acquired the spotless eye of truth, and he believed in Buddha, whose doctrine gave him peace of mind and comfort in the hour of affliction. 1

And it happened that an epidemic swept over the country in which he lived, so that many died, and the people were terrified. Some of them trembled with fright, and in anticipation of their fate were smitten with all the horrors of death before they died, while others began to be merry, shouting loudly, "Let us enjoy ourselves to-day, for we know not whether to-morrow we shall live"; yet was their laughter no genuine gladness, but a mere pretence and affectation. 2

Among all these worldly men and women trembling with anxiety, the Buddhist poet lived in the time of the pestilence, as usual, calm and undisturbed, helping wherever he could and ministering unto the sick, soothing their pains by medicine and religious consolation. 3

And a man came to him and said: 4

"My heart is nervous and excited, for I see people die. I am not anxious about others, but I tremble because of myself. Help me; cure me of my fear." 5

And the poet said: "There is help for him who has compassion on others, but there is no help for thee so long as thou clingest to thine own self alone. Hard times try the souls of men and teach them righteousness and charity. Canst thou witness these sad sights around thee and still be filled with selfishness? Canst thou see thy brothers, sisters, and friends suffer, yet not forget the petty cravings and lust of thy own heart?" 6

Observing the desolation in the soul of the pleasure-seeking man, the Buddhist poet composed this song and taught it to the brethren in the vihâra: 7

"Unless you take refuge in Buddha and find rest in
Nirvâna
Everything is vanity—desolation and vanity.
To see the world is idle, and to enjoy life is empty.
The world, including man, is but like a phantom, and
the hope of heaven is as a mirage. 8

The worldling seeks pleasures and fattens himself like a caged fowl.
But the Buddhist saint flies up to the sun like the wild crane.
The fowl in the coop has her food, but she will soon be boiled in the pot.
No provisions are given to the wild crane, but the heavens and the earth are his." 9

And the poet Che said: "The times are hard and teach the people a lesson; yet do they not heed it." And he composed another poem on the vanity of worldliness: 10

"It is good to reform, and it is good to exhort people to reform.
The things of the world will be all swept away.
Let others be busy and buried with care.
My mind all unvexed shall be pure. 11

After pleasures they hanker and find no satisfaction;
Riches they covet and can never have enough.
They are like unto puppets held up by a string.
When the string breaks they come down with a shock. 12

In the domain of death there are neither great nor small;
Neither gold nor silver is used, nor precious jewels.
No distinction is made between the high and the low.
And daily the dead are buried beneath the fragrant sod. 13

Look at the sun setting behind the western hills.
You lie down to rest, but soon the cock will announce the returning morn.
Reform to-day and do not wait until it be too late.
Do not say it is early, for the time quickly passes by. 14

It is good to reform and it is good to exhort people to
reform,
It is good to lead a life of righteousness and take refuge in Buddha's name.
Your talents may reach to the skies, your wealth may
be untold—
But all is vain unless you attain the peace of Nirvâna." 15

XLIV. PRECEPTS FOR THE NOVICES.

The novices of the order came to Buddha and asked him concerning the precepts which they had to practise, and the Blessed One said: 1

"Those who wish to enter upon the path so as to be truly converted and become faithful followers of Buddha must attend to four things: Firstly they must keep companionship with the good. Secondly, they must hear the law. Thirdly, they must seek enlightenment by reflexion, and fourthly, they must practise virtue. These, O novices, are the four stages of the path. 2

"Lest there be any doubt about your habits of life, I prescribe to you ten precepts. 3

"The ten precepts prescribed to novices are: abstinence from destroying life; abstinence from stealing: abstinence from impurity; abstinence from lying; abstinence from intoxicating liquors; abstinence from eating at forbidden times; abstinence from dancing and seeing spectacles; abstinence from garlands, scents, unguents, ornaments, and finery; abstinence from the use of high or broad beds; abstinence from accepting gold or silver. 4

"I prescribe, O bhikshus, these ten precepts for the exercise of the novices." 5

XLV. RULES FOR THE ORDER.

And Buddha said: 1
"Who is the good man? The religious man is
good. And who is religious? He who agrees with
truth. 2
"Who is the strong man? The patient man is
strong, for he has conquered self and all the petulance
of self. He is calm, enduring, and blameless. 3
"Who is the wise man? He who has obtained in-
sight into the nature of his own being. He keeps his
mind free from the pollution of selfishness and leads a
life of truth." 4
And the Blessed One addressed the bhikshus and
gave them these rules of restriction: 5
"Do not destroy life. Do not take that which is not
given. Do not tell lies. Abstain from intoxication.
Commit no adultery. 6
"These are the five commandments which I give
unto you all, and for those who take the vow I enjoin in
addition the following three rules: 7
"Do not eat food at night. Do not wear garlands
or perfumes. Do not sleep in soft couches but on mats
spread on the ground. 8
"Moreover he who is of a pious mind will observe
the Upavasatha or Sabbath and take delight in sus-
taining the order according to his ability." 9

XLVI. THE TEN COMMANDMENTS.

Buddha said: "All acts of living creatures become bad by ten things, and by avoiding the ten things they

become good. There are three sins of the body, four
sins of the tongue, and three sins of the mind. 1

"The three sins of the body are, murder, theft,
and adultery. 2

"The four sins of the tongue are, lying, slander,
abuse, and idle talk. 3

"The three sins of the mind are, covetousness,
hatred, and error. 4

"Therefore, I give you these commandments: 5

"Kill not, but have regard for life. 6

"Steal not, neither do ye rob; but help everybody
to be master of the fruits of his labor. 7

"Abstain from all impurity, and lead a life of chas-
tity. 8

"Lie not, but be truthful, and speak the truth with
discretion, not so as to do harm, but in a loving heart
and wisely. 9

"Invent not evil reports, neither do ye repeat them.
Carp not, but look for the good sides of your fellow-
beings, so that you may with sincerity defend them
against their enemies. 10

"Swear not, but speak decently and with dignity. 11

"Waste not the time with empty words, but speak
to the purpose or keep silence. 12

"Covet not, nor envy, but rejoice at the fortunes of
other people. 13

"Cleanse your heart of malice; cast out all anger,
spite, and ill-will; cherish no hatred, not even against
your slanderer, nor against those who do you harm, but
embrace all living beings with kindness and benevo-
lence. 14

"Free your mind of ignorance and be anxious to
learn the truth, especially in the one thing that is
needed, lest you fall a prey either to scepticism or to

errors. Scepticism will make you indifferent and errors will lead you astray so that you shall not find the noble path that leads to life eternal." 15

XLVII. THE PREACHER'S MISSION.

And the Blessed One said to his disciples: 1

"When I have passed away and can no longer address you, and edify your minds with religious discourse, select from among you men of good family and education to preach the truth in my stead. And let those men be invested with the robes of the Tathâgata, let them enter into the abode of the Tathâgata, and occupy the pulpit of the Tathâgata. 2

"The robe of the Tathâgata is sublime forbearance and patience. The abode of the Tathâgata is charity and love of all beings. The pulpit of the Tathâgata is the comprehension of the good law in its abstract meaning as well as in its particular application. 3

"The preacher must propound the truth with unshrinking mind. He must have the power of persuasion rooted in virtue and in strict fidelity to his vows. 4

"The preacher must keep in his proper sphere and be steady in his course. He must not flatter his vanity by seeking the company of the great. Nor must he keep company with persons who are frivolous and immoral. When in temptation, he should constantly think of Buddha and he will conquer. 5

"All who come to hear the doctrine, the preacher must receive with benevolence, and his sermon must be without invidiousness. 6

"The preacher must not be prone to carp at others, or to blame other preachers; nor speak scandal, nor propagate bitter words. He must not mention by name

other disciples to vituperate them and reproach their
demeanor. 7

"Clad in a clean robe, dyed with good color, with
appropriate undergarments, he must ascend the pulpit
with a mind free from blame and at peace with the
whole world. 8

"He must not take delight in quarrelous disputa-
tions or engage in controversies so as to show the
superiority of his talents, but be calm and composed. 9

"No hostile feelings shall reside in his heart, and
he must never abandon the disposition of charity to-
ward all beings. His sole aim must be that all beings
become Buddhas. 10

"Let the preacher apply himself with zeal to his
work, and the Tathâgata will show to him the body of
the holy law in its transcendent glory. He shall be
honored as one whom the Tathâgata has blessed. The
Tathâgata blesses the preacher and also those who
reverently listen to him and joyfully accept the doc-
trine. 11

"All those who receive the truth will find perfect
enlightenment. And, verily, such is the power of the
doctrine that even by the reading of a single stanza,
or by reciting, copying, and keeping in mind a single
sentence of the good law, persons may be converted to
the truth and enter the path of righteousness which
leads to deliverance from evil. 12

"Creatures that are swayed by impure passions,
when they listen to the voice, will be purified. The
ignorant who are infatuated with the follies of the
world will, when pondering on the profundity of the
doctrine, acquire wisdom. Those who act under the
impulse of hatred will, when taking refuge in Buddha,
be filled with good-will and love. 13

"A preacher must be full of energy and cheerful hope, never tiring and never despairing of final success. 14

"A preacher must be like a man who in quest of water digs a well in an arid tract of land. So long as he sees that the sand is dry and white, he knows that the water is still far off. But let him not be troubled or give up the task as hopeless. The work of removing the dry sand must be done so that he can dig down deeper into the ground. And often the deeper he has to dig, the cooler and purer and more refreshing will the water be. 15

"When after some time of digging he sees that the sand becomes moist, he accepts it as a foretoken that the water is near. 16

"So long as the people do not listen to the words of truth, the preacher knows that he has to dig deeper into their hearts; but when they begin to heed his words he apprehends that they will soon attain enlightenment. 17

"Into your hands, O ye men of good family and education who take the vow of preaching the words of the Tathâgata, the Blessed One transfers, intrusts, and commands the good law of truth. 18

"Receive the good law of truth, keep it, read and re-read it, fathom it, promulgate it, and preach it to all beings in all the quarters of the universe. 19

"The Tathâgata is not avaricious, nor narrow-minded, and he is willing to impart the perfect Buddha-knowledge unto all who are ready and willing to receive it. Be ye like unto him. Imitate him and follow his example in bounteously giving, showing, and bestowing the truth. 20

"Gather round you hearers who love to listen to

the benign and comforting words of the law; rouse the unbelievers to accept the truth and fill them with delight and joy. Quicken them, edify them, and lift them higher and higher until they see the truth face to
face in all its splendor and infinite glory." 21

When the Blessed One had thus spoken, the disciples said: 22

"O thou who rejoicest in kindness having its source in compassion, thou great cloud of good qualities and of benevolent mind, thou quenchest the fire that vexeth living beings, thou pourest out nectar, the rain of the law! 23

"We shall do, O Lord, what the Tathâgata commands. We shall fulfil his behest; the Lord shall find us obedient to his words." 24

And this vow of the disciples resounded through the universe, and like an echo it came back from all the Bôdhisattvas who are to be and will come to preach the good law of Truth. 25

And the Blessed One said: "The Tathâgata is like unto a powerful king who rules his kingdom with righteousness, but being attacked by envious enemies goes out to wage war against his foes. When the king sees his soldiers fighting he is delighted with their gallantry and will bestow upon them donations of all kinds. Ye are the soldiers of the Tathâgata, while Mâra, the Evil One, is the enemy who must be conquered. And the Tathâgata will give to his soldiers the city of Nirvâna, the great capital of the good law. And when the enemy is overcome, the Dharma-râja, the great king of truth, will bestow upon all his disciples the most precious crown jewel which brings perfect enlightenment, supreme wisdom, and undisturbed peace." 26

BUDDHA, THE TEACHER.

XLVIII. THE DHARMAPADA.

THIS is the Dharmapada, the path of religion pursued by those who are Buddha's followers: 1

All that we are is the result of what we have thought: it is founded on our thoughts, it is made up of our thoughts. 2

By oneself evil is done; by oneself one suffers; by oneself evil is left undone; by oneself one is purified. Purity and impurity belong to oneself, no one can purify another. 3

You yourself must make an effort. The Tathâgatas are only preachers. The thoughtful who enter the way are freed from the bondage of Mâra. 4

He who does not rouse himself when it is time to rise, who, though young and strong, is full of sloth, whose will and thoughts are weak, that lazy and idle man will never find the way to enlightenment. 5

If a man hold himself dear, let him watch himself carefully; the truth guards him who guards his self. 6

If a man makes himself as he teaches others to be, then, being himself subdued, he may subdue others; one's own self is indeed difficult to subdue. 7

If one man conquers in battle a thousand times a thousand men, and if another conquer himself, he is the greatest of conquerors. 8

It is the habit of fools, be they laymen or members of the clergy, to think, "this is done by *me*. May others be subject to *me*. In this or that transaction a prominent part should be played by *me*." Fools do not care for the duty to be performed or the aim to be reached, but think of their self alone. Everything is but a pedestal of their vanity. 9

Bad deeds, and deeds hurtful to ourselves, are easy to do; what is beneficial and good, that is very difficult to do. 10

If anything is to be done, let a man do it, let him attack it vigorously! 11

Before long, alas! this body will lie on the earth, despised, without understanding, like a useless log; yet our thoughts will endure. They will be thought again, and will produce action. Good thoughts will produce good actions, and bad thoughts will produce bad actions. 12

Earnestness is the path of immortality, thoughtlessness the path of death. Those who are in earnest do not die; those who are thoughtless are as if dead already. 13

Those who imagine truth in untruth, and see untruth in truth, never arrive at truth, but follow vain desires. They who know truth in truth, and untruth in untruth, arrive at truth, and follow true desires. 14

As rain breaks through an ill-thatched house, passion will break through an unreflecting mind. As rain does not break through a well-thatched house, passion will not break through a well-reflecting mind. 15

Well-makers lead the water wherever they like; fletchers bend the arrow; carpenters bend a log of wood; wise people fashion themselves; wise people falter not amidst blame and praise. Having listened to the law, they become serene, like a deep, smooth, and still lake. 16

If a man speaks or acts with an evil thought, pain follows him as the wheel follows the foot of the ox that draws the carriage. 17

An evil deed is better left undone, for a man will repent of it afterwards; a good deed is better done, for having done it one will not repent. 18

If a man commits a sin let him not do it again; let him not delight in sin; pain is the outcome of evil. If a man does what is good, let him do it again; let him delight in it; happiness is the outcome of good. 19

Let no man think lightly of evil, saying in his heart, "It will not come nigh unto me." As by the falling of water-drops a water-pot is filled, so the fool becomes full of evil, though he gather it little by little. 20

Let no man think lightly of good, saying in his heart, "It will not come nigh unto me." As by the falling of water-drops a water-pot is filled, so the wise man becomes full of good, though he gather it little by little. 21

He who lives for pleasure only, his senses uncontrolled, immoderate in his food, idle, and weak, him Mâra, the tempter, will certainly overthrow, as the wind throws down a weak tree. He who lives without looking for pleasures, his senses well-controlled, moderate in his food, faithful and strong, him Mâra will certainly not overthrow, any more than the wind throws down a rocky mountain. 22

The fool who knows his foolishness, is wise at least so far. But a fool who thinks himself wise, he is a fool indeed. 23

To the sinful man sin appears sweet as honey; he looks upon it as pleasant so long as it bears no fruit; but when its fruit ripens, then he looks upon it as sin.

And so the good man looks upon the goodness of the dharma as a burden and an evil so long as it bears no fruit; but when its fruit ripens, then he sees its goodness. 24

A hater may do great harm to a hater, or an enemy to an enemy; but a wrongly-directed mind will do greater mischief unto himself. A mother, a father, or any other relative will do much good; but a well-directed mind will do greater service unto himself. 25

He whose wickedness is very great brings himself down to that state where his enemy wishes him to be. He himself is his greatest enemy. Thus a creeper destroys the life of a tree on which it finds support. 26

Do not direct thy thought to what gives pleasure, that thou mayest not cry out when burning, "This is pain." The wicked man burns by his own deeds, as if burnt by fire. 27

Pleasures destroy the foolish; the foolish man by his thirst for pleasures destroys himself as if he were his own enemy. The fields are damaged by hurricanes and weeds; mankind is damaged by passion, by hatred, by vanity, and by lust. 28

Let no man ever take into consideration whether a thing is pleasant or unpleasant. The love of pleasure begets grief and the dread of pain causes fear; he who is free from the love of pleasure and the dread of pain knows neither grief nor fear. 29

He who gives himself to vanity, and does not give himself to meditation, forgetting the real aim of life and grasping at pleasure, will in time envy him who has exerted himself in meditation. 30

The fault of others is easily perceived, but that of oneself is difficult to perceive. A man winnows his neighbor's faults like chaff, but his own fault he hides, as a cheat hides the false die from the gambler. 31

If a man looks after the faults of others, and is always inclined to take offence, his own passions will grow, and he is far from the destruction of passions. 32

Not about the perversities of others, not about their sins of commission or omission, but about his own misdeeds and negligences alone should a sage be worried. 33

Good people shine from afar, like the snowy mountains; bad people are not seen, like arrows shot by night. 34

If a man by causing pain to others, wishes to obtain pleasure for himself, he, entangled in the bonds of selfishness, will never be free from hatred. 35

Let a man overcome anger by love, let him overcome evil by good; let him overcome the greedy by liberality, the liar by truth! 36

For hatred does not cease by hatred at any time; hatred ceases by love, this is an old rule. 37

Speak the truth, do not yield to anger; give, if thou art asked; by these three steps thou wilt become divine. 38

Let a wise man blow off the impurities of his self, as a smith blows off the impurities of silver, one by one, little by little, and from time to time. 39

Lead others, not by violence, but by law and equity. 40

He who possesses virtue and intelligence, who is just, speaks the truth, and does what is his own business, him the world will hold dear. 41

As the bee collects nectar and departs without injuring the flower, or its color or scent, so let a sage dwell in the village. 42

If a traveller does not meet with one who is his better, or his equal, let him firmly keep to his solitary journey; there is no companionship with a fool. 43

Long is the night to him who is awake; long is a mile to him who is tired; long is life to the foolish who do not know the true religion. 44

Better than living a hundred years, not seeing the highest religion, is one day in the life of a man who sees the highest religion. 45

Some form their dharma arbitrarily and fabricate it artificially; they advance complex speculations and imagine that good results are attainable only by the acceptance of their theories; yet the truth is but one; there are not many different truths in the world. Having reflected on the various theories, we have gone into the yoke with him who has shaken off all sin. But shall we be able to proceed together with him? 46

The best of ways is the eightfold. This is the way, there is no other that leads to the purifying of intelligence. Go on this way! Everything else is the deceit of Mâra, the tempter. If you go on this way, you will make an end of pain! Says the Tathâgata, The way was preached by me, when I had understood the removal of the thorn in the flesh. 47

Not only by discipline and vows, not only by much learning, do I earn the happiness of release which no worldling can know. Bhikshu, be not confident as long as thou hast not attained the extinction of thirst. The extinction of sinful desire is the highest religion. 48

The gift of religion exceeds all gifts; the sweetness of religion exceeds all sweetness; the delight in religion exceeds all delights; the extinction of thirst overcomes all pain. 49

Few are there among men who cross the river and

reach the goal. The great multitudes are running up and down the shore; but there is no suffering for him who has finished his journey. 50

As the lily will grow full of sweet perfume and delight upon a heap of rubbish, thus the disciple of the truly enlightened Buddha shines forth by his wisdom among those who are like rubbish, among the people that walk in darkness. 51

Let us live happily then, not hating those who hate us! among men who hate us let us dwell free from hatred! 52

Let us live happily then, free from all ailments among the ailing! among men who are ailing let us dwell free from ailments! 53

Let us live happily, then, free from greed among the greedy! among men who are greedy let us dwell free from greed! 54

The sun is bright by day, the moon shines by night, the warrior is bright in his armor, thinkers are bright in their meditation; but among all the brightest with splendor day and night is Buddha, the Awakened, the Holy, the Blessed. 55

XLIX. THE TWO BRAHMANS.

At one time when the Blessed One was journeying through Kôsala he came to the Brahman village which is called Manasâkrita. There he stayed in a mango grove. 1

And two young Brahmans came to him who were of different schools. One was named Vâsishtha and the other Bhâradvâja. And Vâsishtha said to the Blessed One: 2

"We have a dispute as to the true path. I say the

straight path which leads unto a union with Brahma is that which has been announced by the Brahman Paushkarasâdi, while my friend says the straight path which leads unto a union with Brahma is that which has been announced by the Brahman Târukshya. 3

"Now, regarding your high reputation, O shramana, and knowing that you are called the Enlightened One, the teacher of men and gods, the Blessed Buddha, we have come to ask you, are all these paths saving paths? There are many roads all around our village, and all lead to Manasâkrita. Is it just so with the paths of the Brahmans? Are all paths saving paths?" 4

And the Blessed One proposed these questions to the two Brahmans: "Do you think that all paths are right?" 5

Both answered and said: "Yes, Gautama, we think so." 6

"But tell me," continued Buddha, "has any one of the Brahmans, versed in the Vêdas, seen Brahma face to face?" 7

"No, Sir!" was the reply. 8

"But, then," said the Blessed One, "has any teacher of the Brahmans, versed in the Vêdas, seen Brahma face to face?" 9

The two Brahmans said: "No, Sir." 10

"But, then," said the Blessed One, "has any one of the authors of the Vêdas seen Brahma face to face?" 11

Again the two Brahmans denied the question, and the Blessed One proposed an illustration; he said: 12

"It is as if a man should make a staircase in the place where four roads cross, to mount up into a mansion. And people should ask him, 'Where, good

friend, is this mansion, to mount up into which you
are making this staircase; do you know whether it is
in the east, or in the south, or in the west, or in the north?
Whether it is high, or low, or of medium size?' And
when so asked he should answer, 'I know it not.' And
people should say to him, 'But, then, good friend, you
are making a staircase to mount up into something—
taking it for a mansion—which all the while you know
not, neither have you seen it.' And when so asked he
should answer, 'That is exactly what I do.' What
would you think of him? Would you not say that the
talk of that man was foolish talk?" 13

"In sooth, Gautama," said the two Brahmans, "it
would be foolish talk!" 14

The Blessed One continued: "Then the Brahmans
should say, 'We show you the way unto a union of
what we know not and what we have seen not.' This
being the substance of Brahman lore, does it not fol-
low that their task is vain?" 15

"It does follow," replied Bhâradvâja. 16

Said the Blessed One: "Thus it is impossible that Brahmans versed in the three Vêdas should be able to show the way to a state of union with that which they neither know nor have seen. Just as when a string of blind men are clinging one to the other. Neither can the foremost see, nor can those in the middle see, nor can the hindmost see. Even so, methinks, the talk of the Brahmans versed in the three Vêdas is but blind talk; it is ridiculous, consists of mere words, and is a
vain and empty thing." 17

"Now suppose," added the Blessed One, "that a man should come hither to the bank of the river, and, having some business on the other side, should want to cross. Do you suppose that if he were to invoke the other bank of the river to come over to him on this side, the bank would come on account of his praying?" 18

"Certainly not, Gautama." 19

"Yet this is the way of the Brahmans. They omit the practice of those qualities which really make a man a Brahman, and say, 'Indra, we call upon you; Sôma, we call upon you; Varuna, we call upon you; Brahma, we call upon you.' Verily, it is not possible that these Brahmans, on account of their invocations, prayers, and praises, should after death be united with Brahma." 20

"Now tell me," continued Buddha, "what do the Brahmans say of Brahma? Is his mind full of lust?" 21

And when the Brahmans denied the question, Buddha asked: "Is Brahma's mind full of malice, sloth, or pride?" 22

'No, sir!" was the reply. 23

And Buddha went on: "But are the Brahmans free of these vices?" 24

"No, sir!" said Vâsishtha. 25

The Holy One said: "The Brahmans cling to the five things leading to worldliness and yield to the temptations of the senses; they are entangled in the five hindrances, lust, malice, sloth, pride, and doubt. How can they be united to that which is most unlike their nature? Therefore the threefold wisdom of the Brahmans is a waterless desert, a pathless jungle, and a hopeless desolation." 26

When Buddha had thus spoken, one of the Brahmans said: "We are told, Gautama, that the Shâkyamuni knows the path to a union with Brahma." 27

And the Blessed One said: "What do you think, O Brahmans, of a man born and brought up in Mana-

sâkrita? Would he be in doubt about the directest way
from this spot to Manasâkrita?" 28

"Certainly not, Gautama." 29

"Thus," replied Buddha, "the Tathâgata knows
the straight path that leads to a union with Brahma.
He knows it as one who has entered the world of
Brahma and has been born in it. There can be no
doubt in him." 30

And the two young Brahmans said: "If you know
the way show it to us." 31

And Buddha said: 32

"The Tathâgata sees the universe face to face and
understands its nature. He proclaims the truth both
in its letter and in its spirit, and his doctrine is lovely
in its origin, lovely in its progress, lovely in its con-
summation. The Tathâgata reveals the higher life in
its purity and perfection. 33

"The Tathâgata lets his mind pervade the four
quarters of the world with thoughts of love. And thus
the whole wide world, above, below, around, and every-
where will continue to be filled with love, far-reaching,
grown great, and beyond measure. 34

"Just as a mighty trumpeter makes himself heard
—and that without difficulty—in all the four quarters
of the earth; even so is the coming of the Tathâgata:
there is not one living creature that the Tathâgata
passes by or leaves aside, but regards them all with
mind set free, and deep-felt love. 35

"And this is the sign that a man follows the right
path: Uprightness is his delight, and he sees danger
in the least of those things which he should avoid. He
trains himself in the commands of morality, he encom-
passeth himself with holiness in word and deed; he
sustains life by means that are quite pure; good is his

conduct, guarded is the door of his senses; mindful and self-possessed, he is altogether happy. 36

"He who walks in the eightfold noble path with unswerving determination is sure to reach Nirvâna. The Tathâgata anxiously watches over his children and with loving care helps them to see the light. 37

"When a hen has eight or ten or twelve eggs, over which she has properly brooded, the wish arises in her heart, 'O would that my little chickens should break open the egg-shell with their claws, or with their beaks, and come forth into the light in safety!' yet all the while those little chickens are sure to break the egg-shell and will come forth into the light in safety. Even so, a brother who with firm determination walks in the noble path is sure to come forth into the light, sure to reach up to the higher wisdom, sure to attain to the highest bliss of enlightenment." 38

L. GUARD THE SIX QUARTERS.

While the Blessed One was staying at the bamboo grove near Râjagriha, he once met on his way Srigâla, a householder, who, clasping his hands, turned to the four quarters of the world, to the zenith above, and to the nadir below. And the Blessed One, knowing that this was done according to the traditional religious superstition to avert evil, asked Srigâla: "Why are you performing these strange ceremonies?" 1

And Srigâla in reply said: "Do you think it strange that I protect my home against the influences of demons? I know thou wouldst fain tell me, O Gautama Shâkyamuni, whom people call the Tathâgata and the Blessed Buddha, that incantations are of no avail and possess no saving power. But listen to me and know, that in performing this rite I honor, reverence, and keep sacred the words of my father." 2

Then the Tathâgata said: 3

"You do well, O Srigâla, to honor, reverence, and keep sacred the words of your father; and it is your duty to protect your home, your wife, your children, and the children of your children against the hurtful influences of evil spirits. I find no fault with the performance of your father's rite. But I find that you do not understand the ceremony. Let the Tathâgata, who is now speaking to you as a spiritual father and loves you not less than did your parents, explain to you the meaning of the six directions. 4

"To guard your home by mysterious ceremonies is not sufficient; you must guard it by good deeds. Turn to your parents in the East, to your teachers in the South, to your wife and children in the West, to your friends in the North, and regulate the zenith of your religious relations above you, and the nadir of your servants below you. 5

"Such is the religion your father wants you to have, and the performance of the ceremony shall remind you of your duties." 6

And Srigâla looked up to the Blessed One with reverence as to his father and said: "Truly, Gautama, thou art Buddha, the Blessed One, the holy teacher. I never knew what I was doing, but now I know. Thou hast revealed to me the truth that was hidden as one who brings a lamp into the darkness. I take my refuge in the Enlightened Teacher, in the truth that enlightens, and in the community of brethren who have found the truth." 7

LI. SIMHA'S QUESTION CONCERNING ANNIHILATION.

At that time many distinguished citizens were sitting together assembled in the town-hall and spoke in many ways in praise of the Buddha, of the Dharma, and of the Sangha. Simha, the general-in-chief, a disciple of the Nirgrantha sect, was sitting among them. And Simha thought: "Truly, the Blessed One must be Buddha, the Holy One. I will go and visit him." 1

Then Simha, the general, went to the place where the Nirgrantha chief, Jnyâtaputra, was; and having approached him, he said: "I wish, Lord, to visit the shramana Gautama." 2

Jnyâtaputra said: "Why should you, Simha, who believe in the result of actions according to their moral merit, go to visit the shramana Gautama, who denies the result of actions? The shramana Gautama, O Simha, denies the result of actions; he teaches the doctrine of non-action; and in this doctrine he trains his disciples." 3

Then the desire to go and visit the Blessed One, which had arisen in Simha, the general, abated. 4

Hearing again the praise of the Buddha, of the Dharma, and of the Sangha, Simha asked the Nirgrantha chief a second time; and again Jnyâtaputra persuaded him not to go. 5

When a third time the general heard some men of distinction extol the merits of the Buddha, the Dharma, and the Sangha, the general thought: "Truly the shramana Gautama must be the Holy Buddha. What are the Nirgranthas to me, whether they give their con-

sent or not? I shall go without asking their permission
to visit him, the Blessed One, the Holy Buddha." 6

And Simha, the general, said to the Blessed One: "I have heard, Lord, that the shramana Gautama denies the result of actions; he teaches the doctrine of non-action, saying that the actions of sentient beings do not receive their reward, for he teaches annihilation and the contemptibleness of all things; and in this doctrine he trains his disciples. Do you teach the doing away of the soul and the burning away of man's being? Pray tell me, Lord, do those who speak thus say the truth, or do they bear false witness against the Blessed One, passing off a spurious dharma as your dharma?" 7

The Blessed One said: 8

"There is a way, Simha, in which one who says so, is speaking truly of me; on the other hand, Simha, there is a way in which one who says the opposite is speaking truly of me, too. Listen, and I will tell you: 9

"I teach, Simha, the not-doing of such actions as are unrighteous, either by deed, or by word, or by thought; I teach the not bringing about of all those conditions of heart which are evil and not good. However, I teach, Simha, the doing of such actions as are righteous, by deed, by word, and by thought; I teach the bringing about of all those conditions of heart which are good and not evil. 10

"I teach, Simha, that all the conditions of heart which are evil and not good, unrighteous actions by deed, by word, and by thought, must be burnt away. He who has freed himself, Simha, from all those conditions of heart which are evil and not good, he who has destroyed them as a palm-tree which is rooted out, so that they cannot grow up again, such a man has accomplished the eradication of self." 11

"I proclaim, Simha, the annihilation of egotism, of lust, of ill-will, of delusion. However, I do not proclaim the annihilation of forbearance, of love, of charity, and of truth. 12

"I deem, Simha, unrighteous actions contemptible, whether they be performed by deed, or by word, or by thought; but I deem virtue and righteousness praiseworthy. 13

And Simha said: "One doubt still lurks in my mind concerning the doctrine of the Blessed One. Will the Blessed One consent to clear the cloud away so that I may understand the dharma as the Blessed One teaches it." 14

The Tathâgata having given his consent, Simha said: "I am a soldier, O Blessed One, and am appointed by the king to enforce his laws and to wage his wars. Does the Tathâgata who teaches kindness without end and compassion with all sufferers, permit the punishment of the criminal? and further, does the Tathâgata declare that it is wrong to go to war for the protection of our homes, our wives, our children, and our property? Does the Tathâgata teach the doctrine of a complete self-surrender, so that I should suffer the evil-doer to do what he pleases and yield submissively to him who threatens to take by violence what is my own? Does the Tathâgata maintain that all strife, including such warfare as is waged for a righteous cause, should be forbidden?" 15

Buddha replied: "The Tathâgata says: He who deserves punishment must be punished, and he who is worthy of favor must be favored. Yet at the same time he teaches to do no injury to any living being but to be full of love and kindness. These injunctions are not contradictory, for whosoever must be punished for the crimes which he has committed, suffers his injury not through the ill-will of the judge but on account of his evil-doing. His own acts have brought upon him the injury that the executer of the law inflicts. When a magistrate punishes, let him not harbor hatred in his breast, yet a murderer, when put to death, should consider that this is the fruit of his own act. As soon as he will understand that the punishment will purify his soul, he will no longer lament his fate but rejoice at it." 16

And the Blessed One continued: "The Tathâgata teaches that all warfare in which man tries to slay his brother is lamentable, but he does not teach that those who go to war in a righteous cause after having exhausted all means to preserve the peace are blameworthy. He must be blamed who is the cause of war. 17

"The Tathâgata teaches a complete surrender of self, but he does not teach a surrender of anything to those powers that are evil, be they men or gods or the elements of nature. Struggle must be, for all life is a struggle of some kind. But he that struggles should look to it lest he struggle in the interest of self against truth and righteousness. 18

"He who struggles in the interest of self, so that he himself may be great or powerful or rich or famous, will have no reward, but he who struggles for righteousness and truth, will have great reward, for even his defeat will be a victory. 19

"Self is not a fit vessel to receive any great success; self is small and brittle and its contents will soon be spilt for the benefit, and perhaps also for the curse, of others. 20

"Truth, however, is large enough to receive the

yearnings and aspirations of all selfs, and when the selfs break like soap-bubbles, their contents will be preserved and in the truth they will lead a life everlasting. 21

"He who goeth to battle, O Simha, even though it be in a righteous cause, must be prepared to be slain by his enemies, for that is the destiny of warriors; and should his fate overtake him he has no reason for complaint. 22

"But he who is victorious should remember the instability of earthly things. His success may be great, but be it ever so great the wheel of life may turn again and bring him down into the dust. 23

"However, if he moderates himself and, extinguishing all hatred in his heart lifts his down-trodden adversary up and says to him, 'come. now and make peace and let us be brothers,' he will gain a victory that is not a transient success, for its fruits will remain forever. 24

"Great is a successful general, O Simha, but he who has conquered self is the greater victor. 25

"The doctrine of the conquest of self, O Simha, is not taught to destroy the souls of men, but to preserve them. He who has conquered self is more fit to live, to be successful, and to gain victories than he who is the slave of self. 26

"He whose mind is free from the illusion of self, will stand and not fall in the battle of life. 27

"He whose intentions are righteousness and justice, will meet with no failure, but be successful in his enterprises and his success will endure. 28

"He who harbors in his heart love of truth will live and not die, for he has drunk the water of immortality. 29

"Struggle then, O general, courageously; and fight your battles vigorously, but be a soldier of truth and the Tathâgata will bless you." 30

When the Blessed One had spoken thus, Simha, the general, said: "Glorious Lord, glorious Lord! Thou hast revealed the truth. Great is the doctrine of the Blessed One. Thou, indeed, art the Buddha, the Tathâgata, the Holy One. Thou art the teacher of mankind. Thou showest us the road of salvation, for this indeed is true deliverance. He who follows thee will not miss the light to enlighten his path. He will find blessedness and peace. I take my refuge, Lord, in the Blessed One, and in his doctrine, and in his brotherhood. May the Blessed One receive me from this day forth while my life lasts as a disciple who has taken refuge in him." 31

And the Blessed One said: "Consider first, Simha, what you are doing. It is becoming that persons of rank like you do nothing without due consideration." 32

Simha's faith in the Blessed One increased. He replied: "Had other teachers, Lord, succeeded in making me their disciple, they would carry around their banners through the whole city of Vaishâlî, shouting: 'Simha, the general has become our disciple! For the second time, Lord, I take my refuge in the Blessed One, and in the Dharma, and in the Sangha; may the Blessed One receive me from this day forth while my life lasts as a disciple who has taken his refuge in him." 33

Said the Blessed One: "For a long time, Simha, offerings have been given to the Nirgranthas in your house. You should therefore deem it right also in the future to give them food when they come to you on their alms-pilgrimage." 34

And Simha's heart was filled with joy. He said: "I have been told, Lord: 'The shramana Gautama says: "To me alone and to nobody else gifts should be given. My pupils alone and the pupils of no one else should receive offerings."' But the Blessed One exhorts me to give also to the Nirgranthas. Well, Lord, we shall see what is seasonable. For the third time, Lord, I take my refuge in the Blessed One, and in his dharma, and in his fraternity." 35

LII. ALL EXISTENCE IS SPIRITUAL.

And there was an officer among the retinue of Simha who had heard of the discourse between the Blessed One and the general, and there was some doubt left in his heart. 1

This man came to the Blessed One and said: "It is said, O Lord, that the shramana Gautama denies the existence of the soul. Do they who say so speak the truth, or do they bear false witness against the Blessed One?" 2

And the Blessed One said: "There is a way in which those who say so are speaking truly of me; on the other hand, there is a way in which those who say so do not speak truly of me. 3

"The Tathâgata teaches that there is no self. He who says that the soul is his self and that the self is the thinker of our thoughts and the actor of our deeds, teaches a wrong doctrine which leads to confusion and darkness. 4

"On the other hand, the Tathâgata teaches that there is mind. He who understands by soul mind, and says that mind exists, teaches the truth which leads to clearness and enlightenment." 5

The officer said: "Does, then, the Tathâgata maintain that two things exist? that which we perceive with our senses and that which is mental?" 6

Said the Blessed One: "Verily, I say unto you, your mind is mental, but that which you perceive with your senses is also mental. There is nothing within the world or without which either is not mind or cannot become mind. There is a spirituality in all existence, and the very clay upon which we tread can be changed into children of truth." 7

LIII. IDENTITY AND NON-IDENTITY.

Kûtadanta, the head of the Brahmans in the village of Dânamati having approached the Blessed One respectfully, greeted him and said: "I am told, O shramana, that thou art Buddha, the Holy One, the All-knowing, the Lord of the world. But if thou wert Buddha, wouldst thou not come like a king in all thy glory and power?" 1

Said the Blessed One: "Thy eyes are holden. If the eye of thy mind were undimmed thou couldst see the glory and the power of truth." 2

Said Kûtadanta: "Show me the truth and I shall see it. But thy doctrine is without consistency. If it were consistent, it would stand; but as it is not, it will pass away." 3

The Blessed One replied: "The truth will never pass away." 4

Kûtadanta said: "I am told that thou teachest the law, yet thou tearest down religion. Thy disciples despise rites and abandon immolation, but reverence for the gods can be shown only by sacrifices. The very nature of religion consists in worship and sacrifice." 5

Said Buddha: "Greater than the immolation of bullocks is the sacrifice of self. He who offers to the gods his sinful desires will see the uselessness of slaughtering animals at the altar. Blood has no cleansing power, but the eradication of lust will make the heart pure. Better than worshipping gods is obedience to the laws of righteousness." 6

Kûtadanta being of a religious disposition, and anxious about the future of his soul, had sacrificed countless victims. Now he saw the folly of atonement by blood. Not yet satisfied, however, with the teachings of the Tathâgata, Kûtadanta continued: "Thou believest, O Master, that the soul is reborn; that it migrates in the evolution of life; and that subject to the law of karma we must reap what we sow. Yet teachest thou the non-existence of the soul! Thy disciples praise utter self-extinction as the highest bliss of Nirvâna. If I am merely a combination of the samskâras, my existence will cease when I die. If I am merely a compound of sensations and ideas and desires, whither can I go at the dissolution of the body? Where is the infinite bliss of which thy followers speak? It is an empty word and a self-delusion, for nothingness stares me in the face when I consider thy doctrines." 7

Said the Blessed One: 8

"O Brahman, thou art religious and earnest. Thou art seriously concerned about thy soul. Yet is thy work in vain because thou art lacking in the one thing that is needed. 9

"Only through ignorance and delusion do men indulge in the dream that their souls are separate and self-existent entities. 10

"Thy heart, O Brahman, is cleaving still to self; thou art anxious about heaven but thou seekest the

pleasures of self in heaven, and thus thou canst not
see the bliss of truth and the immortality of truth. 11

"Verily I say unto you: The Blessed One has not
come to teach death, but to teach life, and thou dost
not discern the nature of living and dying. 12

"This body will be dissolved and no amount of
sacrifice will save it. Therefore, seek thou the life that
is of the mind. Where self is, truth cannot be; yet
when truth comes, self will disappear. Therefore, let
thy mind rest in the truth; propagate the truth, put
thy whole soul in it, and let it spread. In the truth
thou shalt live forever. 13

"Self is death and truth is life. The cleaving to
self is a perpetual dying, while moving in the truth is
partaking of Nirvâna which is life everlasting." 14

Kûtadanta said: "Where, O venerable Master, is
Nirvâna?" 15

'Nirvâna is wherever the precepts are obeyed,"
replied the Blessed One. 16

"Do I understand you right," rejoined the Brahman, "that Nirvâna is not a place and being nowhere
it is without reality?" 17

"You do not understand me right," said the Blessed One, "Now listen and answer these questions:
Where does the wind dwell?" 18

"Nowhere," was the reply. 19

Buddha retorted: "Then, sir, there is no such
thing as wind." 20

Kûtadanta made no reply; and the Blessed One
asked again: "Answer me, O Brahman, where does
wisdom dwell? Is wisdom a locality?" 21

"Wisdom has no allotted dwelling-place," replied
Kûtadanta. 22

Said the Blessed One: "Do you mean to say that

there is no wisdom, no enlightenment, no righteousness, and no salvation, because Nirvâna is not a locality? As a great and mighty wind which passeth over the world in the heat of the day, so the Tathâgata comes to blow over the minds of mankind with the breath of his love, so cool, so sweet, so calm, so delicate; and those tormented by fever assuage their suffering and rejoice at the refreshing breeze." 23

Said Kûtadanta: "I feel, O Lord, that thou proclaimest a great doctrine, but I cannot grasp it. Forbear with me that I ask again: Tell me, O Lord, if there be no âtman, how can there be immortality? The activity of the mind passeth, and our thoughts are gone when we have done thinking." 24

Buddha replied: "Our thinking is gone, but our thoughts continue. Reasoning ceases, but knowledge remains." 25

Said Kûtadanta: "How is that? Is not reasoning and knowledge the same?" 26

The Blessed One explained the distinction by an illustration: "It is as when a man wants, during the night, to send a letter, and, after having his clerk called, has a lamp lit, and gets the letter written. Then, when that has been done, he extinguishes the lamp. But though the lamp has been put out the writing is still there. Thus does reasoning cease and knowledge remain; and in the same way mental activity ceases, but experience, wisdom, and all the fruits of our acts endure." 27

Kûtadanta continued: "Tell me, O Lord, pray tell me, where, if the samskâras are dissolved, is the identity of my self. If my thoughts are propagated, and if my soul migrates, my thoughts cease to be *my* thoughts and my soul ceases to be *my* soul. Give me an illustration, but pray, O Lord, tell me, where is the identity of my self?" 28

Said the Blessed One: "Suppose a man were to light a lamp; would it burn the night through?" 29

"Yes, it might do so," was the reply. 30

"Now, is it the same flame that burns in the first watch of the night as in the second?" 31

Kûtadanta hesitated. He thought "yes, it is the same flame," but fearing the complications of a hidden meaning, and trying to be exact, he said: "No, it is not." 32

"Then," continued the Blessed One, "there are two flames, one in the first watch and the other in the second watch." 33

"No, sir," said Kûtadanta. "In one sense it is not the same flame, but in another sense it is the same flame. It burns of the same kind of material, it emits the same kind of light, and it serves the same purpose." 34

"Very well," said Buddha, "and would you call those flames the same that have burned yesterday and are burning now in the same lamp, filled with the same kind of oil, illuminating the same room?" 35

"They may have been extinguished during the day," suggested Kûtadanta. 36

Said the Blessed One: "Suppose the flame of the first watch had been extinguished during the second watch, would you call it the same if it burns again in the third watch?" 37

Replied Kûtadanta: "In one sense it is a different flame, in another it is not." 38

The Tathâgata asked again: "Has the time that elapsed during the extinction of the flame anything to do with its identity or non-identity?" 39

"No, sir," said the Brahman, "it has not. There is a difference and an identity, whether many years elapsed or only one second, and also whether the lamp has been extinguished in the meantime or not." 40

"Well, then, we agree that the flame of to-day is in a certain sense the same as the flame of yesterday, and in another sense it is different at every moment. Moreover, the flames of the same kind, illuminating with equal power the same kind of rooms, are in a certain sense the same." 41

"Yes, sir," replied Kûtadanta. 42

The Blessed One continued: "Now, suppose there is a man who feels like you, thinks like you, and acts like you, is he not the same man as you?" 43

"No, sir," interrupted Kûtadanta. 44

Said Buddha: "Dost thou deny that the same logic holds good for thyself that holds good for the things of the world?" 45

Kûtadanta bethought himself and rejoined slowly: "No. I do not. The same logic holds good universally; but there is a peculiarity about my self which renders it altogether different from everything else and also from other selves. There may be another man who feels exactly like me, thinks like me, and acts like me; suppose even he had the same name and the same kind of possessions, he would not be myself." 46

"True, Kûtadanta," answered Buddha, "he would not be thyself. Now, tell me, is the person who goes to school one, and that same person when he has finished his schooling another? Is it one who commits a crime, another who is punished by having his hands and feet cut off?" 47

"They are the same," was the reply. 48

"Then sameness is constituted by continuity only?"
asked the Tathâgata. 49

"Not only by continuity," said Kûtadanta, "but
also and mainly by identity of character." 50

"Very well," concluded Buddha, "then you agree that persons can be the same, in the same sense as two flames of the same kind are called the same; and thou must recognise that in this sense another man of the same character and product of the same karma is
the same as thou." 51

'Well, I do," said the Brahman. 52

Buddha continued: "And in this same sense alone art thou the same to-day as yesterday. Thy nature is not constituted by the matter of which thy body consists, but by the forms of the body, of the sensations, of the thoughts. Thy soul is the combination of the samskâras. Wherever they are, thou art. Whithersoever they go, thy soul goes. Thus thou wilt recognise in a certain sense an identity of thy self, and in another sense thou wilt not. But he who does not recognise the identity should deny all identity, and should say that the questioner is no longer the same person as he who a minute after receives the answer. Now consider the continuation of thy personality, which is preserved in thy karma. Dost thou call it death and
annihilation, or life and continued life." 53

"I call it life and continued life," rejoined Kûtadanta, "for it is the continuation of my existence, but I do not care for that kind of continuation. All I care for is the continuation of self in the other sense, which makes of every man, whether identical with me or not,
an altogether different person." 54

"Very well," said Buddha. "This is what thou desirest and this is the cleaving to self. This is thy error, and it implicates thee into unnecessary anxieties and wrong-doing, into grief and cares of all kind. He who cleaves to self must pass through the endless migrations of death, he is constantly dying. For the nature of self is a perpetual death." 55

"How is that?" asked Kûtadanta. 56

"Where is thy self?" asked Buddha. And when Kûtadanta made no reply, he continued: "Thy self to which thou cleavest is a constant change. Years ago thou wast a small babe; then, thou wast a boy; then a youth, and now, thou art a man. Is there any identity of the babe and the man? There is an identity in a certain sense only. Indeed there is more identity between the flames of the first and the third watch, even though the lamp might have been extinguished during the second watch. Now which is the true self, that of yesterday, that of to-day, or that of to-morrow, for the preservation of which thou dost clamor?" 57

Kûtadanta was bewildered. "Lord of the world," he said, "I see my error, but I am confused still." 58

The Tathâgata continued: "It is by a process of evolution that samskâras come to be. There is no samskâra which has sprung into being without a gradual becoming. Thy samskâras are the product of thy deeds in former existences. The combination of thy samskâras is thy soul. Wheresoever they are impressed thither thy soul migrates. In thy samskâras thou wilt continue to live and thou wilt reap in future existences the harvest sown now and in the past." 59

"Verily, O Lord," rejoined Kûtadanta, "this is no fair retribution. I cannot recognise the justice that others after me will reap what I am sowing now." 60

The Blessed One waited a moment and then replied: "Is all teaching in vain? Dost thou not understand that those others are thou thyself? Thou thyself wilt reap what thou sowest, not others. 61

"Think of a man who is ill-bred and destitute, suffering from the wretchedness of his condition. As a boy he was slothful and indolent, and when he grew up he had not learned a craft to earn a living. Wouldst thou say, his misery is not the product of his own action, because the adult is no longer the same person as was the boy? 62

"Verily, I say unto you: Not in the heavens, not in the midst of the sea, not if thou hidest thyself away in the clefts of the mountains, wilt thou find a place where thou canst escape the fruit of thy evil actions. 63

"At the same time thou art sure to receive the blessings of thy good actions. 64

"Him, who has been long travelling and who returns home in safety, the welcome of kinsfolk, friends, and acquaintances, awaits. So, the fruits of his good works bid welcome the man who has walked in the path of righteousness, when he passes over from the present life into the hereafter." 65

Kûtadanta said: "I have faith in the glory and excellency of thy doctrines. My eye cannot as yet endure the light; but I now understand that there is no self, and the truth dawns upon me. Sacrifices cannot save, and invocations are idle talk. But how shall I find the path to life everlasting? I know all the Vêdas by heart and have not found the truth." 66

Said Buddha: "Learning is a good thing; but it availeth not. True wisdom can be acquired by practice only. Practise the truth that thy brother is the same as thou. Walk in the noble path of righteous-

ness and thou wilt understand that while there is death
in self, there is immortality in truth." 67

Said Kûtadanta: "Let me take my refuge in the
Blessed One, in the dharma, and in the brotherhood.
Accept me as thy disciple and let me partake of the
bliss of immortality." 68

LIV. BUDDHA, NOT GAUTAMA.

And the Blessed One said: 1

"Those only who do not believe, call me Gautama
Siddhârtha, but you call me Buddha, the Blessed One,
and Teacher. And this is right, for I have even in
this life entered Nirvâna, and the life of Gautama Sid-
dhârtha has been extinguished. 2

"Self has disappeared, and the truth has taken its
abode in me. This body of mine is Gautama's body
and it will be dissolved in due time, and after its dis-
solution no one, neither God nor man, will see Gau-
tama Siddhârtha again. But Buddha will not die;
Buddha will continue to live in the holy body of the
law. 3

"The extinction of the Blessed One will be by that
passing away in which nothing remains that could tend
to the formation of another self. Nor will it be pos-
sible to point out the Blessed One as being here or
there. But it will be like a flame in a great body of
blazing fire. That flame has ceased; it has vanished
and it cannot be said that it is here or there. In the
body of the dharma, however, the Blessed One can be
pointed out; for the dharma has been preached by the
Blessed One. 4

'Ye are my children, I am your father; through
me ye have been released from your sufferings. 5

"I myself having reached the other shore, help others to cross the stream; I myself having attained salvation, am a saviour of others; being comforted, I comfort others and lead them to the place of refuge. 6

"I shall fill with joy all the beings whose limbs languish; I shall give happiness to those who are dying from distress; I shall extend to them succor and deliverance. 7

"I was born into the world as the king of truth for the salvation of the world. 8

"The subject on which I meditate is truth. The practice to which I devote myself is truth. The topic of my conversation is truth. My thoughts are always in the truth. For lo! my self has become the truth. I am the truth. 9

"Whosoever comprehendeth the truth, he will see the Blessed One, for the truth has been preached by the Blessed One." 10

LV. ONE ESSENCE, ONE LAW, ONE AIM.

And the Tathâgata addressed the venerable Kâshyapa, to dispel the uncertainty and doubt of his mind, and he said: 1

"All things are made of one essence, yet things are different according to the forms which they assume under different impressions. As they form themselves so they act, and as they act so they are. 2

"It is, Kâshyapa, as if a potter made different vessels out of the same clay. Some of these pots are to contain sugar, others rice, others curds and milk; others still are vessels of impurity. There is no diversity in the clay used; the diversity of the pots is only due to the moulding hands of the potter who

shapes them for the various uses that circumstances
may require. 3

"And as all things originate from one essence, so
they are developing according to one law and they are
destined to one aim which is Nirvâna. 4

"Nirvâna, comes to you, Kâshyapa, if you thor-
oughly understand, and if you live according to your
understanding, that all things are of one essence and
that there is but one law. Hence, there is but one
Nirvâna as there is but one truth, not two or three. 5

"And the Tathâgata is the same unto all beings,
differing in his attitude only in so far as all beings are
different. 6

"The Tathâgata recreates the whole world like a
cloud shedding its waters without distinction. He has
the same sentiments for the high as for the low, for
the wise as for the ignorant, for the noble-minded as
for the immoral. 7

"The great cloud full of rain comes up in this wide
universe covering all countries and oceans to pour down
its rain everywhere, over all grasses, shrubs, herbs,
trees of various species, families of plants of different
names growing on the earth, on the hills, on the moun-
tains, or in the valleys. 8

"Then, Kâshyapa, the grasses, shrubs, herbs, and
wild trees suck the water emitted from that great cloud
which is all of one essence and has been abundantly
poured down; and they will, according to their nature,
acquire a proportionate development, shooting up and
producing blossoms and fruits in their season. 9

"Rooted in one and the same soil, all those fami-
lies of plants and germs are quickened by water of the
same essence. 10

"The Tathâgata, however, O Kâshyapa, knows

the law whose essence is salvation, and whose end is the peace of Nirvâna. He is the same to all, and yet knowing the requirements of every single being, he does not reveal himself to all alike. He does not impart to them at once the fulness of omniscience, but pays attention to the disposition of various beings." 11

LVI. THE LESSON GIVEN TO RÂHULA.

Before Râhula, the son of Gautama Siddhârtha and Yashôdharâ, attained to the enlightenment of true wisdom, his conduct was not always marked by a love of truth, and the Blessed One sent him to a distant vihâra to govern his mind and to guard his tongue. 1

After some time the Blessed One repaired to the place, and Râhula was filled with joy. 2

And the Blessed One ordered the boy to bring him a basin with water and wash his feet, and Râhula obeyed. 3

When Râhula had washed the Tathâgata's feet, the Blessed One asked: "Is the water now fit for drinking?" 4

"No, my Lord," replied the boy, "the water is defiled." 5

Then the Blessed One said: "Now consider your own case. Although you are my son, and the grandchild of a king, although you are a shramana who has voluntarily given up everything, you are unable to guard your tongue from untruth, and thus defile your mind." 6

And when the water had been poured away, the Blessed One asked again: "Is this vessel now fit for holding water to drink?" 7

"No, my Lord," replied Râhula, "the vessel, too, has become unclean." 8

And the Blessed One said: "Now consider your own case. Although you wear the yellow robe, are you fit for any high purpose when you have become unclean like this vessel?" 9

Then the Blessed One, lifting up the empty basin and whirling it round, asked: "Are you not afraid lest it should fall and break?" 10

"No, my Lord," replied Râhula, "the vessel is but cheap, and its loss will not amount to much." 11

"Now consider your own case," said the Blessed One. "You are whirled about in endless eddies of transmigration, and your body being made of the same substance as other material things that will crumble to dust, there is no loss if it be broken. He who is given to speaking untruths is an object of contempt to the wise." 12

Râhula was filled with shame, and the Blessed One addressed him once more: "Listen, and I will tell you a parable: 13

"There was a king who had a very powerful elephant, able to cope with five hundred ordinary elephants. When going to war, the elephant was armed with sharp swords on his tusks, with scythes on his shoulders, spears on his feet, and an iron ball at his tail. The elephant-master rejoiced to see the noble creature so well equipped, and, knowing that a slight wound by an arrow in the trunk would be fatal, he had taught the elephant to keep his trunk well coiled up. But during the battle the elephant stretched forth his trunk to seize a sword. 14

"His master was frightened and consulted with

the king, and they decided that the elephant was no longer fit to be used in battle. 15

"O Râhula! if men would only guard their tongues all would be well! Be like the fighting elephant who guards his trunk against the arrow that strikes in the middle. 16

"By love of truth the sincere escape iniquity. Like the elephant well subdued and quiet, who permits the king to mount on his trunk, thus the man that reveres righteousness will endure faithfully throughout his life." 17

Râhula hearing these words was filled with deep sorrow; he never again gave any occasion for complaint, and forthwith he sanctified his life by earnest exertions. 18

LVII. THE SERMON ON ABUSE.

And the Blessed One observed the ways of society and noticed how much misery came from malignity and foolish offences done only to gratify vanity and self-seeking pride. 1

And Buddha said: "If a man foolishly does me wrong, I will return to him the protection of my ungrudging love; the more evil comes from him, the more good shall go from me; the fragrance of goodness always comes to me, and the harmful air of evil goes to him." 2

A foolish man learning that Buddha observed the principle of great love which commends to return good for evil, came and abused him. Buddha was silent, pitying his folly. 3

The man having finished his abuse, Buddha asked him, saying: "Son, if a man declined to accept a present made to him, to whom would it belong?" And

he answered: "In that case it would belong to the
man who offered it." 4

"My son," said Buddha, "you have railed at me,
but I decline to accept your abuse, and request you to
keep it yourself. Will it not be a source of misery to
you? As the echo belongs to the sound, and the
shadow to the substance, so misery will overtake the
evil-doer without fail." 5

The abuser made no reply, and Buddha contin-
ued: 6

"A wicked man who reproaches a virtuous one is
like one who looks up and spits at heaven; the spittle
soils not the heaven, but comes back and defiles his
own person. 7

"The slanderer is like one who flings dust at another
when the wind is contrary; the dust does but return on
him who threw it. The virtuous man cannot be hurt,
and the misery that the other would inflict comes back
on himself." 8

The abuser went away ashamed, but he came again
and took refuge in the Buddha, the Dharma, and the
Sangha. 9

LVIII. BUDDHA REPLIES TO THE DÊVA.

On a certain day when the Blessed One dwelt at
Jêtavana, the garden of Anâthapindika, a celestial dêva
came to him in the shape of a Brahman whose coun-
tenance was bright and whose garments were white
like snow. The dêva asked questions which the Bles-
sed One answered. 1

The dêva said: "What is the sharpest sword?
What is the deadliest poison? What is the fiercest
fire? What is the darkest night?" 2

The Blessed One replied: "A word spoken in wrath is the sharpest sword; covetousness is the deadliest poison; passion is the fiercest fire; ignorance is the darkest night." 3

The dêva said: "Who gains the greatest benefit? Who loses most? Which armor is invulnerable? What is the best weapon?" 4

The Blessed One replied: "He is the greatest gainer who gives to others, and he loses most who receives from others without giving a compensation. Patience is an invulnerable armor; wisdom is the best weapon." 5

The dêva said: "Who is the most dangerous thief? What is the most precious treasure? Who is most successful in taking away by violence not only on earth, but also in heaven?" 6

The Blessed One replied: "Evil thought is the most dangerous thief; virtue is the most precious treasure. Immortality is most successful in taking away by violence not only on earth but also in heaven." 7

The dêva said: "What is attractive? What is disgusting? What is the most horrible pain? What is the greatest enjoyment?" 8

The Blessed One replied: "Good is attractive; evil is disgusting. A bad conscience is the most tormenting of all pains; deliverance is the height of bliss." 9

The dêva asked: "What causes ruin in the world? What breaks off friendships? What is the most violent fever? Who is the best physician?" 10

The Blessed One replied: "Ignorance causes the ruin of the world. Envy and selfishness break off friendships. Hatred is the most violent fever, and Buddha is the best physician." 11

The dêva then asked and said: "Now I have only one doubt to be solved; pray, clear it away: What is it fire can neither burn, nor moisture corrode, nor wind crush down, but is able to reform the whole world?" 12

The Blessed One replied: "Blessing! The blessing of a good deed is secure from the attack of a malignant man who desires to take it away." 13

The dêva, having heard the words of the Blessed One, was full of exceeding joy. Clasping his hands, he bowed down before him in reverence, and disappeared suddenly from the presence of Buddha. 14

LIX. WORDS OF INSTRUCTION.

Thus I have heard. The bhikshus came to the Blessed One, and having saluted him with clasped hands they said: 1

"O Master, thou all-seeing, we all wish to learn; our ears are ready to hear, thou art our teacher, thou art incomparable. Cut off our doubt, inform us of the blessed dharma, O thou of great understanding; speak in the midst of us, O thou who art all-seeing, as is the thousand-eyed Lord of the gods. 2

"We will ask the muni of great understanding, who has crossed the stream, gone to the other shore, is blessed and of a firm mind: How does a bhikshu wander rightly in the world, after having gone out from his house and driven away desire?" 3

Buddha said: 4

"Let the bhikshu subdue his passion for human and celestial pleasures, then, having conquered existence, he will command the dharma. Such a one will wander rightly in the world. 5

"He whose lusts have been destroyed, who is free

from pride, who has overcome all the ways of passion, is subdued, perfectly happy,and of a firm mind. Such a one will wander rightly in the world. 6

"Faithful is he who is possessed of knowledge, seeing the way that leads to Nirvâna, he who is no partisan, he who is pure and victorious, and has removed the veil from his eyes. Such a one will wander rightly in the world." 7

Said the bhikshus: "Certainly, O Bhagavat, it is so: whichever bhikshu lives in this way, subdued and having overcome all bonds, such a one will wander rightly in the world." 8

The Blessed One said: 9

"Whatever is to be done by him who aspires to attain the tranquillity of Nirvâna let him be able and upright, conscientious and gentle, and not proud. 10

"Let no one deceive another, let no one despise another, let no one out of anger or resentment wish to harm another. 11

"Happy is the solitude of the peaceful who know and behold the truth. Happy is he who stands firm by holding himself in check alway. Happy is he whose every sorrow, whose every desire is at an end. The conquest of the stubborn vanity of self is truly supreme happiness. 12

"Let a man's pleasure be the dharma, let him delight in the dharma, let him stand fast in the dharma, let him know how to inquire into the dharma, let him not raise any dispute that pollutes the dharma, and let him spend his time in pondering on the well-spoken truths of the dharma. 13

"A treasure that is laid up in a deep pit profits nothing and may easily be lost. The real treasure that is laid up through charity and piety, temperance, self-control, or deeds of merit, is hid secure and cannot pass away. It is never gained by despoiling or wronging others, and no thief can steal it. A man, when he dies, must leave the fleeting wealth of the world, but this treasure of virtuous acts he takes with him. Let the wise do good deeds; they are a treasure that can never be lost." 14

And the bhikshus praised the wisdom of the Tathâgata: 15

"Thou hast past beyond pain; thou art holy, O Enlightened One, we consider thee one that has destroyed his passions. Thou art glorious, thoughtful, and of great understanding. O thou who puts an end to pain, thou hast carried us across our doubt. 16

"Because thou sawest our longing and carriedest us across our doubt, adoration be to thee, O muni, who hast attained the highest gain in the ways of wisdom. 17

"The doubt we had before, thou hast cleared away, O thou clearly-seeing; surely thou art a muni, perfectly enlightened, there is no obstacle for thee. 18

"And all thy troubles are scattered and cut off; thou art calm, subdued, firm, truthful. 19

"Adoration be to thee, O noble muni, adoration be to thee, O thou best of beings; in the world of men and gods there is none equal to thee. 20

"Thou art Buddha, thou art the Master, thou art the muni that conquers Mâra; after having cut off desire thou hast crossed over and carriest this generation to the other shore." 21

LX. AMITÂBHA.

One of the disciples came to the Blessed One with a trembling heart and his mind full of doubt. And he asked the Blessed One: "O Buddha, our Lord and

Master, why do we give up the pleasures of the world, if you forbid us to work miracles and to attain the supernatural? Is not Amitâbha, the infinite light of revelation, the source of innumerable miracles?" 1

And the Blessed One, seeing the anxiety of a truth-seeking mind, said: "O shrâvaka, thou art a novice among the novices, and thou art swimming on the surface of samsâra. How long will it take thee to grasp the truth? Thou hast not understood the words of the Tathâgata. The law of karma is irrefragable, and supplications have no effect, for they are empty words." 2

Said the disciple: "So you say there are no miraculous and wonderful things?" 3

And the Blessed One replied: 4

"Is it not a wonderful thing, mysterious and miraculous to the worldling, that a sinner can become a saint, that he who attains to true enlightenment will find the path of truth and abandon the evil ways of selfishness? 5

"The bhikshu who renounces the transient pleasures of the world for the eternal bliss of holiness, performs the only miracle that can truly be called a miracle. 6

"A holy man changes the curses of karma into blessings. The desire to perform miracles arises either from covetousness or from vanity. 7

"That mendicant does right who does not think: 'People should salute me'; who, though despised by the world, yet cherishes no ill-will towards it. 8

"That mendicant does right to whom omens, meteors, dreams, and signs are things abolished; he is free from all their evils. 9

"Amitâbha, the unbounded light, is the source of the spiritual existence of Buddhahood. The deeds of sorcerers and miracle-mongers are frauds, but what is more wondrous, more mysterious, more miraculous than Amitâbha?" 10

"But, Master," continued the shrâvaka, "is the promise of the happy region vain talk and a myth?" 11

"What is this promise?" asked Buddha; and the disciple replied: 12

"There is in the West a paradisian country called the Pure Land, exquisitely adorned with gold and silver and precious gems. There are pure waters with golden sands, surrounded by pleasant walks and covered with large lotus flowers. Joyous music is heard, and flowers rain down three times a day. There are singing birds whose harmonious notes proclaim the praises of religion, and in the minds of those who listen to their sweet sounds, remembrance arises of the Buddha, the law, and the brotherhood. No evil birth is possible there, and even the name of hell is unknown. He who fervently and with a pious mind repeats the words 'Amitâbha Buddha' will be transported to the happy region of this pure land, and when death draws nigh, Buddha, with a company of saintly followers, will stand before him, and there will be perfect tranquillity." 13

"In truth," said Buddha, "there is such a happy paradise. But the country is spiritual and it is accessible only to those that are spiritual. You say, It lies in the West. This means, look for it where he who enlightens the world resides. The sun sinks down and leaves us in utter darkness, the shades of night steal over us, and Mâra, the evil one, buries our bodies in the grave. Sunset is nevertheless no extinction, and where we imagine we see extinction there is boundless light and inexhaustible life." 14

"Your description," Buddha continued, "is beautiful; yet it is insufficient and does little justice to the glory of the pure land. The worldly can speak of it in a worldly way only, they use worldly similes and worldly words. But the pure land in which the pure live is more beautiful than you can say or imagine. 15

"However, the repetition of the name Amitâbha Buddha is meritorious only if you speak it with such a devout attitude of mind as will cleanse your heart and attune your will to do works of righteousness. He only can reach the happy land whose soul is filled with the infinite light of truth. He only can live and breathe in the spiritual atmosphere of the western paradise who has attained enlightenment. 16

"Verily I say unto you, the Tathâgata lives in the pure land of eternal bliss even now while he is still in the body; and the Tathâgata preaches the law of religion unto you and unto the whole world, so that you and your brethren may attain the same peace and the same happiness." 17

Said the disciple: "Teach me, O Lord, the meditations to which I must devote myself in order to let my mind enter into the paradise of the pure land." 18

Buddha said: "There are five meditations. 19

"The first meditation is the meditation of love in which you must so adjust your heart that you long for the weal and welfare of all beings, including the happiness of your enemies. 20

"The second meditation is the meditation of pity, in which you think of all beings in distress, vividly representing in your imagination their sorrows and anxieties so as to arouse a deep compassion for them in your soul. 21

"The third meditation is the meditation of joy in

which you think of the prosperity of others and rejoice with their rejoicings. 22

"The fourth meditation is the meditation on impurity, in which you consider the evil consequences of corruption, the effects of sin and diseases. How trivial often the pleasure of the moment and how fatal its consequences! 23

"The fifth meditation is the meditation on serenity, in which you rise above love and hate, tyranny and oppression, wealth and want, and regard your own fate with impartial calmness and perfect tranquillity. 24

"A true follower of the Tathâgata does not found his trust upon austerities or rituals but giving up the idea of self relies with his whole heart upon Amitâbha, which is the unbounded light of truth." 25

The Blessed One after having explained his doctrine of Amitâbha, the immeasurable light which makes him who receives it a Buddha, looked into the heart of his disciple and saw still some doubts and anxieties. And the Blessed One said: "Ask me, my son, the questions which weigh upon your soul." 26

And the disciple said: "Can a humble monk, by sanctifying himself, acquire the talents of supernatural wisdom called abhijnyâ and the supernatural powers called riddhi? Show me the riddhi-pâda, the path to the highest wisdom? Open to me the dhyânas which are the means of acquiring samâdhi, the fixity of mind which enraptures the soul." 27

And the Blessed One said: "Which are the abhijnyâs?" 28

The disciple replied: "There are six abhijnyâs: (1) The celestial eye; (2) the celestial ear; (3) the body at will or the power of transformation; (4) the knowledge of the destiny of former dwellings, so as to know former states of existence; (5) the faculty of reading the thoughts of others; and (6) the knowledge of comprehending the finality of the stream of life." 29

And the Blessed One replied: "These are wondrous things; but verily, every man can attain them. Consider the abilities of your own mind, you were born about two hundred leagues from here and can you not, in your thought, in an instant travel to your native place and remember the details of your father's home? Do you not see with your mind's eye the roots of the tree which is shaken by the wind without being overthrown? Does not the collector of herbs see in his mental vision, whenever he pleases, any plant with its roots, its stem, its fruits, its leaves, and even the uses to which it can be applied? Cannot the man who understands languages recall to his mind any word whenever he pleases, knowing its exact meaning and import? How much more does the Tathâgata understand the nature of all things; he looks into the hearts of men and reads their thoughts. He knows the evolution of beings in their wearisome transmigrations and foresees their ends." 30

Said the disciple: "Which are the dhyânas through which we must pass to reach abhijnyâ?" 31

And Buddha replied: "There are four dhyânas. The first dhyâna is seclusion in which you must free your mind from sensuality; the second dhyâna is a tranquillity of mind full of joy and gladness; the third dhyâna is a taking delight in things spiritual; the fourth dhyâna is a state of perfect purity and peace in which the mind is above all gladness and grief." 32

Said the disciple: "Forbear with me, O Blessed One, for I have faith without understanding and I am seeking the truth. Teach me, O Blessed One, O Ta-

thâgata, my Lord and Master, teach me the riddhi-
pâdâ." 33

And the Blessed One said: "There are four means
by which riddhi is acquired; (1) Prevent bad quali-
ties from arising. (2) Put away bad qualities which
have arisen. (3) Produce goodness that does not as
yet exist. And (4) increase the goodness that does
exist. 34

"Search with sincerity, and persevere in your
search. In the end you will find the truth." 35

LXI. THE TEACHER UNKNOWN.

And the Blessed One said to Ânanda: 1

"There are various kinds of assemblies, O Ânanda;
assemblies of nobles, of Brahmans, of householders,
of bhikshus, and of other beings. When I used to enter
into an assembly, I always became, before I seated
myself, in color like unto the color of my audience,
and in voice like unto their voice. Then with religious
discourse, I instructed, quickened, and gladdened
them. 2

"My doctrine is like the ocean, having the same
eight wonderful qualities. 3

"Both the ocean and my doctrine become gradually deeper. Both preserve their identity under all changes. Both cast out dead bodies upon the dry land. As the great rivers, when falling into the main, lose their names and are thenceforth reckoned as the great ocean, so all the castes, having renounced their lineage and entered the Sangha, become brethren and are reckoned the sons of Shâkyamuni. The ocean is the goal of all streams and of the rain from the clouds, yet is it never overflowing and never emptied: so the dharma is embraced by many millions of people, yet it neither increases nor decreases. As the great ocean has only one taste, the taste of salt, so my doctrine has only one flavor, the flavor of emancipation. Both the ocean and the dharma are full of gems and pearls and jewels, and both afford a dwelling-place for mighty beings. 4

"These are the eight wonderful qualities in which my doctrine resembles the ocean. 5

"My doctrine is pure and it makes no discrimination between noble and ignoble, rich and poor. 6

"My doctrine is like unto water which cleanses all without distinction. 7

"My doctrine is like unto fire which consumes all things that exist between heaven and earth, great and small. 8

"My doctrine is like unto the heavens, for there is room in it, ample room for the reception of all, for men and women, boys and girls, the powerful and the lowly. 9

"But when I spoke, they knew me not and would say, 'Who may this be who thus speaks, a man or a god?' Then having instructed, quickened, and gladdened them with religious discourse, I would vanish away. But they knew me not, even when I vanished away." 10

PARABLES AND STORIES.

LXII. PARABLES.

AND the Blessed One thought: "I have taught the truth which is excellent in the beginning, excellent in the middle, and excellent in the end; it is glorious in its spirit and glorious in its letter. But simple as it is, the people cannot understand it. I must speak to them in their own language, I must adapt my thoughts to their thoughts. They are like unto children, and love to hear tales. Therefore, I will tell them stories to explain the glory of the dharma. If they cannot grasp the truth in the abstract arguments by which I have reached it, they may nevertheless come to understand it, if it is illustrated in parables." 1

LXIII. THE BURNING MANSION.

There was a wealthy householder who possessed a large but old mansion; its rafters were worm-eaten, its pillars rotten, its roof dry and combustible. And it happened on one day that there was a smell of fire. The householder ran out doors and saw the thatch all ablaze. He was horror-struck, for he loved his children dearly, and knew that, ignorant of the danger, they were romping about in the burning mansion. 1

The distracted father thought to himself, "What shall I do? The children are ignorant, and it will be useless to warn them of the danger. If I run in to catch them and carry them out in my arms, they will run away, and while I might save one of them, the others would perish in the flames." Suddenly an idea came to him. "My children love toys," he thought; "if I promise them playthings of wonderful beauty, they will listen to me." 2

Then he shouted aloud: "Children, come out and see the exquisite feast your father has prepared for you. Here are toys for you finer than you have ever seen. Come quickly, before it is too late!" 3

And lo! from the blazing ruins the children came out in full haste. The word "toys" had caught their minds. Then the fond father in his joy bought them the most precious playthings, and, when they saw the destruction of the house, they understood the good intention of their father, and praised the wisdom which had saved their lives. 4

The Tathâgata knows that the children of the world love the tinsel of worldly pleasures; he describes the bliss of righteousness, thus endeavoring to save their souls from perdition, and he will give them the spiritual treasures of truth. 5

LXIV. THE MAN BORN BLIND.

There was a man born blind and he said: "I do not believe in the world of light and appearance. There are no colors, bright or sombre. There is no sun, no moon, no stars. No one has witnessed these things." 1

His friends remonstrated with him, but he clung to his opinion: "What you say that you see," he objected, "are illusions. If colors existed I should be able to touch them. They have no substance and are unreal." 2

In those days there was a physician who was called to see the blind man, and he mixed four simples and cured him of his disease. 3

The Tathâgata is the physician, and the four simples are the four noble truths. 4

LXV. THE LOST SON.

There was a householder's son who went away into a distant country, and while the father accumulated immeasurable riches, the son became miserably poor. And the son while searching for food and clothing happened to come to the country in which his father lived. And the father saw him in his wretchedness, for he was ragged and brutalised by poverty, and ordered some of his servants to call him. 1

When the son saw the palace to which he was conducted, he thought, "I must have evoked the suspicion of a powerful man, and he will throw me into prison." Full of apprehension he made his escape before he had seen his father. 2

Then the father sent messengers out after his son, and he was caught and brought back in spite of his cries and lamentations. And his father ordered the servants to deal tenderly with his son, and he appointed a laborer of his son's rank and education to employ the lad as a helpmate on the estate. And the son was pleased with his new situation. 3

From the window of his palace the father watched his boy, and when he saw that he was honest and industrious, he promoted him higher and higher. 4

After many years, he summoned his son and called together all his servants, and made the secret known to them. Then the poor man was exceedingly glad and he was full of joy at meeting his father. 5

Little by little must the minds of men be trained for higher truths. 6

LXVI. THE GIDDY FISH.

There was a bhikshu who had great difficulty in keeping his senses and passions under control; so, resolving to leave the order, he came to the Blessed One to ask him for a release from the vows. And the Blessed One said to the bhikshu: 1

"Take heed, my son, lest you fall a prey to the passions of your misguided heart. For I see that in former existences, you have suffered much from the evil consequences of lust, and unless you learn to conquer your sensual desires, you will in this life be ruined through your folly. 2

"Listen to a story of another existence of yours, as a fish. 3

"The fish could be seen swimming lustily in the river, playing with his mate. She, moving in front, suddenly perceived the meshes of a net, and slipping around escaped the danger; but he, blinded by love, shot eagerly after her and fell straight into the mouth of the net. The fisherman pulled the net up, and the fish, who complained bitterly of his sad fate, saying, 'this indeed is the bitter fruit of my folly,' would surely have died if Bôdhisattva had not chanced to come by, and, understanding the language of the fish, took pity on him. He bought the poor creature and said to him: 'My good fish, had I not caught sight of you this day, you would have lost your life. I shall save you, but henceforth sin no more.' With these words he threw the fish into the water. 4

"Make the best of the time of grace that is offered you in your present existence, and fear the dart of lust which, if you guard not your senses, will lead you into destruction." 5

LXVII. THE CRUEL CRANE OUTWITTED.

A tailor who used to make robes for the brotherhood was wont to cheat his customers, and thus prided himself on being smarter than other men. But once, on entering upon an important business transaction with a stranger, he found his master in fraudulent practices, and suffered a heavy loss. 1

And the Blessed One said: This is no isolated incident in the greedy tailor's fate; in other incarnations he suffered similar losses, and by trying to dupe others ultimately ruined himself. 2

This same greedy character lived many generations ago as a crane near a pond, and when the dry season set in he said to the fish with a bland voice: "Are you not anxious for your future welfare? There is at present very little water and still less food in this pond. What will you do should in this drought the whole pond become dry?" 3

"Yes, indeed," said the fish, "what should we do?" 4

Replied the crane: "I know a fine, large lake, which never becomes dry. Would you not like to be carried to that place in my beak?" When the fish began to distrust the honesty of the crane, he proposed to have one of them sent over to the lake to see it; and one of them, a big carp, at last decided to take the risk for the sake of the others, and the crane carried him to a beautiful lake and brought him back in safety. Then all doubt vanished, and the fish gained confidence in the crane, and now the crane took the fish one by one out of the pond and devoured them on a big varana-tree. 5

There was also a lobster in the pond, and when it listed the crane to eat him too, he said to him: "I have taken all the fish away and put them in a fine, large lake. Come along. I shall take you, too!" 6

"But how will you take hold of me to carry me along?" asked the lobster. 7

"I shall bite hold of you with my beak," said the crane. 8

"You will let me fall if you carry me like that. I will not go with you!" replied the lobster. 9

"You need not fear," rejoined the crane; "I shall hold you quite tight all the way." 10

Then said the lobster to himself: "If this crane once gets hold of a fish, he will certainly never let him go in a lake! Now if he should really put me into the lake it would be splendid; but if he does not, then I will cut his throat and kill him!" So he said to him: "Look here, friend, you will not be able to hold me tight enough; but we lobsters have a famous grip. If you let me catch hold of you round the neck with my claws, I shall be glad to go with you." 11

And the crane did not see that the lobster was trying to outwit him, and agreed. So the lobster caught hold of his neck with his claws as securely as with a pair of blacksmith's pincers, and called out: "Off with you now!" 12

The crane took him and showed him the lake, and then turned off toward the varana-tree. "My dear uncle!" cried the lobster, "the lake lies that way, but you are taking me this way." 13

Answered the crane: "Do you think so? Am I your dear uncle? You mean me to understand, I suppose, that I am your slave, who has to lift you up and carry you about with him, where you please! Now cast your eye upon that heap of fish-bones at the root of yonder varana-tree. Just as I have eaten those fish, every one of them, just so I will devour you as well!" 14

"Ah! those fishes got eaten through their own stupidity," answered the lobster, "but I am not going to let you kill me. On the contrary, it is you that I am going to destroy. For you, in your folly, have not seen that I have outwitted you. If we die, we both die together; for I will cut off this head of yours and cast it to the ground!" And so saying, he gave the crane's neck a grip with his claws as with a vise. 15

Then gasping, and with tears trickling from his eyes, and trembling with the fear of death, the crane beseeched him, saying: "O, my Lord! Indeed I did not intend to eat you. Grant me my life!" 16

"Very well! fly down and put me into the lake," replied the lobster. 17

And the crane turned round and stepped down into the lake, to place the lobster on the mud at its edge. But the lobster cut the crane's neck through as clean as one would cut a lotus-stalk with a hunting-knife, and then entered the water! 18

When the Teacher had finished this discourse, he added: "Not now only was this man outwitted in this way, but in other existences, too, he was outwitted, in the same way." 19

LXVIII. FOUR KINDS OF MERIT.

There was a rich man who used to invite all the Brahmans of the neighborhood to his house, and, giving them rich gifts, offer great sacrifices to the gods. 1

And the Blessed One said: "If a man each month repeat a thousand sacrifices and give offerings without ceasing, he is not equal to him who but for a moment fixes his mind upon righteousness." 2

The world-honored Buddha continued: "There are four kinds of offering: first, when the gifts are large and the merit small; secondly, when the gifts are small and the merit large; thirdly, when the gifts are large and the merit large; and fourthly, when the gifts are small and the merit is also small. 3

"The first is the case of the deluded man who takes away life for the purpose of sacrificing to the gods, accompanied by carousing and feasting. Here the gifts are great, but the merit is small indeed. 4

"The gifts are small and the merit is also small, when from covetousness and an evil heart a man keeps to himself a part of that which he intends to offer. 5

"The merit is great, however, while the gift is small, when a man makes his offering from love and with a desire to grow in wisdom and in kindness. 6

"Lastly, the gift is large and the merit is large, when a wealthy man, in an unselfish spirit and with the wisdom of a Buddha, gives donations and founds institutions for the best of mankind to enlighten the minds of his fellow-men and to administer unto their needs." 7

LXIX. THE LIGHT OF THE WORLD.

There was a certain Brahman in Kaushâmbî, a wrangler and well versed in the Vedas. As he found no one whom he regarded his equal in debate he used to carry a lighted torch in his hand, and when asked for the reason of his strange conduct, he replied: "The world is so dark that I carry this torch to light it up, as far as I can." 1

A shramana sitting in the market-place heard these

words and said: "My friend, if your eyes are blind to the sight of the omnipresent light of the day, do not call the world dark. Your torch adds nothing to the glory of the sun and your good intention to illumine the minds of others is as futile as it is arrogant." 2

On this the Brahman asked: "Where is the sun of which thou speakest?" And the shramana replied: "The wisdom of the Tathâgata is the sun of the soul. His radiancy is glorious by day and night, and he whose faith is strong will not lack light on the path to Nirvâna where he will inherit bliss everlasting." 3

LXX. LUXURIOUS LIVING.

While Buddha was preaching his doctrine for the conversion of the world in the neighborhood of Shrâvastî, a man of great wealth who suffered from many ailments came to him with clasped hands and said: "World-honored Buddha, pardon me for my want of respect in not saluting you as I ought to, but I suffer greatly from obesity, excessive drowsiness, and other complaints, so that I cannot move without pain." 1

The Tathâgata, seeing the luxuries with which the man was surrounded asked him: "Have you a desire to know the cause of your ailments?" And when the wealthy man expressed his willingness to learn, the Blessed One said: "There are five things which produce the condition of which you complain: opulent dinners, love of sleep, hankering after pleasure, thoughtlessness, and lack of occupation. Exercise self-control at your meals, and take upon yourself some duties that will exercise your abilities and make you useful to your fellow-men. In following this advice you will prolong your life." 2

The rich man remembered the words of Buddha and after some time having recovered his lightness of body and youthful buoyancy returned to the World-honored One and, coming afoot without horses and attendants, said to him: "Master you have cured my bodily ailments; I come now to seek enlightenment of my soul." 3

And the Blessed One said: "The worldling nourishes his body, but the wise man nourishes his soul. He who indulges in the satisfaction of his appetites works his own destruction; but he who walks in the path will have both the salvation of his soul and prolongation of life." 4

LXXI. THE COMMUNICATION OF BLISS.

Annabhâra, the slave of Sumana, having just cut the grass on the meadow, saw a shramana with his bowl begging for food. And throwing down his bundle of grass he ran into the house and returned with the rice that had been provided for his own food. 1

The shramana ate the rice and gladdened him with words of religious comfort. 2

The daughter of Sumana having observed the scene from a window called out: "Good! Annabhâra, good! Very good!" 3

Sumana hearing these words inquired what she meant, and on being informed about Annabhâra's devotion and the words of comfort he had received from the shramana, went to his slave and offered him money to divide the bliss of his offering. 4

"My Lord," said Annabhâra, "let me first ask the venerable man." And approaching the shramana, he said: "My master has asked me to share with him the bliss of the offering I made you of my allowance of rice. Is it right that I should divide it with him?" 5

The shramana replied in a parable. He said: "In a village of one hundred houses a single light was burning. Then a neighbor came with his lamp and lit it; and in this same way the light was communicated from house to house and the brightness in the village was increased. Thus the light of religion may be diffused without stinting him who communicates it. Let the bliss of thy offering also be diffused. Divide it." 6

Annabhâra returned to his master's house and said to him: "I present you, my Lord, with a share of the bliss of my offering. Deign to accept it." 7

Sumana accepted it and offered his slave a sum of money, but Annabhâra replied: "Not so, my Lord; if I accept your money it would appear as if I sold you my share. Bliss cannot be sold; please accept it as a gift." 8

The master replied: "Brother Annabhâra, from this day forth thou shalt be free. Live with me as my friend and accept this present as a token of my respect." 9

LXXII. THE LISTLESS FOOL.

There was a rich Brahman, well advanced in years, who, unmindful of the impermanence of earthly things and anticipating a long life, had built himself a large house. 1

Buddha sent Ânanda to the rich Brahman to inquire for the reasons why he had built a mansion with so many apartments and to preach to him the four noble truths and the eightfold path of salvation. 2

The Brahman showed Ânanda his house and explained to him the purpose of its numerous chambers, but to the instruction of Buddha's teachings he did not listen. 3

Ânanda said: "It is the habit of fools to say, 'I have children and wealth.' He who says so is not even master of himself; how can he claim possession of children, riches, and servants? Many are the anxieties of the worldly, but they know nothing of the changes of the future." 4

Scarcely had Ânanda left, when the old man was struck by apoplexy and fell dead. And Buddha said, for the instruction of those who were ready to learn: "A fool, though he live in the company of the wise, understands nothing of the true doctrine, as a spoon tastes not the flavor of the soup. He thinks of himself only, and unmindful of the advice of good counsellors is unable to deliver himself." 5

LXXIII. RESCUE IN THE DESERT.

There was a disciple of the Blessed One, full of energy and zeal for the truth, who, living under a vow to complete a meditation in solitude, flagged in a moment of weakness; and he said to himself: "The Teacher said there are several kinds of men; I must belong to the lowest class and fear that in this birth there will be neither path nor fruit for me. What is the use of a forest life if I cannot by my constant endeavor attain the insight of meditation to which I have devoted myself?" And he left the solitude and returned to the Jêtavana. 1

When the brethren saw him they said to him: "You have done wrong, O brother, after taking a vow, to give up the attempt of carrying it out;" and they took him to the Master. 2

When the Blessed One saw them he said: "I see, O mendicants, that you have brought this brother here against his will. What has he done?" 3

"Lord, this brother, having taken the vows of so sanctifying a faith, has abandoned the endeavor to accomplish the aim of a member of the order, and has come back to us." 4

Then the Teacher said to him: "Is it true that you have given up trying?" 5

"It is true, O Blessed One!" was the reply. 6

The Master said: "This present life of yours is a time of grace. If you now fail to reach the happy state you will have to suffer remorse in future existences. How is it, brother, that you have proved yourself so irresolute! Why, in former states of existence you were full of determination. By your energy alone the men and bullocks of five hundred waggons obtained water in the sandy desert, and were saved. How is it that you give up trying now?" 7

By these few words that brother was re-established in his resolution! But the others besought the Blessed One, saying: "Lord! Tell us how this was." 8

"Listen, then, O mendicants!" said the Blessed One; and having thus excited their attention, he made manifest a thing concealed by the change of birth. 9

Once upon a time, when Brahmadatta was reigning in Kâshî, Bôdhisattva was born in a merchant's family; and when he grew up, he went about trafficking with five hundred carts. 10

One day he arrived at a sandy desert many leagues across. The sand in that desert was so fine that when taken in the closed fist it could not be kept in the hand. After the sun had risen it became as hot as a mass of burning charcoal, so that no man could walk on it. Those, therefore, who had to travel over it took wood, and water, and oil, and rice in their carts, and travelled during the night. And at daybreak they formed an encampment and spread an awning over it, and, taking their meals early, they passed the day sitting in the shade. At sunset they supped, and when the ground had become cool they yoked their oxen and went on. The travelling was like a voyage over the sea: a desert-pilot had to be chosen, and he brought the caravan safe to the other side by his knowledge of the stars. 11

On this occasion the merchant of our story traversed the desert in that way. And when he had passed over fifty-nine leagues he thought, "Now, in one more night we shall get out of the sand," and after supper he directed the waggons to be yoked, and so set out. The pilot had cushions arranged on the foremost cart, and lay down, looking at the stars, and directing them where to drive. But worn out by want of rest during the long march, he fell asleep, and did not perceive that the oxen had turned round and taken the same road by which they had come. 12

The oxen went on the whole night through. Towards the dawn the pilot woke up, and, observing the stars, called out: "Stop the waggons, stop the waggons!" The day broke just as they stopped and were drawing up the carts in a line. Then the men cried out: "Why this is the very encampment we left yesterday! Our wood and water is all gone! We are lost!" And unyoking the oxen and spreading the canopy over their heads, they lay down in despondency, each one under his waggon. But Bôdhisattva, saying to himself, "If I lose heart, all these will perish," walked about while the morning was yet cool. And on seeing a tuft of kusa-grass, he thought: "This could have grown only by soaking up some water which must be beneath it." 13

And he made them bring a spade and dig in that spot. And they dug sixty cubits deep. And when they had got thus far, the spade of the diggers struck on a rock; and as soon as it struck, they all gave up in despair. But Bôdhisattva thought, "There must be water under that rock," and, descending into the well, he got upon the stone, and, stooping down, applied his ear to it, and tested the sound of it. And he heard the sound of water gurgling beneath. And he got out and called his page. "My lad, if you give up now, we shall all be lost. Do not you lose heart. Take this iron hammer, and go down into the pit, and give the rock a good blow." 14

The lad obeyed, and though they all stood by in despair, he went down full of determination, and struck at the stone. And the rock split in two, and fell below, and no longer blocked up the stream. And water rose till its brim was the height of a palm-tree in the well. And they all drank of the water, and bathed in it. Then they cooked rice and ate it, and fed their oxen with it. And when the sun set, they put a flag in the well, and went to the place appointed. There they sold their merchandise at a good profit and returned to their home, and when they died they passed away according to their deeds. And Bôdhisattva gave gifts and did other virtuous acts, and he also passed away according to his deeds. 15

After the Teacher had told the story he formed the connexion by saying in conclusion, "The caravan-leader was Bôdhisattva, the future Buddha; the page who at that time despaired not, but broke the stone, and gave water to the multitude, was this brother without perseverance; and the other men were the attendants on the Buddha." 16

LXXIV. BUDDHA, THE SOWER.

Bhâradvâja, a wealthy Brahman, was celebrating his harvest-thanksgiving when the Blessed One came with his alms-bowl, begging for food. 1

Some of the people paid him reverence, but the Brahman was angry and said: "O shramana, it would suit you better to go to work than to go begging. I plough and sow, and having ploughed and sown, I eat. If you did likewise, you, too, would have to eat." 2

And the Tathâgata answered him and said: "O Brahman, I, too, plough and sow, and having ploughed and sown, I eat." 3

"Do you profess to be a husbandman?" replied the Brahman. "Where, then, are your bullocks? Where is the seed and the plough?" 4

The Blessed One said: "Faith is the seed I sow: good works are the rain that fertilises it; wisdom and modesty are the plough; my mind is the guiding-rein; I lay hold of the handle of the law; earnestness is the goad I use; and exertion is my draught-ox. This ploughing is ploughed to destroy the weeds of illusion. The harvest it yields is the immortal life of Nirvâna, and thus all sorrow ends." 5

Then the Brahman poured rice-milk into a golden bowl and offered it to the Blessed One, saying: "Let the Teacher of mankind partake of the rice-milk, for the venerable Gautama ploughs a ploughing that bears the fruit of immortality." 6

LXXV. THE OUTCAST.

When Bhagavat dwelt at Shrâvastî in the Jêtavana, he went out with his alms-bowl to beg for food and approached the house of a Brahman priest while the fire of an offering was blazing upon the altar. And the priest said: "Stay there, O shaveling; stay there, O wretched shramana; thou art an outcast." 1

The Blessed One replied: "Who is an outcast? 2

"An outcast is the man who is angry and bears hatred; the man who is wicked and hypocritical, he who embraces error and is full of deceit. 3

"Whosoever is a provoker and is avaricious, has sinful desires, is envious, wicked, shameless, and without fear to commit sins, let him be known as an outcast. 4

"Not by birth does one become an outcast, not by birth does one become a Brahman; by deeds one becomes an outcast, by deeds one becomes a Brahman." 5

LXXVI. THE WOMAN AT THE WELL.

Ânanda, the favorite disciple of Buddha, having been sent by the Lord on a mission, passed by a well near a village, and seeing Prakriti, a girl of the Mâtanga caste, he asked her for water to drink. 1

Prakriti said, "O Brahman, I am too humble and mean to give you water to drink, do not ask any service of me lest your holiness be contaminated, for I am of low caste." 2

And Ânanda replied: "I ask not for caste but for water;" and the Mâtanga girl's heart leaped joyfully and she gave Ânanda to drink. 3

Ânanda thanked her and went away; but she followed him at a distance. 4

Having heard that Ânanda was a disciple of Gautama Shâkyamuni, the girl repaired to the Blessed One and cried: "O Lord help me, and let me live in the place where Ânanda thy disciple dwells, so that I may see him and minister unto him, for I love Ânanda." 5

And the Blessed One understood the emotions of her heart and he said: "Prakriti, thy heart is full of love, but you do not understand your own sentiments. It is not Ânanda whom you love, but his kindness. Receive, then, the kindness you have seen him practise unto you, and in the humility of your station practise it unto others. 6

"Verily there is great merit in the generosity of a king when he is kind to a slave; but there is a greater merit in the slave when ignoring the wrongs which he suffers he cherishes kindness and good-will to all mankind. He will cease to hate his oppressors, and even when powerless to resist their usurpation will with compassion pity their arrogance and supercilious demeanor. 7

"Blessed art thou, Prakriti, for though you are a Mâtanga you will be a model for noblemen and noblewomen. You are of low caste, but Brahmans will learn a lesson from you. Swerve not from the path of justice and righteousness and you will outshine the royal glory of queens on the throne." 8

LXXVII. THE PEACEMAKER.

It is reported that two kingdoms were on the verge of war, the possession of a certain embankment being disputed by them. 1

And Buddha seeing the kings with their armies
ready to fight, requested them to tell him the cause of
their quarrels. Having heard the complaints on both
sides, he said: 2

"I understand that the embankment has value for
some of your people, has it any intrinsic value aside
from its service to your men?" 3

"It has no intrinsic value whatever," was the re-
ply. The Tathâgata continued: "Now when you go
to battle is it not sure that many of your men will be
slain and you yourselves, O kings, are liable to lose
your lives?" 4

And they said: "Verily, it is sure that many will
be slain and our own lives be jeopardised." 5

"The blood of men, however," said Buddha, "has
it less intrinsic value than a mound of earth?" 6

"No," the kings said, "the lives of men and
above all the lives of kings, are priceless." 7

Then the Tathâgata concluded: "Are you going to
stake that which is priceless against that which has no
intrinsic value whatever?" 8

The wrath of the two monarchs abated, and they
came to a peaceable agreement. 9

LXXVIII. THE HUNGRY DOG.

There was a great king who oppressed his people
and was hated by his subjects; yet when the Tathâgata
came into his kingdom, the king desired much to see
him; so he went to the place where the Blessed One
stayed and asked: "O Shâkyamuni, can you teach a
lesson to the king that will divert his mind and benefit
him at the same time?" 1

And the Blessed One said: "I shall tell you the
parable of the hungry dog: 2

"There was a wicked tyrant; and the god Indra, assuming the shape of a hunter, came down upon earth with the demon Mâtalî, the latter appearing as a dog of enormous size. Hunter and dog entered the palace, and the dog howled so wofully that the royal buildings shook by the sound to their very foundations. The tyrant had the awe-inspiring hunter brought before his throne and inquired after the cause of the terrible bark. The hunter said, "The dog is hungry," whereupon the frightened king ordered food for him. All the food prepared at the royal banquet disappeared rapidly in the dog's jaws, and still he howled with portentous significance. More food was sent for, and all the royal store-houses were emptied, but in vain. Then the tyrant grew desperate and asked: 'Will nothing satisfy the cravings of that woful beast?' 'Nothing,' replied the hunter, 'nothing except perhaps the flesh of all his enemies.' 'And who are his enemies?' anxiously asked the tyrant. The hunter replied: 'The dog will howl as long as there are people hungry in the kingdom, and his enemies are those who practise injustice and oppress the poor.' The oppressor of the people, remembering his evil deeds, was seized with remorse, and for the first time in his life he began to listen to the teachings of righteousness." 3

Having ended his story, the Blessed One addressed the king, who had turned pale, and said to him: 4

"The Tathâgata can quicken the spiritual ears of the powerful, and when thou, great king, hearest the dog bark, think of the teachings of Buddha, and you may still learn to pacify the monster." 5

LXXIX. THE DESPOT.

Brahmadatta râja happened to see a beautiful woman, the wife of a merchant, and, conceiving a passion for her, ordered a precious jewel secretly to be dropped into the merchant's carriage. The jewel was missed, searched for, and found. The merchant was arrested on the charge of stealing, and the king pretended to listen with great attention to the defence, and with seeming regret ordered the merchant to be executed, while his wife was consigned to the royal harem. 1

Brahmadatta decided to attend the execution in person, for such sights used to give him pleasure, but when the doomed man looked with deep compassion at his infamous judge, a flash of Buddha's wisdom lit up the king's passion-beclouded mind; and while the executioner raised the sword for the fatal stroke, Brahmadatta felt the merchant's soul enter into his own being, and he imagined he saw himself on the block. 2

"Hold, executioner!" shouted Brahmadatta, "it is the king whom you slay!" 3

Too late! The executioner had done the bloody deed. 4

The king fell back in a swoon, and when he awoke a change had come over him. He had ceased to be the cruel despot and henceforth led a life of holiness and rectitude. 5

O ye that commit murders and robberies! The veil of Mâyâ is upon your eyes. If you could see things as they are, not as they appear, you would no longer inflict injuries and pain on your own souls. You do not see that you will have to atone for your evil deeds, for what you sow that you will reap. 6

LXXX. VÂSAVADATTA.

There was a courtesan in Mathurâ named Vâsavadattâ. She happened to see Upagupta, one of Buddha's disciples, a tall and beautiful youth, and fell desperately in love with him. Vâsavadattâ sent an invitation to the young man, but he replied: "The time has not yet arrived when Upagupta will visit Vâsavadattâ." 1

The courtesan was astonished at the reply, and she sent again for him, saying: "Vâsavadattâ desires love, not gold, from Upagupta." But Upagupta made the same enigmatic reply and did not come. 2

A few months later Vâsavadattâ had a love-intrigue with the chief of the artisans, and at that time a wealthy merchant came to Mathurâ, who fell in love with Vâsavadattâ. Seeing his wealth, and fearing the jealousy of her other lover, she contrived the death of the chief of the artisans, and concealed his body under a dunghill. 3

When the chief of the artisans had disappeared, his relatives and friends searched for him and found his body. Vâsavadattâ, however, was tried by a judge, and condemned to have her ears and nose, her hands and feet cut off, and flung into a graveyard. 4

Vâsavadattâ had been a passionate girl, but kind to her servants, and one of her maids followed her, and out of love for her former mistress ministered unto her in her agonies, and chased away the crows. 5

Now the time had arrived when Upagupta decided to visit Vâsavadattâ. 6

When he came, the poor woman ordered her maid to collect and hide under a cloth her severed limbs; and he greeted her kindly, but she said with petulance: "Once this body was fragrant like the lotus, and I offered you my love. In those days I was covered with pearls and fine muslin. Now I am mangled by the executioner and covered with filth and blood." 7

"Sister," said the young man, "it is not for my pleasure that I approach you. It is to restore to you a nobler beauty than the charms which you have lost. 8

"I have seen with mine eyes the Tathâgata walking upon earth and teaching men his wonderful doctrine. But you would not have listened to the words of righteousness while surrounded with temptations, while under the spell of passion and yearning for worldly pleasures. You would not have listened to the teachings of the Tathâgata, for your heart was wayward, and you set your trust on the sham of your transient charms. 9

"The charms of a lovely form are treacherous, and quickly lead into temptations, which have proved too strong for you. But there is a beauty which will not fade, and if you but listen to the doctrine of our Lord, the Buddha, you will find that peace which you never would have found in the restless world of sinful pleasures." 10

Vâsavadattâ became calm and a spiritual happiness soothed the tortures of her bodily pain; for where there is much suffering there is also great bliss. 11

Having taken refuge in the Buddha, the Dharma, and the Sangha, she died in pious submission to the punishment of her crime. 12

LXXXI. THE MARRIAGE-FEAST IN JÂMBÛNADA.

There was a man in Jâmbûnada who was to be married the next day, and he thought, "Might Buddha, the Blessed One, be present at the wedding." 1

And the Blessed One passed by his house and met him, and when he read the silent wish in the heart of the bridegroom, he consented to enter. 2

When the Holy One appeared with the retinue of his many bhikshus, the host, whose means were limited, received them as best he could, saying: "Eat, my Lord, and all your congregation, according to your desire." 3

While the holy men ate, the meats and drinks remained undiminished, and the host thought to himself: "How wondrous is this. I should have had plenty for all my relatives and friends. Would that I had invited them all." 4

When this thought was in the host's mind, all his relatives and friends entered the house; and although the hall in the house was small there was room in it for all of them. They sat down at the table and ate, and there was more than enough for all of them. 5

The Blessed One was pleased to see so many guests full of good cheer and he quickened them and gladdened them with words of truth, proclaiming the bliss of righteousness: 6

"The greatest happiness which a mortal man can imagine is the bond of marriage that ties together two loving hearts. But there is a greater happiness still: it is the embrace of truth. Death will separate husband and wife, but death will never separate him who has espoused the truth. 7

"Therefore be married unto the truth and live with the truth in holy wedlock. The husband who loves his wife and desires for a union that shall be everlasting must be faithful to her so as to be like truth itself, and she will rely upon him and revere him and minister unto him. And the wife who loves her husband and desires for a union that shall be everlasting must be faithful to him so as to be like truth itself; and he will place his trust in her, he will honor her, he will provide for her. Verily, I say unto you, their wedlock will be holiness and bliss, and their children will become like unto their parents and will bear witness to their happiness. 8

"Let no man be single, let every one be wedded in holy love to the truth. And when Mâra, the destroyer, comes to separate the visible forms of your being, you will continue to live in the truth, and you will partake of the life everlasting, for the truth is immortal." 9

There was no one among the guests but was strengthened in his spiritual life, and recognised the sweetness of a life of righteousness; and they took refuge in the Buddha, the Dharma, and the Sangha. 10

LXXXII. A PARTY IN SEARCH FOR A THIEF.

Having sent out his disciples, the Blessed One himself wandered from place to place until he reached Uruvilvâ. 1

On his way he sat down in a grove to rest, and it happened that in that same grove there was a party of thirty friends who were enjoying themselves with their wives; and while they were sporting, some of their goods were stolen. 2

Then the whole party went in search of the thief and, meeting the Blessed One sitting under a tree, saluted him and said: "Pray, Lord, did you see the thief pass by with our goods?" 3

And the Blessed One said: "Which is better for you, that you go in search for the thief or for yourselves?" And the youths cried: "In search for ourselves!" 4

"Well, then," said the Blessed One, "sit down and I will preach you the truth." 5

And the whole party sat down and they listened eagerly to the words of the Blessed One. Having grasped the truth, they praised the doctrine and took refuge in the Buddha. 6

LXXXIII. IN THE REALM OF YAMARÂJA.

There was a Brahman, a religious man and fond in his affections but without deep wisdom; he had a very promising son of great skill, who, when seven years old, was struck with a fatal disease and died. The unfortunate father was unable to control himself; he threw himself upon the corpse and lay there as one dead. 1

The relatives came and buried the dead child and when the father came to himself, he was so immoderate in his grief that he behaved like an insane person. He no longer gave way to tears but wandered about asking for the residence of Yamarâja, the king of death, to beg of him humbly that his child might be allowed to return alive. 2

Having arrived at a great Brahman temple the sad father went through certain religious rites and fell asleep. While wandering on in his dream he came to a deep mountain pass where he met a number of shramanas who had acquired supreme wisdom. "Kind sirs," he said, "can you not tell me where the residence of Yamarâja is?" And they asked him, "Good friend, why do you want to know?" Whereupon he told them his sad story and explained his intentions. Pitying his self-delusion, the shramanas said: "No mortal man can reach the place where Yama reigns, but some four hundred miles westward lies a great city in which many good spirits live; every eighth day of the month Yama visits the place, and there you may see him who is the king of death and ask him for a boon." 3

The Brahman rejoicing at the news went to the city and found it as the shramanas had told him. And he was admitted to the dread presence of Yama, the King of Death, who, on hearing his request, said: "Your son lives now in the eastern garden disporting himself; go there and ask him to follow you." 4

Said the happy father: "How does it happen that my son, without having performed one good work, is now living in paradise?" Yamarâja replied: "He has obtained celestial happiness not for performing good deeds, but because he died in faith and love to the Lord and Master, the most glorious Buddha. Buddha says: 'The heart of love and faith spreads as it were a beneficent shade from the world of men to the world of gods.' This glorious utterance is like the stamp of a king's seal upon a royal edict." 5

The happy father hastened to the place and saw his beloved child playing with other children, all transfigured by the peace of the blissful existence of a heavenly life. He ran up to his boy and cried with tears running down his cheeks: "My son, my son, do you not remember me, your father who watched over you with loving care and tended you in your sickness? Return home with me to the land of the living." But the boy, while struggling to go back to his playmates, upbraided him for using such strange expressions as father and son. "In my present state," he said, "I know no such words, for I am free from delusion." 6

On this, the Brahman departed, and when he woke

from his dream he bethought himself of the Blessed Master of mankind, the great Buddha, and resolved to go to him, lay bare his grief, and seek consolation. 7

Having arrived at the Jêtavana, the Brahman told his story and how his boy had refused to recognise him and to go home with him. 8

And the World-honored One said: "Truly you are self-deluded. When man dies the body is dissolved into its elements, but the spirit is not entombed. It leads a higher mode of life in which all the relative terms of father, son, wife, mother, are at an end, just as a guest who leaves his lodging has done with it, as though it were a thing of the past. Men concern themselves most about that which passes away; but the end of life quickly comes as a burning torrent sweeping away the transient in a moment. They are like a blind man set to look after a burning lamp. A wise man, understanding the transiency of worldly relations, destroys the cause of grief, and escapes from the seething whirlpool of sorrow. Religious wisdom lifts a man above the pleasures and pains of the world and gives him peace everlasting." 9

The Brahman asked the permission of the Blessed One to enter into the community of his bhikshus, so as to acquire that heavenly wisdom which alone can give comfort to an afflicted heart. 10

LXXXIV. THE MUSTARD SEED.

There was a rich man who found his gold suddenly transformed into charcoal; and he took to his bed and refused all food. A friend, hearing of his sickness, visited the rich man and heard the cause of his grief. And the friend said: "You made no good use of your wealth. When you hoarded it up, it was not better than charcoal. Now hear my advice. Spread mats in the bazaar; pile up this charcoal, and pretend to trade with it." 1

The rich man did as his friend had told him, and when his neighbors asked him, "Why do you sell charcoal?" he said: "I offer my goods for sale." 2

After some time a young girl named Krishâ Gautamî, an orphan and very poor, passed by, and seeing the rich man in the bazaar, said: "My lord, why do you thus pile up gold and silver for sale." 3

And the rich man said: "Will you please hand me that gold and silver?" And Krishâ Gautamî took up a handful of charcoal, and lo! it changed back into gold. 4

Considering that Krishâ Gautamî had the mental eye of spiritual knowledge and saw the real worth of things, the rich man gave her in marriage to his son, and he said: "With many, gold is no better than charcoal, but with Krishâ Gautamî charcoal becomes pure gold." 5

And Krishâ Gautamî had an only son, and he died. In her grief she carried the dead child to all her neighbors, asking them for medicine, and the people said: "She has lost her senses. The boy is dead." 6

At length Krishâ Gautamî met a man who replied to her request: "I cannot give you medicine for your child, but I know a physician who can." 7

And the girl said: "Pray tell me, sir; who is it?" And the man replied: "Go to Shâkyamuni, the Buddha." 8

Krishâ Gautamî repaired to Buddha and cried: "Lord and Master, give me the medicine that will cure my boy." 9

Buddha answered: "I want a handful of mustard-seed." And when the girl in her joy promised to procure it, Buddha added: "The mustard-seed must be taken from a house where no one has lost a child, husband, parent, or friend." 10

Poor Krishâ Gautamî now went from house to house, and the people pitied her and said: "Here is mustard-seed; take it!" But when she asked, "Did a son or daughter, a father or mother, die in your family?" They answered her: "Alas! the living are few, but the dead are many. Do not remind us of our deepest grief." And there was no house but some beloved one had died in it. 11

Krishâ Gautamî became weary and hopeless, and sat down at the wayside, watching the lights of the city, as they flickered up and were extinguished again. At last the darkness of the night reigned everywhere. And she considered the fate of men, that their lives flicker up and are extinguished. And she thought to herself: "How selfish am I in my grief! Death is common to all; yet in this valley of desolation there is a path that leads him who has surrendered all selfishness to immortality." 12

Putting away the selfishness of her affection for her child, Krishâ Gautamî had the dead body buried in the forest. Returning to Buddha, she took refuge in him and found comfort in the dharma, which is a balm that will soothe all the pains of our troubled hearts. 13

Buddha said: 14

The life of mortals in this world is troubled and brief and combined with pain. For there is not any means by which those that have been born can avoid dying; after reaching old age there is death; of such a nature are living beings. 15

As ripe fruits are early in danger of falling, so mortals when born are always in danger of death. 16

As all earthen vessels made by the potter end in being broken, so is the life of mortals. 17

Both young and adult, both those who are fools and those who are wise, all fall into the power of death; all are subject to death. 18

Of those who, overcome by death, depart from life, a father cannot save his son, nor relatives their relations. 19

Mark! while relatives are looking on and lamenting deeply, one by one of the mortals is carried off, like an ox that is led to the slaughter. 20

So the world is afflicted with death and decay, therefore the wise do not grieve, knowing the terms of the world. 21

In whatever manner people think a thing will come to pass, it is often different when it happens, and great is the disappointment; see, such are the terms of the world. 22

Not from weeping nor from grieving will any one obtain peace of mind; on the contrary, his pain will be the greater and his body will suffer. He will make himself sick and pale, yet the dead are not saved by his lamentation. 23

People pass away, and their fate after death will be according to their deeds. 24

Even if a man live a hundred years, or even more, he will at last be separated from the company of his relatives, and leave the life of this world. 25

He who seeks peace should draw out the arrow of lamentation, and complaint, and grief. 26

He who has drawn out the arrow and has become

composed will obtain peace of mind; he who has overcome all sorrow will become free from sorrow, and be blessed. 27

LXXXV. FOLLOWING THE MASTER OVER THE STREAM.

South of Shrâvastî there was a great river, very deep and wide, on the banks of which lay a hamlet of five hundred houses. Its inhabitants had not yet heard the good tidings of salvation and were still immersed in worldliness and selfish pursuits. 1

Thinking of the salvation of men, the world-honored Buddha resolved to go to the village and preach to the people. Accordingly, he came to the riverside and sat down beneath a tree, and the villagers seeing the glory of his appearance approached him with reverence; but when he began to preach to them, they believed him not. 2

When the world-honored Buddha had left Shrâvastî, Shâriputra felt a desire to see the Lord and to hear him preach. Coming to the river where the water was deep and the current strong, he said to himself: "This stream shall not prevent me. I shall go and see the Blessed One," and he walked across the water, approached the Master and saluted him. 3

The people of the village were astonished to see Shâriputra, wondering how he had crossed the stream where there was neither a bridge nor a ferry, and how he could walk on its surface without sinking. 4

And Shâriputra replied: "I lived in ignorance until I heard the voice of Buddha. As I was anxious to hear the doctrine of salvation, I crossed the river and I walked over its troubled waters because I had faith. Faith, nothing else, enabled me to do so, and now I am here in the bliss of the Master's presence." 5

The World-honored One added: "Shâriputra, thou hast spoken well. Faith like thine, alone can save the world from the yawning gulf of migration and enable men to walk dryshod to the other shore." 6

And the Blessed One urged to the villagers the necessity of ever advancing in the conquest of sorrow and of casting off all shackles so as to cross the river of worldliness and attain deliverance from death. 7

Hearing the words of the Tathâgata, the villagers were filled with joy and believing in the doctrines of the Blessed One embraced the five rules and took refuge in his name. 8

LXXXVI. THE SICK BHIKSHU.

An old bhikshu of a surly disposition was afflicted with a loathsome disease the sight and smell of which was so nauseating that no one would come near him or help him in his distress. And it happened that the World-honored One came to the vihâra in which the unfortunate man lay; hearing of the case he ordered warm water to be prepared and went to the sick-room to administer unto the sores of the patient with his own hand, saying to his disciples: 1

"The Tathâgata has come into the world to befriend the poor, to succor the unprotected, to nourish those in bodily affliction, both the followers of the dharma and unbelievers, to give sight to the blind and enlighten the minds of the deluded, to stand up for the rights of orphans as well as the aged, and in so doing to set an example to others. This is the consummation of his work, and thus he attains the great goal of life as the rivers that lose themselves in the ocean." 2

The World-honored One administered unto the sick bhikshu daily so long as he stayed in that place. And the governor of the city came to Buddha to do him reverence, and having heard of the service which the Lord did in the vihâra asked the Blessed One about the previous existence of the sick monk, and Buddha said: 3

"In days gone by there was a wicked king who used to extort from his subjects all he could get; and he ordered one of his officers to lay the lash on a man of eminence. The officer little thinking of the pain he inflicted upon others, obeyed; but when the victim of the king's wrath begged for mercy, he felt compassion and laid the whip lightly upon him. Now the king was reborn as Dêvadatta, who was abandoned by all his followers, because they were no longer willing to stand his severity and he died miserable and full of penitence. The officer is the sick bhikshu, who having often given offence to his brethren in the vihâra was left without assistance in his distress. The eminent man, however, who begged for mercy was Bôdhisattva; he has been reborn as the Tathâgata. It is now my lot to help the wretched man as he had mercy on me." 4

And the World-honored One repeated these lines: "He who inflicts pain on the gentle, or falsely accuses the innocent, will inherit one of the ten great calamities. But he who has learned to suffer with patience will be purified and will be the chosen instrument for the alleviation of suffering." 5

The diseased bhikshu on hearing these words turned to Buddha and confessing his ill-natured temper repented and with a heart cleansed from sin did reverence unto the Lord. 6

THE LAST DAYS.

LXXXVII. THE CONDITIONS OF WELFARE.

WHEN the Blessed One was residing on the mount called Vulture's Peak, near Râjagriha, Ajâtashatru the king of Magadha, who reigned in the place of Bimbisâra, planned an attack on the Vriji, and he said to Varshakâra, his prime minister: "I will root out the Vriji, mighty though they be. I will destroy the Vriji; I will bring them to utter ruin! Come now, O Brahman, and go to the Blessed One; inquire in my name for his health, and tell him my purpose. Bear carefully in mind what the Blessed One may say, and repeat it to me, for the Buddhas speak nothing untrue." 1

When Varshakâra, the prime minister, had greeted the Blessed One and delivered his message, the venerable Ânanda stood behind the Blessed One and fanned him, and the Blessed One said to him: "Have you heard, Ânanda, that the Vriji hold full and frequent public assemblies?" 2

"Lord, so I have heard," replied he. 3

"So long, Ânanda," said the Blessed One, "as the Vriji hold these full and frequent public assemblies, they may be expected not to decline, but to prosper. So long as they meet together in concord, so long as they honor their elders, so long as they respect womanhood, so long as they remain religious, performing all proper rites, so long as they extend the rightful protection, defence and support to the holy ones, the Vriji may be expected not to decline, but to prosper." 4

Then the Blessed One addressed Varshakâra and said: "When I staid, O Brahman, at Vaishâlî, I taught the Vriji these conditions of welfare, that so long as they should remain well instructed, so long as they will continue in the right path, so long as they should live up to the precepts of righteousness, we could expect them not to decline, but to prosper." 5

As soon as the king's messenger had gone, the Blessed One had the brethren, that were in the neighborhood of Râjagriha, assembled in the service-hall, and addressed them, saying: 6

"I will teach you, O bhikshus, the conditions of the welfare of a community. Listen well, and I will speak. 7

"So long, O bhikshus, as the brethren hold full and frequent assemblies, meeting in concord, rising in concord, and attending in concord to the affairs of the Sangha, so long as they, O brethren, do not abrogate that which experience has proved to be good, and introduce nothing except such things as have been carefully tested, so long as their elders practise justice, so long as the brethren esteem, revere, and support their elders, and hearken unto their words, so long as the brethren are not under the influence of craving, but delight in the blessings of religion, so that good and holy men shall come to them and dwell among them in quiet, so long as the brethren shall not be addicted to sloth and idleness, so long as the brethren shall exercise themselves in the sevenfold higher wisdom of mental activity, search after truth, energy, joy,

modesty, self-control, earnest contemplation, and equanimity of mind, so long the Sangha may be expected
not to decline, but to prosper. 8

"Therefore, O bhikshus, be full of faith, modest in heart, afraid of sin, anxious to learn, strong in energy, active in mind, and full of wisdom." 9

LXXXVIII. UPRIGHT CONDUCT.

While the Blessed One stayed at Vulture's Peak he held a broad religious conversation with the brethren on the nature of upright conduct, and he repeated this
sermon in a great many places all over the country. 1

And the Blessed One said: 2

"Great is the fruit, great is the advantage of earnest contemplation, when set round with upright conduct. 3

"Great is the fruit, great is the advantage of intellect, when set round with earnest contemplation. 4

"The mind set round with intelligence is freed from the great evils of sensuality, selfishness, delusion, and ignorance." 5

LXXXIX. PÂTALIPUTRA.

When the Blessed One had stayed as long as convenient at Nâlandâ, he went to Pâtaliputra, the frontier town of Magadha; and when the disciples at Pâtaliputra heard of his arrival, they invited him to their village rest-house. And the Blessed One robed himself, took his bowl and went with the brethren to the rest-house. There he washed his feet, entered the hall, and seated himself against the centre pillar, with his face towards the east. The brethren, also, having washed their feet, entered the hall, and took their seats round the Blessed One, against the western wall, facing the east. And the lay devotees of Pâtaliputra, having also washed their feet, entered the hall, and took their seats opposite the Blessed One, against the eastern wall, facing towards the west. 1

Then the Blessed One addressed the lay-disciples of Pâtaliputra, and he said: 2

"Fivefold, O householders, is the loss of the wrong-doer through his want of rectitude. In the first place, the wrong-doer, devoid of rectitude, falls into great poverty through sloth; in the next place, his evil repute gets noised abroad; thirdly, whatever society he enters, whether of Brahmans, nobles, heads of houses, or shramanas, he enters shyly and confusedly; fourthly, he is full of anxiety when he dies; and lastly, on the dissolution of the body after death, his mind remains in an unhappy state. Wherever his karma continues, there will be suffering and woe. This, O householders, is the fivefold loss of the evil-doer! 3

"Fivefold, O householders, is the gain of the well-doer through his practice of rectitude. In the first place the well-doer, strong in rectitude, acquires property through his industry; in the next place, good reports of him are spread abroad; thirdly, whatever society he enters, whether of nobles, Brahmans, heads of houses, or members of the order, he enters with confidence and self-possession; fourthly, he dies without anxiety; and, lastly, on the dissolution of the body after death, his mind remains in a happy state. Wherever his karma continues, there will be heavenly bliss and peace. This, O householders, is the fivefold gain of the well-doer." 4

When the Blessed One had taught the disciples, and incited them, and roused them, and gladdened them far into the night with religious edification, he dismissed them, saying, "The night is far spent, O householders. It is time for you to do what you deem most fit." 5

"Be it so, Lord!" answered the disciples of Pâtaliputra, and rising from their seats, they bowed to the Blessed One, and keeping him on their right hand as they passed him, they departed thence. 6

While the Blessed One stayed at Pâtaliputra, the king of Magadha sent a messenger to the governor of Pâtaliputra to raise fortifications for the security of the town. 7

And the Blessed One seeing the laborers at work predicted the future greatness of the place, saying: "The men who build the fortress act as if they had consulted higher powers. For this city of Pâtaliputra will be a dwelling-place of busy men and a centre for the exchange of all kinds of goods. But three dangers hang over Pâtaliputra, that of fire, that of water, that of dissension." 8

When the governor heard of the prophecy of Pâtaliputra's future, he greatly rejoiced and named the city-gate through which Buddha had gone towards the river Ganges, "The Gautama Gate." 9

Meanwhile the people living on the banks of the Ganges arrived in great numbers to pay reverence to the Lord of the world; and many persons asked him to do them the honor to cross over in their boats. But the Blessed One considering the number of the boats and their beauty did not want to show any partiality, and by accepting the invitation of one to offend all the others. He therefore crossed the river without any boat, signifying thereby that the rafts of asceticism and the gaudy gondolas of religious ceremonies were not staunch enough to weather the storms of the ocean of Samsâra, while the boat of wisdom is the safest vessel to reach the shore of Nirvâna. 10

And as the city gate was called after the name of the Tathâgata so the people called this passage of the river "Gautama Ford." 11

XC. SHÂRIPUTRA'S FAITH.

The Blessed One proceeded with a great company of the brethren to Nâlandâ; and there he stayed in a mango grove. 1

Now the venerable Shâriputra came to the place where the Blessed One was, and having saluted him, took his seat respectfully at his side, and said: "Lord! such faith have I in the Blessed One, that methinks there never has been, nor will there be, nor is there now any other, who is greater or wiser than the Blessed One, that is to say, as regards the higher wisdom." 2

Replied the Blessed One: "Grand and bold are the words of thy mouth, Shâriputra: verily, thou hast burst forth into a song of ecstasy! Surely then thou hast known all the Blessed Ones who in the long ages of the past have been holy Buddhas?" 3

"Not so, O Lord!" said Shâriputra. 4

And the Lord continued: "Then thou hast perceived all the Blessed Ones who in the long ages of the future shall be holy Buddhas?" 5

"Not so, O Lord!" 6

"But at least then, O Shâriputra, thou knowest me as the holy Buddha now alive, and hast penetrated my mind." 7

"Not even that, O Lord!" 8

"You see then, Shâriputra, that you know not the hearts of the holy Buddhas of the past nor the hearts of those of the future. Why, therefore, are your words so grand and bold? Why do you burst forth into such a song of ecstasy?" 9

"O Lord! I have not the knowledge of the hearts of Buddhas that have been and are to come, and now are. I only know the lineage of the faith. Just, Lord, as a king might have a border city, strong in its foundations, strong in its ramparts and with one gate alone; and the king might have a watchman there, clever, expert, and wise, to stop all strangers and admit only friends. And he, on going over the approaches all about the city, might not be able to observe all the joints and crevices in the ramparts of that city as to know where such a small creature as a cat could get out. That might well be. Yet all living beings of larger size that entered or left the city, would have to pass through that gate. Thus only is it, Lord, that I know the lineage of the faith. I know that the holy Buddhas of the past, putting away all lust, ill-will, sloth, pride, and doubt, knowing all those mental faults which make men weak, training their minds in the four kinds of mental activity, thoroughly exercising themselves in the sevenfold higher wisdom, received the full fruition of Enlightenment. And I know that the holy Buddhas of the times to come will do the same. And I know that the Blessed One, the holy Buddha of to-day, has done so now." 10

"Great is thy faith, O Shâriputra," replied the Blessed One, "but take heed that it be well grounded." 11

XCI. THE MIRROR OF TRUTH.

The Blessed One proceeded to the village Nâdika with a great company of brethren and there he stayed at the Brick Hall. And the venerable Ânanda went to the Blessed One and mentioning to him the names of the brethren and sisters that had died, anxiously inquired about their fate after death, whether they had been reborn in animals or in hell, or as ghosts, or in any place of woe. 1

And the Blessed One replied to Ânanda and said: 2

"Those who have died after the complete destruction of the three bonds of lust, of covetousness and of the egotistical cleaving to existence, need not fear the state after death. They will not be reborn in a state of suffering; their minds will not continue as a karma of evil deeds or sin, but are assured of final salvation. 3

"When they die, nothing will remain of them but their good thoughts, their righteous acts, and the bliss that proceeds from truth and righteousness. As rivers must at last reach the distant main, so their minds will be reborn in higher states of existence and continue to be pressing on to their ultimate goal which is the ocean of truth, the eternal peace of Nirvâna. 4

"Men are anxious about death and their fate after death; but there is nothing strange in this, Ânanda, that a human being should die. However, that you should inquire about them, and having heard the truth still be anxious about the dead, this is wearisome to the Blessed One. I will, therefore, teach you the mirror of truth: 5

"'Hell is destroyed for me, and rebirth as an animal, or a ghost, or in any place of woe. I am converted; I am no longer liable to be reborn in a state of suffering, and am assured of final salvation.' 6

"What, then, Ânanda, is this mirror of truth? It is the consciousness that the elect disciple is in this world possessed of faith in the Buddha, believing the Blessed One to be the Holy One, the Fully-enlightened One, wise, upright, happy, world-knowing, supreme, the Bridler of men's wayward hearts, the Teacher of gods and men, the blessed Buddha. 7

"It is further the consciousness that the disciple is possessed of faith in the truth, believing the truth to have been proclaimed by the Blessed One, for the benefit of the world, passing not away, welcoming all, leading to salvation, to which through truth the wise will attain, each one by his own efforts. 8

"And, finally, it is the consciousness that the disciple is possessed of faith in the order, believing in the efficacy of a union among those men and women who are anxious to walk in the noble eightfold path, believing this church of the Buddha, of the righteous, the upright, the just, the law-abiding, to be worthy of honor, of hospitality, of gifts, and of reverence; to be the supreme sowing-ground of merit for the world; to be possessed of the virtues beloved by the good, virtues unbroken, intact, unspotted, unblemished, virtues which make men truly free, virtues which are praised by the wise, are untarnished by the desire of selfish aims, either now or in a future life, or by the belief in the efficacy of outward acts, and are conducive to high and holy thought. 9

"This is the mirror of truth which teaches the straightest way to enlightenment which is the common goal of all living creatures. He who possesses the mirror of truth is free from fear, will find comfort in the tribulations of life, and his life will be a blessing to all his fellow-creatures." 10

XCII. AMBAPÂLÎ.

Then the Blessed One proceeded with a great number of brethren to Vaishâlî, and he stayed at the grove of the courtesan Ambapâlî. And he said to the brethren: "Let a brother, O bhikshus, be mindful and thoughtful. Let a brother, whilst in the world, overcome the grief which arises from bodily craving, from the lust of sensations, and from the errors of wrong reasoning. Whatever you do, act always in full presence of mind. Be thoughtful in eating and drinking, in walking or standing, in sleeping or waking, in talking or in being silent." 1

Now the courtesan Ambapâlî heard that the Blessed One had arrived and was staying at her mango grove; and she went in a carriage as far as the ground was passable for carriages, and there she alighted. Thence proceeding on foot to the place where the Blessed One was, she took her seat respectfully on one side. As a prudent woman goes forth to perform her religious duties, so she appeared in a simple dress without any ornaments, yet beautiful to look upon. 2

And the Blessed One thought to himself: "This woman moves in worldly circles and is a favorite of kings and princes; yet is her heart composed and quieted. Young in years, rich, surrounded by pleasures, she is thoughtful and steadfast. This, indeed, is rare in the world. Women, as a rule, are scant in wisdom and deeply immersed in vanity; but she, although living in luxury, has acquired the wisdom of a master, taking delight in piety, and able to receive the truth in its completeness." 3

When she was seated, the Blessed One instructed, aroused, and gladdened her with religious discourse. 4

As she listened to the law, her face brightened with delight. Then she rose and said to the Blessed One: "May the Blessed One do me the honor of taking his meal, together with the brethren, at my house to-morrow?" And the Blessed One gave, by silence, his consent. 5

Now, the Licchavi, a wealthy family of princely descent, hearing that the Blessed One had arrived at Vaishâlî and was staying at Ambapâlî's grove, mounted their magnificent carriages, and proceeded with their retinue to the place where the Blessed One was. And the Licchavi were gorgeously dressed in bright colors and decorated with costly jewels. 6

And Ambapâlî drove up against the young Licchavi, axle to axle, wheel to wheel, and yoke to yoke, and the Licchavi said to Ambapâlî, the courtesan: "How is it, Ambapâlî, that you drive up against us thus?" 7

"My lords," said she, "I have just invited the Blessed One and his brethren for their to-morrow's meal." 8

And the princes replied: "Ambapâlî! give up this meal to us for a hundred thousand." 9

"My Lord, were you to offer all Vaishâlî with its subject territory, I would not give up so great an honor!" 10

Then the Licchavi went on to Ambapâlî's grove. 11

When the Blessed One saw the Licchavi approaching in the distance, he addressed the brethren, and said: "O brethren, let those of the brethren who have never seen the gods gaze upon this company of the

Licchavi, for they are dressed gorgeously, like immortals." 12

And when they had driven as far as the ground was passable for carriages, the Licchavi alighted and went on foot to the place where the Blessed One was, taking their seats respectfully by his side. And when they were thus seated, the Blessed One instructed, roused, and gladdened them with religious discourse. 13

Then they addressed the Blessed One and said: "May the Blessed One do us the honor of taking his meal, together with the brethren, at our palace to-morrow?" 14

"O Licchavi," said the Blessed One, "I have promised to dine to-morrow with Ambapâlî, the courtesan." 15

Then the Licchavi, expressing their approval of the words of the Blessed One, arose from their seats and bowed down before the Blessed One, and, keeping him on their right hand as they passed him, they departed thence; but when they came home, they cast up their hands, saying: "A worldly woman has outdone us; we have been left behind by a frivolous girl!" 16

And at the end of the night Ambapâlî, the courtesan, made ready in her mansion sweet rice and cakes, and announced through a messenger the time to the Blessed One, saying, "The hour, Lord, has come, and the meal is ready!" 17

And the Blessed One robed himself early in the morning, took his bowl, and went with the brethren to the place where Ambapâlî's dwelling-house was: and when they had come there they seated themselves on the seats prepared for them. And Ambapâlî, the courtesan, set the sweet rice and cakes before the order, with the Buddha at their head, and waited upon them till they refused to take more. 18

And when the Blessed One had finished his meal, the courtezan had a low stool brought, and sat down at his side, and addressed the Blessed One, and said: "Lord, I present this mansion to the order of bhikshus, of which Buddha is the chief." And the Blessed One accepted the gift; and after instructing, rousing, and gladdening her with religious edification, he rose from his seat and departed thence. 19

XCIII. BUDDHA'S FAREWELL ADDRESS.

When the Blessed One had remained as long as he wished at Ambapâlî's grove, he went to Vênuvana, near Vaishâlî. There the Blessed One addressed the brethren, and said: "O mendicants, do you take up your abode for the rainy season round about Vaishâlî, each one according to the place where his friends and near companions may live. I shall enter upon the rainy season here at Vênuvana." 1

When the Blessed One had thus entered upon the rainy season there fell upon him a dire sickness, and sharp pains came upon him even unto death. But the Blessed One, mindful and self-possessed, bore them without complaint. 2

Then this thought occurred to the Blessed One, "It would not be right for me to pass away from life without addressing the disciples, without taking leave of the order. Let me now, by a strong effort of the will, bend this sickness down again, and keep my hold on life till the allotted time have come." 3

And the Blessed One, by a strong effort of the will, bent the sickness down, and kept his hold on life till the time he fixed upon should come. And the sickness abated. 4

Thus the Blessed One began to recover; and when he had quite got rid of the sickness, he went out from the monastery, and sat down on a seat spread out in the open air. And the venerable Ânanda, accompanied by many other disciples, approached where the Blessed One was, saluted him, and taking a seat respectfully on one side, said: "I have beheld, Lord, how the Blessed One was in health, and I have beheld how the Blessed One had to suffer. And though at the sight of the sickness of the Blessed One my body became weak as a creeper, and the horizon became dim to me, and my faculties were no longer clear, yet notwithstanding I took some little comfort from the thought that the Blessed One would not pass away from existence until at least he had left instructions as touching the order." 5

And the Blessed One addressed Ânanda for the sake of the order and said: 6

"What, then, Ânanda, does the order expect of me? I have preached the truth without making any distinction between exoteric and esoteric doctrine; for in respect of the truth, Ânanda, the Tathâgata has no such thing as the closed fist of a teacher, who keeps some things back. 7

"Surely, Ânanda, should there be any one who harbours the thought, 'It is I who will lead the brotherhood,' or, 'The order is dependent upon me,' he should lay down instructions in any matter concerning the order. Now the Tathâgata, Ânanda, thinks not that it is he who should lead the brotherhood, or that the order is dependent upon him. 8

"Why, then, should the Tathâgata leave instructions in any matter concerning the order? 9

"I am now grown old, O Ânanda, and full of years, my journey is drawing to its close, I have reached the sum of my days, I am turning eighty years of age. 10

"Just as a worn-out cart can only with much difficulty be made to move along, so the body of the Tathâgata can only be kept going with much additional care. 11

"It is only, Ânanda, when the Tathâgata, ceasing to attend to any outward thing, becomes plunged in that devout meditation of heart which is concerned with no bodily object, it is only then that the body of the Tathâgata is at ease. 12

"Therefore, O Ânanda, be ye lamps unto yourselves. Rely on yourselves, and do not rely on external help. 13

"Hold fast to the truth as a lamp. Seek salvation alone in the truth. Look not for assistance to any one besides yourselves. 14

"And how, Ânanda, can a brother be a lamp unto himself, rely on himself only and not on any external help, holding fast to the truth as his lamp and seeking salvation in the truth alone, looking not for assistance to any one besides himself? 15

"Herein, O Ânanda, let a brother, as he dwells in the body, so regard the body that he, being strenuous, thoughtful, and mindful, may, whilst in the world, overcome the grief which arises from the body's cravings. 16

"While subject to sensations let him continue so to regard the sensations that he, being strenuous, thoughtful, and mindful, may, whilst in the world, overcome the grief which arises from the sensations. 17

"And so, also, when he thinks or reasons, or feels, let him so regard his thoughts that being strenuous, thoughtful, and mindful he may, whilst in the world, overcome the grief which arises from the craving due to ideas, or to reasoning, or to feeling. 18

"Those who, either now or after I am dead, shall be a lamp unto themselves, relying upon themselves only and not relying upon any external help, but holding fast to the truth as their lamp, and seeking their salvation in the truth alone, shall not look for assistance to any one besides themselves, it is they, Ânanda, among my bhikshus, who shall reach the very topmost height! But they must be anxious to learn." 19

XCIV. BUDDHA ANNOUNCES HIS DEATH.

Said the Tathâgata to Ânanda: "In former years, Ânanda, Mâra, the Evil One, approached the holy Buddha three times to tempt him." 1

When Bôdhisattva left the palace, Mâra stood in the gate and stopped him: "Depart not, O my Lord," exclaimed Mâra, "in seven days from now the wheel of empire will appear, and will make you sovereign over the four continents and the two thousand adjacent islands. Therefore, stay, my Lord." 2

Bôdhisattva replied: "Well do I know that the wheel of empire will appear to me; but it is not sovereignty that I desire. I will become a Buddha and make all the world shout for joy. 3

"Again, Ânanda, the Evil One approached the Tathâgata when, after a practice of severe self-mortification, having bathed his body, he left the Nairanjana river. Mâra said: 'Thou art emaciated from fasts, and death is near. What good is thy exertion? Deign to live, and thou wilt be able to do good works.' 4

"Then the Blessed One made reply: 'O thou friend of the indolent, thou wicked one; for what purpose hast thou come? 5

"Let the flesh waste away, if but the mind becomes more tranquil and attention more steadfast. 6

"What is life in this world? Death in battle is better to me than that I should live defeated.' 7

"And Mâra left the Tathâgata, saying: 'For seven years I followed the Blessed One step by step, but I found no fault in the Enlightened One.' 8

"A third time, Ânanda, the tempter approached the Blessed One when he was resting under the shepherd's Nyagrôdha tree on the bank of the river Nairanjana, immediately after having reached the great enlightenment. Then Mâra, the Evil One, came to the place where the Blessed One was, and, standing beside him, he addressed him in the words: 'Pass away now, Lord, from existence! Let the Blessed One now die! Now is the time for the Blessed One to pass away!' 9

"And when Mâra had thus spoken, the Blessed One said: 'I shall not die, O Evil One, until not only the brethren and sisters of the order, but also the lay-disciples of both sexes, shall have become true hearers, wise and well trained, ready and learned, versed in the Scriptures, fulfilling all the greater and lesser duties, correct in life, walking according to the precepts—until they, having thus themselves learned the doctrine, shall be able to give information to others concerning it, preach it, make it known, establish it, open it, minutely explain it, and make it clear—until they, when others start vain doctrines, shall be able to vanquish and refute them, and so to spread the wonder-working truth abroad! I shall not die until the pure religion of truth shall have become successful, prosperous, widespread, and popular in all its full extent—until, in a word, it shall have been well proclaimed among men!' 10

"Thus three times did Mâra approach me in former years. And now, Ânanda, Mâra, the Evil One, came again to-day to the place where I was, and, standing beside me, addressed me in the same words: 'Pass away, Lord, from existence.' And when he had thus spoken, Ânanda, I answered him and said: 'Make thyself happy; the final extinction of the Tathâgata shall take place before long.'" 11

And the venerable Ânanda addressed the Blessed One and said: "Vouchsafe, Lord, to remain with us, O Blessed One! for the good and the happiness of the great multitudes, out of pity for the world, for the good and the gain of mankind!" 12

Said the Blessed One: "Enough now, Ânanda, beseech not the Tathâgata!" 13

And again, a second time, the venerable Ânanda besought the Blessed One in the same words. And he received from the Blessed One the same reply. 14

And again, the third time, the venerable Ânanda besought the Blessed One to live longer; and the Blessed One said: "Hast thou faith, Ânanda?" 15

Said Ânanda: "I have, my Lord!" 16

And the Blessed One, seeing the quivering eyelids of Ânanda, read the deep grief in the heart of his beloved disciple, and he asked again: "Hast thou, indeed, faith, Ânanda?" 17

And Ânanda said: "I have faith, my Lord." 18

Then the Blessed One continued: "If thou hast

faith, Ânanda, in the wisdom of the Tathâgata, why, then, Ânanda, dost thou trouble the Tathâgata even until the third time? Have I not formerly declared to you that it is in the very nature of all things, near and dear unto us, that we must separate from them, and leave them? How then, Ânanda, can it be possible for me to remain, since everything that is born, or brought into being, and organised, contains within itself the inherent necessity of dissolution? How, then, can it be possible that this body of mine should not be dissolved? No such condition can exist! And this mortal existence, O Ânanda, has been relinquished, cast away, renounced, rejected, and abandoned by the Tathâgata." 19

And the Blessed One said to Ânanda: "Go now, Ânanda, and assemble in the Service Hall such of the brethren as reside in the neighborhood of Vaishâlî." 20

Then the Blessed One proceeded to the Service Hall, and sat down there on the mat spread out for him. And when he was seated, the Blessed One addressed the brethren, and said: 21

"O brethren, ye to whom the truth has been made known, having thoroughly made yourselves masters of it, practise it, meditate upon it, and spread it abroad, in order that pure religion may last long and be perpetuated, in order that it may continue for the good and happiness of the great multitudes, out of pity for the world, and to the good and gain of all living beings! 22

"Star-gazing and astrology, forecasting lucky or unfortunate events by signs, prognosticating good or evil, all these are things forbidden. 23

"He who lets his heart go loose without restraint shall not attain Nirvâna; therefore, must we hold the heart in check, and retire from worldly excitements and seek tranquillity of mind. 24

"Eat your food to satisfy your hunger, and drink to satisfy your thirst. Satisfy the necessities of life like the butterfly that sips the flower, without destroying its fragrance or its texture. 25

"It is through not understanding and grasping the four truths, O brethren, that we have gone astray so long, and wandered in this weary path of transmigrations, both you and I, until we have found the truth. 26

"Practise the earnest meditations I have taught you. Continue in the great struggle against sin. Walk steadily in the roads of saintship. Be strong in moral powers. Let the organs of your spiritual sense be quick. When the seven kinds of wisdom enlighten your mind, you will find the noble, eightfold path that leads to Nirvâna. 27

"Behold, O brethren, the final extinction of the Tathâgata will take place before long. I now exhort you, saying: 'All component things must grow old and be dissolved again. Seek ye for that which is permanent, and work out your salvation with diligence.'" 28

XCV. CHUNDA, THE SMITH.

And the Blessed One went to Pâvâ. 1

When Chunda, the worker in metals, heard that the Blessed One had come to Pâvâ and was staying in his mango grove, he came to Buddha and respectfully invited him and the brethren to take their meal at his house. And Chunda prepared rice-cakes and a quantity of dried boar's flesh. 2

When the Blessed One had eaten the food prepared by Chunda, the worker in metals, there fell upon him a dire sickness, and sharp pain came upon him even unto death. But the Blessed One, mindful and self-possessed, bore it without complaint. 3

And the Blessed One addressed the venerable Ânanda, and said: "Come, Ânanda, let us go on to Kushinagara." 4

On his way the Blessed One grew tired, and he went aside from the road to rest at the foot of a tree, and said: "Fold, I pray you, Ânanda, the robe, and spread it out for me. I am weary, Ânanda, and must rest awhile!" 5

"Be it so, Lord!" said the venerable Ânanda; and he spread out the robe folded fourfold. 6

The Blessed One seated himself, and when he was seated he addressed the venerable Ânanda, and said: "Fetch me, I pray you, Ânanda, some water. I am thirsty, Ânanda, and would drink." 7

When he had thus spoken, the venerable Ânanda said to the Blessed One: "But just now, Lord, five hundred carts have gone over and have stirred the water; but a river, O Lord, is not far off. Its water is clear and pleasant, cool and transparent, and it is easy to get down to it. There the Blessed One may both drink water and cool his limbs." 8

A second time the Blessed One addressed the venerable Ânanda, saying: "Fetch me, I pray you, Ânanda, some water. I am thirsty, Ânanda, and would drink." 9

And a second time the venerable Ânanda said: "Let us go to the river." 10

Then the third time the Blessed One addressed the venerable Ânanda, and said: "Fetch me, I pray you, Ânanda, some water. I am thirsty, Ânanda, and would drink." 11

"Be it so, Lord!" said the venerable Ânanda in assent to the Blessed One; and, taking a bowl, he went down to the streamlet. And lo! the streamlet, which, stirred up by wheels, had become muddy, when the venerable Ânanda came up to it, flowed clear and bright and free from all turbidity. And he thought: "How wonderful, how marvellous is the great might and power of the Tathâgata!" 12

Ânanda brought the water in the bowl to the Lord, saying: "Let the Blessed One take the bowl. Let the Happy One drink the water. Let the Teacher of men and gods quench his thirst." 13

Then the Blessed One drank of the water. 14

Now, at that time a man of low caste, named Pukkasha, a young Malla, a disciple of Ârâda Kâlâma, was passing along the high road from Kushinagara to Pâvâ. 15

And Pukkasha, the young Malla, saw the Blessed One seated at the foot of a tree. On seeing him, he went up to the place where the Blessed One was, and when he had come there, he saluted the Blessed One and took his seat respectfully on one side. Then the Blessed One instructed, edified, and gladdened Pukkasha, the young Malla, with religious discourse. 16

Aroused and gladdened by the words of the Blessed One, Pukkasha, the young Malla, addressed a certain man who happened to pass by, and said: "Fetch me, I pray you, my good man, two robes of cloth of gold, burnished and ready for wear." 17

"Be it so, sir!" said that man in assent to Pukkasha, the young Malla; and he brought two robes of cloth of gold, burnished and ready for wear. 18

And the Malla, Pukkasha, presented the two robes of cloth of gold, burnished and ready for wear, to the

Blessed One, saying: "Lord, these two robes of burnished cloth of gold are ready for wear. May the Blessed One show me favor and accept them at my hands!" 19

The Blessed One said: "Pukkasha, robe me in one, and Ânanda in the other." 20

And the Tathâgata's body appeared shining like a flame, and he was beautiful above all expression. 21

And the venerable Ânanda said to the Blessed One: "How wonderful a thing is it, Lord, and how marvellous, that the color of the skin of the Blessed One should be so clear, so exceedingly bright! When I placed this robe of burnished cloth of gold on the body of the Blessed One, lo! it seemed as if it had lost its splendor!" 22

The Blessed One said: "There are two occasions on which a Tathâgata's appearance becomes clear and exceeding bright. In the night, Ânanda, in which a Tathâgata attains to the supreme and perfect insight, and in the night in which he passes finally away in that utter passing away which leaves nothing whatever of his earthly existence to remain." 23

And the Blessed One addressed the venerable Ânanda, and said: "Now it may happen, Ânanda, that some one should stir up remorse in Chunda, the smith, by saying: 'It is evil to thee, Chunda, and loss to thee, that the Tathâgata died, having eaten his last meal from thy provision.' Any such remorse, Ânanda, in Chunda, the smith, should be checked by saying: 'It is good to thee, Chunda, and gain to thee, that the Tathâgata died, having eaten his last meal from thy provision. From the very mouth of the Blessed One, O Chunda, have I heard, from his own mouth have I received this saying, "These two offerings of food are

of equal fruit and of much greater profit than any other: the offerings of food which a Tathâgata accepts when he has attained perfect enlightenment and when he passes away by the utter passing away in which nothing whatever of his earthly existence remains behind—these two offerings of food are of equal fruit and of equal profit, and of much greater fruit and much greater profit than any other. There has been laid up by Chunda, the smith, a karma redounding to length of life, redounding to good birth, redounding to good fortune, redounding to good fame, redounding to the inheritance of heaven and of great power."' In this way, Ânanda, should be checked any remorse in
Chunda, the smith." 24

Then the Blessed One, perceiving that death was near, uttered these words: "He who gives away shall have real gain. He who subdues himself shall be free of passions. The righteous man casts off sin; and by rooting out lust, bitterness, and illusion, do we reach
Nirvâna."' 25

XCVI. MAITRÊYA.

The Blessed One proceeded with a great company of the brethren to the shâla grove of the Mallas, the Upavartana of Kushinagara on the further side of the river Hiranyavatî, and when he had arrived he addressed the venerable Ânanda, and said: "Make ready for me, I pray you, Ânanda, the couch with its head to the north, between the twin shâla trees. I am weary,
Ânanda, and wish to lie down." 1

"Be it so, Lord!" said the venerable Ânanda, and he spread a couch with its head to the north, between the twin shâla trees. And the Blessed One laid him-
self down, and he was mindful and self-possessed. 2

Now, at that time the twin shâla trees were full of bloom with flowers out of season; and heavenly songs came wafted from the skies, out of reverence for the successor of the Buddhas of old. And Ânanda was filled with wonder that the Blessed One was thus honored. But the Blessed One said: "Not by such events, Ânanda, is the Tathâgata rightly honored, held sacred, or revered. But the brother or the sister, the devout man or the devout woman, who continually fulfils all the greater and the lesser duties, walking according to the precepts, it is they who rightly honor, hold sacred, and revere the Tathâgata with the worthiest homage. Therefore, O Ânanda, be ye constant in the fulfilment of the greater and of the lesser duties, and walk according to the precepts; thus, Ânanda, will ye honor the Master." 3

Then the venerable Ânanda went into the vihâra, and stood leaning against the lintel of the door, weeping at the thought: "Alas! I remain still but a learner, one who has yet to work out his own perfection. And the Master is about to pass away from me—he who is so kind!" 4

Now, the Blessed One called the brethren, and said: "Where, O brethren, is Ânanda?" 5

And one of the brethren went and called Ânanda. And Ânanda came and said to the Blessed One: "Deep darkness reigned for want of wisdom; the world of sentient creatures was groping for want of light; then the Tathâgata lit up the lamp of wisdom, and now it will be extinguished again, ere he has brought it out." 6

And the Blessed One said to the venerable Ânanda, as he sat there by his side: 7

"Enough, Ânanda! Do not let yourself be troubled;

do not weep! Have I not already, on former occasions, told you that it is in the very nature of all things most near and dear unto us that we must separate from them and leave them? 8

"The foolish man conceives the idea of 'self,' the wise man sees there is no ground on which to build the idea of 'self,' thus he has a right conception of the world and well concludes that all compounds amassed by sorrow will be dissolved again, but the truth will remain. 9

"Why should I preserve this body of flesh, when the body of the excellent law will endure? I am resolved; having accomplished my purpose and attended to the work set me, I look for rest! This is the one thing needed. 10

"For a long time, Ânanda, have you been very near to me by thoughts and acts of such love as never varies and is beyond all measure. You have done well, Ânanda! Be earnest in effort and you too shall soon be free from the great evils, from sensuality, from selfishness, from delusion, and from ignorance!" 11

And Ânanda, suppressing his tears, said to the Blessed One: "Who shall teach us when thou art gone?" 12

And the Blessed One replied: "I am not the first Buddha who came upon earth, nor shall I be the last. I came to teach you the truth, and I have founded on earth the kingdom of truth. Gautama Siddhârtha will die, but Buddha will live, for Buddha is the truth, and the truth cannot die. He who believes in the truth and lives it, is my disciple, and I shall teach him. The truth will be propagated, and the kingdom of truth will increase for about five hundred years. Then for a while the clouds of error will darken the light, and in due time another Buddha will arise, and he will reveal to you the selfsame eternal truth which I have taught you." 13

Ânanda said: "How shall we know him?" 14

The Blessed One said: "The Buddha that will come after me will be known as Maitrêya, which means 'he whose name is kindness.'" 15

XCVII. BUDDHA'S DEATH.

Then the Mallas, with their young men and maidens and their wives, being grieved, and sad, and afflicted at heart, went to the Upavartana, the shâla grove of the Mallas, and wanted to see the Blessed One, in order to partake of the bliss that devolves upon those who are in the presence of the Holy One. 1

And the Blessed One addressed them and said: 2

"Seeking the way, you must exert yourselves and strive with diligence. It is not enough to have seen me! Walk as I have commanded you; free yourself of the tangled net of sorrow. Walk in the path with steadfast aim. 3

"A sick man may be cured by the healing power of medicine and will be rid of all his ailments without beholding the physician. 4

"He who does not do what I command sees me in vain. This brings no profit. Whilst he who lives far off from where I am and yet walks righteously is ever near me. 5

"A man may dwell beside me, and yet, being disobedient, be far away from me. Yet he who obeys the dharma will always enjoy the bliss of the Tathâgata's presence." 6

Then the mendicant Subhadra went to the shâla

grove of the Mallas and said to the venerable Ânanda: "I have heard from fellow mendicants of mine, who were deep stricken in years and teachers of great experience: 'Sometimes and full seldom do Tathâgatas appear in the world, the holy Buddhas.' Now it is said that to-day in the last watch of the night, the final passing away of the shramana Gautama will take place. My mind is full of uncertainty, yet have I faith in the shramana Gautama and trust he will be able so to present the truth that I may get rid of my doubts. O that I might be allowed to see the shramana Gautama!" 7

When he had thus spoken the venerable Ânanda said to the mendicant Subhadra: "Enough! friend Subhadra. Trouble not the Tathâgata. The Blessed One is weary." 8

Now the Blessed One overheard this conversation of the venerable Ânanda with the mendicant Subhadra. And the Blessed One called the venerable Ânanda, and said: "Ânanda! Do not keep out Subhadra. Subhadra may be allowed to see the Tathâgata. Whatever Subhadra will ask of me, he will ask from a desire of knowledge, and not to annoy me, and whatever I may say in answer to his questions, that he will quickly understand." 9

Then the venerable Ânanda said to Subhadra the mendicant: "Step in, friend Subhadra; for the Blessed One gives you leave." 10

When the Blessed One had instructed Subhadra, and aroused and gladdened him with words of wisdom and comfort, Subhadra said to the Blessed One: 11

"Glorious Lord, glorious Lord! Most excellent are the words of thy mouth, most excellent! They set up that which has been overturned, they reveal that which has been hidden. They point out the right road to the wanderer who has gone astray. They bring a lamp into the darkness so that those who have eyes to see can see. Thus, Lord, the truth has been made known to me by the Blessed One and I take my refuge in the Blessed One, in the Truth, and in the Order. May the Blessed One accept me as a disciple and true believer, from this day forth as long as life endures." 12

And Subhadra, the mendicant, said to the venerable Ânanda: "Great is your gain, friend Ânanda, great is your good fortune, that for so many years you have been sprinkled with the sprinkling of discipleship in this brotherhood at the hands of the Master himself!" 13

Now the Blessed One addressed the venerable Ânanda, and said: "It may be, Ânanda, that in some of you the thought may arise, 'The word of the Master is ended, we have no teacher more!' But it is not thus, Ânanda, that you should regard it. It is true that no more shall I receive a body, for all future sorrow is now forever passed away. But while Gautama Siddhârtha is gone, Buddha remains. The truth and the rules of the order which I have set forth and laid down for you all, let them, after I am gone, be a teacher unto you. When I am gone, Ânanda, let the order, if it should so wish, abolish all the lesser and minor precepts." 14

Then the Blessed One addressed the brethren, and said: "There may be some doubt or misgiving in the mind of a brother as to the Buddha, or the truth, or the path. Do not have to reproach yourselves afterwards with the thought, 'We did not inquire of the Blessed One when we were face to face with him.' Therefore inquire now, O brethren, inquire freely." 15

And the brethren remained silent. 16

Then the venerable Ânanda said to the Blessed One: "Verily, I believe that in this whole assembly of the brethren there is not one brother who has any doubt or misgiving as to the Buddha, or the truth, or the path!" 17

Said the Blessed One: "It is out of the fullness of faith that thou hast spoken, Ânanda! But, Ânanda, the Tathâgata knows for certain that in this whole assembly of the brethren there is not one brother who has any doubt or misgiving as to the Buddha, or the truth, or the path! For even the most backward, Ânanda, of all these brethren has become converted, and is assured of final salvation." 18

Then the Blessed One addressed the brethren and said: "If ye now know the dharma, the cause of all suffering, and the path of salvation, O disciples, will ye then say: 'We respect the Master, and out of reverence for the Master do we thus speak!'" 19

The brethren replied: "That we shall not, O Lord." 20

And the Holy One continued: 21

"Of those beings who live in ignorance, shut up and confined, as it were, in an egg, I have first broken the egg-shell of ignorance and alone in the universe obtained the most exalted, universal Buddhahood. Thus, O disciples, I am the eldest, the noblest of beings. 22

"But what ye speak, O disciples, is it not even that which ye have yourselves known, yourselves seen, yourselves realised?" 23

Ânanda and the brethren said: "It is, O Lord." 24

Once more the Blessed One began to speak: "Behold now, brethren," said he, "I exhort you, saying, 'Decay is inherent in all component things, but the truth will remain forever!' Work out your salvation with diligence!" This was the last word of the Tathâgata. Then the Tathâgata fell into a deep meditation, and having lost consciousness passed peacefully away. 25

When the Blessed One entered Nirvâna there arose, at his passing out of existence, a mighty earthquake, terrible and awe-inspiring: and the thunders of heaven burst forth, and of those of the brethren who were not yet free from passions some stretched out their arms and wept, and some fell headlong on the ground, in anguish at the thought: "Too soon has the Blessed One died! Too soon has the Happy One passed away from existence! Too soon has the Light of the world gone out!" 26

Then the venerable Anuruddha exhorted the brethren and said: "Enough, my brethren! Weep not, neither lament! Has not the Blessed One formerly declared this to us, that it is in the very nature of all things near and dear unto us, that we must separate from them and leave them, since everything that is born, brought into being, and organised, contains within itself the inherent necessity of dissolution? How then can it be possible that the body of the Tathâgata should not be dissolved? No such condition can exist! Those who are free from passion will bear the loss, calm and self-possessed, mindful of the truth he has taught us." 27

And the venerable Anuruddha and the venerable Ânanda spent the rest of the night in religious discourse. 28

Then the venerable Anuruddha said to the venerable Ânanda: "Go now, brother Ânanda, and inform the Mallas of Kushinagara saying, 'The Blessed One has passed away: do, then, whatsoever seemeth to you fit!'" 29

And when the Mallas had heard this saying they were grieved, and sad, and afflicted at heart. 30

Then the Mallas of Kushinagara gave orders to their attendants, saying, "Gather together perfumes and garlands, and all the music in Kushinagara!" And the Mallas of Kushinagara took the perfumes and garlands, and all the musical instruments, and five hundred garments, and went to the shâla grove where the body of the Blessed One lay. There they passed the day in paying honor and reverence to the remains of the Blessed One, with dancing, and hymns, and music, and with garlands and perfumes, and in making canopies of their garments, and preparing decorative wreaths to hang thereon. And they burned the remains of the Blessed One as they would do to the body of a king of kings. 31

When the funeral pyre was lit, the sun and moon withdrew their shining, the peaceful streams on every side were torrent-swollen, the earth quaked, and the sturdy forests shook like aspen leaves, whilst flowers and leaves untimely fell to the ground, like scattered rain, so that all Kushinagara became strewn knee-deep with mandâra flowers raining down from heaven. 32

When the burning ceremonies were over, Dêvaputra said to the multitudes that were assembled round the pyre: 33

"Behold, O brethren, the earthly remains of the Blessed One have been dissolved, but the truth which he has taught us lives in our minds and cleanses us from all sin. 34

"Let us, then, go out into the world, as compassionate and merciful as our great master, and preach to all living beings the four noble truths and the eightfold path of righteousness, so that all mankind may attain to a final salvation, taking refuge in the Buddha, the Dharma, and the Sangha." 35

And when the Blessed One had entered into Nirvâna, and the Mallas had burned the body with such ceremonies as would indicate that he was the great king of kings, ambassadors came from all the empires that at the time had embraced his doctrine, to claim a share of the relics; and the relics were divided into eight parts and eight dâgôbas were erected for their preservation. One dâgôba was erected by the Mallas and seven others by the seven kings of those countries, the people of which had taken refuge in Buddha. 36

CONCLUSION.

XCVIII. THE THREE PERSONALITIES OF BUDDHA.

WHEN the Blessed One had passed away into Nirvâna, the disciples came together and consulted what to do in order to keep the dharma pure and uncorrupted by heresies. 1

And Upâli rose, saying: 2

"Our great Master used to say to the brethren: 'O bhikshus! after my Nirvâna you must reverence and obey the law. Regard the law as your master. The law is like unto a light that shines in the darkness, pointing out the way; it is also like unto a precious jewel to gain which you must shun no trouble, and be ready to bring any sacrifice, even, should it be needed, your own lives. Obey the dharma which I have revealed to you; follow it carefully and regard it in no way different from myself.' 3

"Such were the words of the Blessed One. 4

"The law, accordingly, which Buddha has left us as a precious inheritance has now become the visible body of the Tathâgata. Let us, therefore, revere it and keep it sacred. For what is the use of erecting dâgôbas for relics, if we neglect the spirit of the Master's teachings." 5

And Anuruddha arose and said: 6

"Let us bear in mind, O brethren, that Gautama Siddhârtha was the visible appearance of the truth itself. He was the Holy One and the Perfect One and the Blessed One, because the eternal truth had taken abode in his body. The great Shâkyamuni is the bodily incarnation of the truth, and he has revealed the truth
to us. 7

"The Tathâgata taught us that the truth existed before he was born into this world, and will exist after
he has entered into the bliss of Nirvâna. 8

"The Tathâgata said: 9

"'The Blessed One is the truth; and as such he is omnipresent and eternal, endowed with excellencies innumerable, above all human nature, and ineffable in
his holiness.' 10

"Now, let us bear in mind that not this or that law which he has given us in the dharma is Buddha, but the truth, the truth which is eternal, omnipresent, im-
mutable, and most excellent. 11

"Many laws of the dharma are temporary and were prescribed because they suited the occasion and were needed for some transient emergency. The truth, how-
ever, is not temporary. 12

"The truth is not arbitrary or a matter of opinion, but can be investigated, and he who earnestly searches
for the truth will find it. 13

"The truth is hidden to the blind, but he who has the mental eye sees the truth. The truth is Buddha's essence, and the truth will remain the ultimate standard by which we can discern false and true doc-
trines. 14

"Let us, then, revere the truth; let us inquire into the truth and state it, and let us obey the truth. For the truth is Buddha our Master, our Teacher, our Lord." 15

And Kâshyapa rose and said: 16

"Truly you have spoken well, O brethren. Neither is there any conflict of opinion on the meaning of our religion. For the Blessed One possesses three personalities, and every one of them is of equal importance to us. 17

"There is the Dhârma Kâya. There is the Nirmâna Kâya. There is the Sambhôga Kâya. 18

"Buddha is the all-excellent truth, eternal, omnipresent, and immutable. This is the Sambhôga Kâya which is in a state of perfect bliss. 19

"Buddha is the all-loving teacher assuming the shape of the beings whom he teaches. This is the Nirmâna Kâya, his apparitional body. 20

"Buddha is the all-blessed dispensation of religion. He is the spirit of the Sangha and the meaning of the commands which he has left us in his sacred word, the dharma. This is the Dharma Kâya, the body of the most excellent law. 21

"If Buddha had not appeared to us as Gautama Shâkyamuni, how could we have the sacred traditions of his doctrine? And if the generations to come did not have the sacred traditions preserved in the Sangha, how could they know anything of the great Shâkyamuni? And neither we nor others would know anything about the most excellent truth which is eternal, omnipresent, and immutable. 22

"Let us then keep sacred and revere the traditions; let us keep sacred the memory of Gautama Shâkyamuni, so that both may serve us to find the truth; for he whose spiritual eye is open will discover it, and it is the same to every one who possesses the comprehension of a Buddha to recognise it and to expound it." 23

Then the brethren decided to convene a synod in Râjagriha in order to lay down the pure doctrines of the Blessed One, to collect and collate the sacred writings, and establish a canon which should serve as a source of instruction for future generations. 24

XCIX. THE PURPOSE OF BEING.

When in the cycle of forming universes the first tangible shapes of sun and earth and moon appeared, Truth moved in the cosmic dust and filled the whole world with blazing light. Yet there was no eye to see the light, no ear to listen to the truth, no mind to perceive its meaning; and in the immeasurable spaces of existence no place was found where the truth could abide in all its glory. 1

In the due course of evolution sentiency appeared and sense-perception arose. There was a new realm of soul-life, full of yearning, with powerful passions and of unconquerable energy. And the world split in twain: there were pleasures and pains, self and not-self, friends and foes, hatred and love. The truth vibrated through the world of sentiency, but in all its infinite potentialities no place could be found where the truth could abide in all its glory. 2

And reason came forth in the struggle for life. Reason began to guide the instinct of self, and reason took the sceptre of the creation and overcame the strength of the brutes and the power of the elements. Yet reason seemed to add new fuel to the flame of hatred, increasing the turmoil of conflicting passions; and brothers slew their brothers for the sake of satisfying the lust of a fleeting moment. And the truth repaired to the domains of reason, but in all its recesses no place was found where the truth could abide in all its glory. 3

Now reason, as the helpmate of self, implicated all living beings more and more in the meshes of lust, hatred, and envy, and from lust, hatred, and envy the evils of sin originated. Men broke down under the burdens of life, until the saviour appeared, the great Buddha, the Holy Teacher of men and gods. 4

And Buddha taught men the right use of sentiency, and the right application of reason; and he taught men to see things as they are, without illusions, and they learned to act according to truth. He taught righteousness and thus changed rational creatures into humane beings, just, kind-hearted, and faithful. And now at last a place was found where the truth might abide in all its glory, and this place is the soul of mankind. 5

Buddha, O Blessed One, O Holy One, O Perfect One, thou hast revealed the truth, and the truth has appeared upon earth and the kingdom of truth has been founded. 6

There is no room for truth in space, infinite though it be. 7

There is no room for truth in sentiency, neither in its pleasures nor in its pains; sentiency is the first footstep of truth, but there is no room in it for the truth, though it may beam with the blazing glow of beauty and life. 8

Neither is there any room for truth in rationality. Rationality is a two-edged sword and serves the purpose of love equally as well as the purpose of hatred. Rationality is the platform on which the truth stand.

eth. No truth is attainable without reason. Nevertheless, in mere rationality there is no room for truth, though it be the instrument that masters the things of the world. 9

The throne of truth is righteousness; and love and justice and good-will are its ornaments. 10

Righteousness is the place in which truth dwells, and here in the souls of mankind aspiring after the realisation of righteousness, there is ample space for a rich and ever richer revelation of the truth. 11

This is the Gospel of the Blessed One. This is the revelation of the Enlightened One. This is the bequest of the Holy One. 12

Those who accept the truth and have faith in the truth, take refuge in the Buddha, the Dharma, and the Sangha. 13

Receive us, O Buddha, as thy disciples from this day hence, so long as our life lasts. 14

Comfort, O holy Teacher, compassionate and all-loving, the afflicted and the sorrow-laden, illumine those who go astray, and let us all gain more and more in comprehension and in holiness. 15

The truth is the end and aim of all existence, and the worlds originate so that the truth may come and dwell therein. 16

Those who fail to aspire for the truth have missed the purpose of life. 17

Blessed is he who rests in the truth, for all things will pass away, but the truth abideth forever. 18

The world is built for the truth, but false combinations of thought misrepresent the true state of things and bring forth errors. 19

Errors can be fashioned as it pleases those who cherish them; therefore they are pleasant to look

upon, but they are unstable and contain the seeds of
dissolution. 20

Truth cannot be fashioned. Truth is one and the
same; it is immutable. 21

Truth is above the power of death, it is omni-
present, eternal, and most glorious. 22

Illusions, errors, and lies are the daughters of Mâra,
and great power is given unto them to seduce the
minds of men and lead them astray upon the path of
sin. 23

The nature of delusions, errors, and lies is death;
and sin is the way to perdition. 24

Delusions, errors, and lies are like huge, gaudy
vessels, the rafters of which are rotten and worm-
eaten, and those who embark in them are fated to be
shipwrecked. 25

There are many who say: "Come error, be thou
my guide," and when they are caught in the meshes of
selfishness, lust, and evil desires, misery is begot. 26

Yet does all life yearn for the truth and the truth
only can cure our diseases and give peace to our un-
rest. 27

Truth is the essence of life, for truth endureth be-
yond the death of the body. Truth is eternal and will
still remain even though heaven and earth shall pass
away. 28

There are not many different truths in the world,
for truth is one and the same at all times and in every
place. 29

Truth teaches us the noble eightfold path of right-
eousness, and it is a straight path easily found by the
truth loving. Happy are those who walk in it. 30

C. THE PRAISE OF ALL THE BUDDHAS.

All the Buddhas are wonderful and glorious.
There is not their equal upon earth.
They reveal to us the path of life.
And we hail their appearance with pious reverence. 1

All the Buddhas teach the same truth.
The Truth points out the way to those who have gone wrong.
The Truth is our hope and comfort.
We gratefully accept its illimitable light. 2

All the Buddhas are one in essence,
Which is omnipresent in all modes of being,
Sanctifying the bonds that tie all souls together,
And we rest in its bliss as our final refuge. 3

TABLE OF REFERENCE.

THE GOSPEL OF BUDDHA CHAPTER AND VERSE	SOURCES	PARALLELISMS
I–III	*E A*	
Descent from heaven omitted	*L V* .... *rGya*, iii–v	Klopstock's *Messias* Gesang I.
IV	*Fo*, *vv*. 1–147	
IV, 6	*B St*, *p*. 64	Mark vii, 32, 37 Matth. xi, 5
IV, 9	*Fo*, *vv*. 22–24......	Matth. ii, 1
IV, 12	*Fo*, *vv*. 39–40......	Luke ii, 36
IV, 17	*R B* 150; *R H B* 52	Pseudo Matth. 23
IV, 27	*Fo*, *v*. 147.........	Luke ii, 52
Omitted	*R H B*, *pp*. 103–108.	Matth. ii, 16
V	*H M*, *p*. 156; *R B*, *p*. 83; *rGya*, xii	
	Fo, *vv*. 152–156....	Luke ii, 46–47
V, 9	*Fo*, *v*. 164.........	Matth. iii, 16
VI	*Fo*, *vv*. 191–322	
VI, 19–20	*B St*, *pp*. 79–80 .... *R B*, *p*. 23	Luke xi, 27–28
VII	*Fo*, *vv*. 335–417	
VII, 7	*B St*, *p*. 5–6	
VII, 18–19	*B St*, *p*. 18	Matth. xxiv, 35 Luke xxi, 33 Luke xvi, 17
VIII	*Fo*, *vv*. 778–918	
VIII, 15	*D P*, *v*. 178	
IX	*Fo*, *vv*. 919–1035	
IX, 6	*M V*, i, 6, §§ 36–38 [*S B*, xiii, *p*. 100]	

THE GOSPEL OF BUDDHA CHAPTER AND VERSE	SOURCES	PARALLELISMS
IX, 14	*QKM*, *pp.* 83–86 ..	Evolution theory
IX, 15	*QKM*, *p.* 133	
IX, 16	*QKM*, *p.* 111	
X	*Fo*, *vv* 1000–1023	
X, 11	*Fo*, *v.* 1024 .... *Fo*, *vv.* 1222–1224..	Luke vii, 19 Matth. ii, 3
XI [See LXXXIX, 1–6]	*Fo*, *vv.* 1026–1110..	Luke iv, 2 Matth. iv, 1–7 Mark i, 13
XII	*Fo*, 1111–1199	
XII, 8	*QKM*, *p.* 79 *SDP*, vii [*SB*, xxi, *p.* 172]	
XII, 11–15	*SDP*, iii [*SB*, xxi, *p.* 90] *MV*, i, 6, §§ 19–28 Cf. *Old*, *G*, *pp.* 227–228, *Old*, *E*, *p.* 211 *RhDB*, *pp.* 106–107	
XII, 16	*B St*, *pp.* 103–104 Cf. *DP*, *pp.* 153–154	
XII, 20	*rGya*, 355	Matth. v, 3–11
XIII	*MV*, i, 4	
XIV	*MV*, i, 5	
XIV, 2	*MV*, i, 3, § 4	
XV	*Fo*, *vv.* 1200–1217 *MV*, i, 6, §§ 1–9	
XVI	*Fo*, 1217–1279 *MV*, i, 6, §§ 10–47	
XVI, 5	*SN*, *v.* 248	
XVI, 6	*RhDB*, *p.* 131	
XVI, 7	*SN*, *v.* 241........	Matth. xv, 10
XVII	*MV*, i, 6, § 10–47	
XVII, 10–12	*Samyuttaka Nikâya*, volume iii, fol. sâ, quoted by *Old*, *G*, 364; *Old*, *E*, *p.* 339	

THE GOSPEL OF BUDDHA CHAPTER AND VERSE	SOURCES	PARALLELISMS
XVIII	*M V*, i, 7, 8, 9..... *Fo*, *vv*. 1280–1296..	John iii, 2
XVIII, 8	*Fo*, *vv*. 1289–1290	
XVIII, 10	*Fo*, *v*. 1292	
XIX	*M V*, i, 11 *Fo*, *vv*. 1297–1300..	Luke ix, 1–6 Luke x, 1–24
XIX,	*Q K M*, *p*. 264 ..... *Q K M*, *p*. 266	Matth. v, 16 Matth. vii, 6
XX	*Fo*, 1300–1334 *M V*, i, 20–21	
XXI	*Fo*, 1335–1379 *M V*, i, 22	
XXI, 19–20	*S N*, *v*. 148. *Metta Sutra*. [An often quoted sentence. *Rh D B*, *p*. 109, Hardy, "Legends and Theories of the Buddhas," *p*. 212.	
XXI, 23	*Rh D B*, *p*. 62	
XXI, 28	*Fo*, *v*. 1733	
XXII	*Fo*, 1380–1381 *M V*, i, 22, §§ 15–18	
XXIII	*Fo*, *vv*. 1382–1431 *M V*, i, 23–24	
XXIII, 3–5	*M V*, i, 23, §§ 13–14	Matth. xxi, 9 Mark xi, 9 John xii, 13
XXIV	*M V*, i, 23 § 5–7	
XXV	*Fo*, 1432–1495	
XXV, 10–20	*E A*,	
XXVI	*Fo*, *vv*. 1496–1521	
XXVI, 4	*Fo*, 1516–1517	Acts xx, 35
XXVII	*Fo*, *vv*. 1534–1610 *H M*, *p*. 204	

THE GOSPEL OF BUDDHA CHAPTER AND VERSE	SOURCES	PARALLELISMS
XXVIII	*HM*, *p.* 203 et seqq. *B St*, *pp.* 125–126	
XXIX	*M V*, i. 54. *H M*, 208–209	
XXX	*Fo*, *vv.* 1522–1533 1611–1671	
XXXI	*MV*, viii, 23–36 [*SB.* xvii, *pp.* 193–194]	
XXXII	*Fo*, *vv.* 1672–1673	
XXXIII	*H M*, *pp.* 353–354	
XXXIV	*S 42 S*............ *Fo*, *vv*, 1757–1766.. *B P*, *p.* 153	Matth. v, 28
XXXIV, 19–11	*Fo*, *vv.* 1762–1763.. *Fo*, *vv.* 1763.......	Eph. vi, 13–17 Mark ix, 47 Matth. v, 29 Matth. xviii, 9
XXXV	*M V.* viii, 15. [*S B*, xvii, *pp.* 219–225.]	
XXXV, 24 [Last part of the verse.]	*Bgt*, *p.* 211........	Luke viii, ii Matth. xiii, 24–27
XXXVI	*M V*, ii	
XXXVII	*M V*, x, 1, 2 §1–2 and end of 2 § 20	
XXXVIII	*M V*, x, 5-6; x, 2 §3-20	
XXXIX	*M V*, v, 4	
XXXIX, 3	*B St*, *p.* 311	
XXXIX, 5	*M V*, v, 4, 2. [*S B.* xvii, *p.* 18.]	Matth. v, 46–47
XL	*Fo*, *vv.* 1713–1734 *H M*, *pp.* 337–340	
XL, 4	*B St*, *p.* 200	
XL, 7	*DP*, *v.* 227; *SB* x, *p.* 58 (cf. *ChD*, *p.* 122)	Matth. xi, 16, 19
XLI	*M V*, vi, 29. [*S B*, xvii, *pp.* 104–105]	

THE GOSPEL OF BUDDHA CHAPTER AND VERSE	SOURCES	PARALLELISMS
XLI, 12–13	*Metta Sutta* *S N*, *v.* 148. [cf. *Rh D B*, *p.* 109]	
XLII	*R B*, *pp.* 68–69. [cf. *Rh D B*, *p.* 71 and *Old*, *G*, 376–378].	Mark iii, 14 Luke ix, 2
	Bgt, 212	Matth. xiii, 3 et seq. Mark iv, 3–20
XLIV	*M V*, i, 56	
XLV	*S 42 S*, 12–13 *Rh D B*, *p.* 139	
XLVI	*S 42 S*, 4	
XLVII	*S D P*, x, xiii, xxvii	
XLVII, 23	*S D P*, xxiv, 22 [*S B* xxi, *p.* 416]	
XLVIII	*D P* in *S B*, x	
XLVIII, 36–37	*D P*, *v.* 5..........	Matth. v, 44
XLVIII, 47	*D P*, *v.* 275.	II Cor. xii, 7
XLVIII, 50	*S N*, 3, 5–6; 12, 7–9; 8, 11.	
XLIX	*Tevijja Sutta* in *S B* xi, *pp.* 157–203	
XLIX, 17	*Tevijja S*, i, 15....	Matth. xv, 14
L	*Sigâlovada Sutta* in *S S P*, *pp.* 297–320 [cf. *Rh D B*, 143]	
LI, 1–14 LI, 31–35	*M V*, vi, 31, [*S B*, xvii, *pp.* 108–113	
LI, 15–30	*E A* [cf. *Q K M*, *pp.* 254–257]	
LII	*E A* [cf. *C B S p.* 15 and also *M Y* v]	
LIII	Compiled from *HM* *pp.* 280 et seq., *Fo* *vv.* 1682–1683, and *QKM*	

THE GOSPEL OF BUDDHA CHAPTER AND VERSE	SOURCES	PARALLELISMS
LIII, 18–23*a*	*QKM, p.* 120	
LIII, 23*b*	*QKM, p.* 148.....	John iii, 8
LIII, 26–27	*QKM, p.* 67	
LIII, 29–32	*QKM, pp.* 73–74	
LIII, 47	*QKM, p.* 63	
LIII, 59	*QKM, p.* 83–86	
LIV, 1–2	*Fo, vv.* 1228, 1208..	Matth. v, 3–11
LIV, 3	*Brahmajâla Sutta,* quoted by *Rh D, p.* 99	John xvi, 16 Matth. xxiv, 23
LIV, 4	*QKM, p.* 114	
LIV, 5	*Fo, v.* 1231	
LIV, 6–8	*rGya, p.* 372	Matth. xi, 28
LIV, 9	*S 42 S,* 16	
LIV, 10	*QKM, p.* 110.....	John xiv, 6 John xviii, 37
LV	*SDP,* v	
LVI	*Mahâ Râhula Sutta*	
LVII	*S 42 S*	
LVIII	*Buddhist Catena*	
LIX	*SN, pp.* 58–62; *p.* 25; *p.* 147; *p.* 54 *MV,* i, 3, § 4 [cf. *Old, E, p.* 118] *Nidhikanda Sutta,* quoted by *Rh DB, p.* 127	Matth. vi, 20
LX, 7–8	*Rh DB, p.* 156	
LX, 12	Beal, *Buddhism of China,* chap. xii	
LX, 18–23	*Rh DB, p.* 170	
LX, 27–28	*EH*	
LX, 29	*QKM, p.* 127	
LX, 31	*Rh DB, pp.* 175–176	
LX, 33	*Rh DB, p.* 173	
LXI	*MPN,* iii. 22 [*SB* xx, *p.* 48–49]	

THE GOSPEL OF BUDDHA CHAPTER AND VERSE	SOURCES	PARALLELISMS
LXI, 3–5	*Chullavagga* ix, 1–4 [*S B* xx, 301–305]	Matth. v, 13
LXI, 6–9	*Sutra Dsanglun* [cf. R. Seydel "*Das Ev. v. Jesu in s. Verh. z. Buddha-Sage*" *pp.* 184–185	Matth. v, 1–2
LXII	*E A*	
LXIII	*S D P*, iii	
LXIV	*D D P*, v	
LXV	*S D P*, iv	Luke xv, 11 et seq.
LXVI	*B St*, *pp.* 211, 299 [See *PT*, ii, 58]	
LXVII	*B St*, *pp.* 315 et seq.	
LXVIII	*Ch D*, *pp.* 88–89	
LXVIII, 6	*Ch D*	Mark xii, 42–44
LXIX	*Ch D*, *p.* 46	The Story of Diogenes and his Lantern
LXX	*Ch D*, *p.* 134	
LXXI	*Bg P*, *pp.* 107 et seq.	
LXXII	*Ch D*, *p.* 77	Luke xii, 20
LXXIII	*B St*, *p.* 147	
LXXIII, 15	*B St*..............	Exodus xvii, 6
LXXIV	*S N*, *pp.* 11–15	Matth. xiii, 3 et seq. Mark iv, 14
LXXV	*S N*, *pp.* 20 et seq.	
LXXVI	*Bf*, *p.* 205	John v, 5 et seq.
LXXVII	*H M*, *pp.* 317–319	
LXXVIII LXXIX	*Jataka Tales*	
LXXX	*Bf*, *pp.* 146 et seq.	
LXXXI	*Fu-Pen-Hing-tsi-King*, tr. by S. Beal	
LXXXI, 7–10	*E A*	John ii, 1 et seq.
LXXXII	*M V*, i, 14	
LXXXIII	*Ch D*, *p.* 130 et seq.	

THE GOSPEL OF BUDDHA CHAPTER AND VERSE	SOURCES	PARALLELISMS
LXXXIII, 5	*B P*, *p*. 16	
LXXXIII, 5, 6, 9	*Ch D* and *S S*	Matth. xxii, 30
LXXXIV, 1–14	*B P*, *pp*. 98 et seqq.	Greek versions quoted by Jacob H. Thiesen, *L K G.*
LXXXIV, 15–28	*S B*, x, *p*. 106	
LXXXV	*Ch D*, *pp*. 50–51....	Matth. v, 25, 29
LXXXV, 6	*Ch D*	Rom. iii, 28
LXXXVI	*Ch D*, *pp*. 94–98	
LXXXVII	*M P N*, i [*S B*, xi, *p*. 1 et seqq.]	
LXXXVIII	*M P N*, ii, 4 and passim	
LXXXIX	*M P N*, i, 19, 22 *M V*, vi, 28	
XC	*M P N*, i, 16	
XCI	*M P N*, ii, 9	
XCI, 6	*M P N*...........	I Cor. 15, 55
XCII	*M P N*, ii, 12–24 *Fo*, *vv*. 1749–1753; 1768–1782.	
XCIII	*M P N*, ii, 27–35	
XCIV, 1–3	*B St*, *p*. 84........	Luke iv, 5–8 [See also Matth. iv, 1–7 and Mark i, 13]
XCIV, 4–7	*S N*, *vv*. 425, 439 ..	Luke iv, 2–4
XCIV, 8	*S N*, *v* 445	John iii, 46
XCIV, 9–22	*M P N*, iii, 43–63	
XCV	*M P N*, iv, 14–57	
XCV, 6	*M P N*, iv, 25	John xix, 28
XCV, 14–22	*M P N*, iv, 47–52 ..	Matth. xvii, 2 Mark ix, 2
XCVI	*M P N*, v, 1–14, concerning Maitrêya see *E H s. v. Rh D B*, *pp*. 180, 200; *Old*, *G*, *p*. 153, etc.	John xiv, 26

THE GOSPEL OF BUDDHA CHAPTER AND VERSE	SOURCES	PARALLELISMS
XCVII	*MPN*, v, 52–69, and vi; *Fo*, *vv*. 2303–2310	
XCVII, 19–20 } XCVII, 23–24 }	*Mahatanhâsakhamya-Sutta*, *Majjhima Nikâya*, vol. i, *p*. 263, quoted by *Old*, *G*, *p*. 349, *E*, *p*. 325	
XCVII, 22	*Suttavibhanga*, *Pârâjika* i, *pp*. 1, 4, quoted by *Old*, *G*, *p*. 349, *E*, *p*. 325.	I Cor. xv, 20
XCVIII	*EA*, embodying later traditions see *EH* and almost any other work on Buddhism	The Christian Trinity dogma.
XCIX	*EA*	
C	*EA*, in imitation of a formula at present in use among Northern Buddhists.	

ABBREVIATIONS IN THE TABLE OF REFERENCE.

Bf.—Burnouf, Introduction à l'histoire du Bouddhisme Indien, Paris, 1844.

Bgt.—The Life or Legend of Gautama, by the R. Rev. P. Bigandet, Second Edition, Rangoon, 1886.

BP.—Buddhaghosha's Parables. Translated by T. Rogers, London, 1870.

BSt.—Buddhist Birth Stories or Jataka Tales. Translated by Rhys Davids, London, 1880.

CBS.—A Catena of Buddhist Scriptures from the Chinese by Samuel Beal London, 1871.

Ch D.—[Chinese Dhammapada.] Texts from the Buddhist Canon, commonly known as Dhammapada. Translated by S. Beal, London and Boston, 1878.

D P.—The Dhammapada. Translated from Pâli by F. Max Müller, Vol. X, Part I, of the Sacred Books of the East. Oxford, 1881.

E A.—Explanatory Addition.

E H.—Handbook of Chinese Buddhism, by Ernest J. Eitel. London, 1888.

Fo.—The Fo-Sho-Hing-Tsan-King. A Life of Buddha by Asvaghosha, translated from Sanskrit into Chinese by Dharmaraksha, A. D. 420, and from Chinese into English by Samuel Beal. Vol. XIX of the Sacred Books of the East. Oxford, 1883.

H M.—A Manual of Buddhism, by R. Spence Hardy. Second Edition. London, 1880.

L K G.—Die Legende von Kisâgotami, by Jakob H. Thiessen. Breslau, 1880.

L V.—Lalita Vistara, translated into German by Dr. S. Lefmann. Berlin, 1874.

M P N.—The Mahâparinibbâna Suttanta. The Book of the Great Decease. Vol. XI of the Sacred Books of the East. Oxford, 1881.

M V.—The Mahâvagga. I–IV in Vol. XIII; V–X in Vol. XVII of the Sacred Books of the East. Oxford, 1881–1882.

M Y.—Outlines of the Mahâyâna as Taught by Buddha, by S. Kuroda. Tokyo, Japan, 1893.

Old G.—German Edition, Buddha, sein Leben, seine Lehre und seine Gemeinde, by H. Oldenberg. Second Edition. Berlin, 1890.

Old E.—English translation, Buddha, His Life, His Doctrine, and His Order by H. Oldenberg. London, 1882.

P T.—Pantschatantra, translated into German by Theodor Benfey. Two vols. Leipsic, 1859.

Q K M.—The Questions of King Milinda, translated from Pâli by T. W. Rhys Davids, Vol. XXXV of the Sacred Books of the East. Oxford, 1890.

R B.—The Life of the Buddha from Thibetan Works, translated by W. W. Rockhill. London, 1884.

rGya.—rGya Tchee Roll Pa, Histoire du Bouddha Sakya Mouni, by Foucaux. Paris, 1868.

R H B.—The Romantic History of Buddha from the Chinese Sanskrit, by S. Beal. London, 1875.

Rh D B.—Buddhism, by T. W. Rhys Davids, in the Series of Non-Christian Religious Systems. London, 1890.

S 42 S.—Sutra of Forty-two Sections. Kyoto, Japan.

S B.—Sacred Books of the East.

S N.—Sutta Nipata, translated from the Pâli by V. Fausböll. Part II, Vol. X, of the Sacred Books of the East. Oxford, 1881.

S S.—A Brief Account of Shin-Shiu, by R. Akamatsu. Kyoto, Japan, 1893.

S S P.—Sept Suttas Pâlis, by M. P. Grimblot. Paris, 1876.

GLOSSARY OF NAMES AND TERMS.

[In the text of the present booklet all unnecessary terms have been avoided. Whenever a good English equivalent could be found, the foreign expression has been dropped. Nevertheless, the introduction not only of many foreign-sounding names, but also of some of the original terms, was unavoidable.

Now we have to state that the Eastern people, at least those of Hindu culture during the golden age of Buddhism in India, adopted the habit of translating not only terms but also names. A German whose name is Schmied is not called Smith in English, but Buddhists, when translating from Pâli into Sanskrit, change Siddhattha into Siddhârtha. The reason of this strange custom lies in the fact that Buddhists originally employed the popular speech and did not adopt the use of Sanskrit until about five hundred years after Buddha. Since the most important names and terms, such as Siddhârtha, Nirvâna, and Dharma, have become familiar to us in their Sanskrit form, while their Pâli equivalents, Siddhattha, Nibbâna, and Dhamma, are little used, *it appeared advisable to prefer the Sanskrit forms*, and *this principle has been carried out in "The Gospel of Buddha," with as much consistency as possible.* However, as there are instances in which the Pâli, for some reason or other, has been preferred by English authors [e. g. Krishâ Gautamî is always called Kisa Gôtamî], we present here in the Glossary both the Sanskrit and the Pâli forms.

Names which have been Anglicised, such as "Brahma, Brahman, Benares, Jain, and karma," have been preserved in their accepted form. If we adopt the rule of transferring Sanskrit and Pâli words in their stem-form, as we do in most cases (e. g. Nirvâna, âtman), we ought to call Brahma "Brahman," and karma "karman." But *usus est tyrannus*. In a popular book it is not wise to swim against the stream.

Following the common English usage of saying "Christ," not "the Christ," we say "Buddha," "Bôdhisattva," not "the Buddha," "the Bôdhisattva."]

Abhi'jñâ, *skt.*, Abhi'ññâ, *p.*, supernatural talent. There are six abhijñâs which Buddha acquired when attaining perfect enlightenment:—(1) the celestial eye, or an intuitive insight of the nature of any object in any universe; (2) the celestial ear, or the ability to understand any sound produced in any universe; (3) the power of assuming any shape or form; (4) knowledge of all forms of pre-existence of one's self and others;

(5) intuitive knowledge of the minds of all beings; and (6) knowledge of the finality of the stream of life.—154, 155.

Achira'vatî, *skt.* and *p.*, a river.—81.

Ajâtasha'tru, *skt.*, Ajâtasa'ttu, *p.*, the son of king Bimbisâra and his successor to the throne of Magadha.—95, 97.

Âjñâ'ta, *skt.*, Aññâ'ta, *p.*, literally "knowing," a cognomen of Kaundiñña, the first disciple of Buddha.—44.

Ambapâ'lî, the courtesan, called "Lady Amra" in Fo-Sho-Hing-Tsan-King. It is difficult for us to form a proper conception of the social position of courtesans at Buddha's time in India. This much is sure, that they were not common prostitutes, but ladies of wealth, possessing great influence. Their education was similar to the hetairæ in Greece, where Aspasia played so prominent a part. Their rank must sometimes have been like that of Madame Pompadour in France at the court of Louis XIV. They rose to prominence, not by birth, but by beauty, education, refinement, and other purely personal accomplishments, and many of them were installed by royal favor. The first paragraphs of Khandhaka VIII of the Mahâvagga [*S. B.*, Vol. XVII, pp. 171–172] gives a fair idea of the important rôle of courtesans in those days. They were not necessarily venal daughters of lust, but, often women of distinction and repute, worldly, but not disrespectable.—201, 202, 203, 204.

Amitâ'bha, *skt.* and *p.*, endowed with boundless light, from *amita*, infinite, immeasurable, and *âbhâ*, ray of light, splendor, the bliss of enlightenment. It is a term of later Buddhism and has been personified as Amitâbha Buddha, or Amita. The invocation of the all-saving name of Amitâbha Buddha is a favorite tenet of the Lotus or Pure Land sect, so popular in China and Japan. Their poetical conception of a paradise in the West is referred to in Chapter LX. Southern Buddhism knows nothing of a personified Amitâbha, and the Chinese travellers Fa-hien and Hiuen-tsang do not mention it. The oldest allusion to Amita is found in the *Amitâyus Sûtra*, translated A. D. 148–170. [See Eitel, *Handbook*, pp. 7–9.]—150, 151, 152, 153.

Âna'nda, *skt.* and *p.*, Buddha's cousin and his favorite disciple. The Buddhistic St. John (Johannes).—69, 70, 76, 100, 168, 169, 174, 175, 192, 199, 200, 205, 206, 207, 208, 209, 210, 212, 213, 214, 215, 216, 217, 218, 219, 220, 221, 222.

Anâthapi'ndika, *skt.* and *p.*, (also called Anâthapi'ndada in *skt.*) literally "One who gives alms (*pinda*) to the unprotected or needy (*anâtha*)." Eitel's etymology "one who gives without keeping (anâtha) a mouthful (pinda) for himself" is not tenable. A wealthy lay devotee famous for his liberality and donor of the Jêtavana vihâra.—59, 60, 61, 63, 64, 70, 71, 146.

Annabhâ'ra, *skt.* and *p.*, literally "he who brings food"; name of Sumana's slave.—167, 168.

Anuru'ddha, a prominent disciple of Buddha, known as the great master of Buddhist metaphysics. He was a cousin of Buddha, being the second son of Amritôdana, a brother of Shuddhôdana.—69, 222, 225.

Ârâ'da, *skt.*, Alâ'ra, *p.*, a prominent Brahman philosopher. His full name is Ârâda Kâlâma.—22, 23, 213.

Ar'hant, *skt.*, A'rahat, *p.*, a saint. (See also Saint in Index.)—82.

A'shvajit, *skt.*, A'ssaji, *p.*, one of Buddha's disciples by whose dignified demeanor Shâriputra is converted.—58.

A'sita, *skt.* and *p.*, a prophet.—8, 9.

Â'tman, *skt.* and *p.*, breath as the principle of life, the soul, self, the ego. To some of the old Brahman schools the âtman constitutes a metaphysical being in man, which is the thinker of his thoughts, the perceiver of his sensations, and the doer of his doings. Buddha denies the existence of an âtman in this sense.—22, 24, 26, 134.

Balâ'ni, or pancha-balâni, *skt.* and *p.*, (the singular is *bala*, power), the five moral powers (also called pancha-indriyâni), which are: Faith, energy, memory or recollection, meditation or contemplation, and wisdom or intuition.

Bena'res, the well-known city in India; Anglicised form of Vârâ'nasî, *skt.*, and Bârâ'nasî, *p.* (See also Kâshî.)—37, 48, 90, 91, 93, 94.

Bha'gavant, *skt.*, Bha'gavat, *p.*, the man of merit, worshipful, the Blessed One. A title of honor given to Buddha.—17, 174.

Bha'llika, *skt.* and *p.*, a merchant.—34, 35.

Bhâradvâ'ja, *skt.* and *p.*, name of a Brahman.—117, 119, 173.

Bhâ'vanâ, *p.*, meditation. There are five principal meditations: metta-bhâvanâ, on love; karunâ-bhâvanâ, on pity; muditâ-bhâvanâ, on joy; asubha-bhâvanâ, on impunity; and upekshâ-bhâvanâ, on serenity. [See Rhys Davids's *Buddhism*, pp. 170–171.]—153.

Bhi'kshu, *skt.*, bhi'kkhu, *p.*, mendicant, monk, friar; the five bhikshus, 27, 37, 38, 39, 40, 42, 43, 44, 49, 57, 59, 66, 75, 76, 77, 78, 80, 81, 82, 84, 85, 86, 87, 88, 90, 94, 95, 98, 100, 101,

104; bhikshus doffed their robes, 80; bhikshus rebuked, 94; bhikshus prospered, 100; the sick bhikshu, 190, 191.

Bhi'kshunî, *skt.*, bhi'kkhunî, *p.*, nun.—81.

Bimbisâ'ra, *skt.* and *p.*, the king of Magadha; often honored with the cognomen "Sai'nya," *skt.*, or "Sê'niya," *p.*, i. e. "the warlike or military."—19, 20, 54, 76, 97.

Bô'dhi, *skt.* and *p.*, knowledge, wisdom, enlightenment.

Bôdhi-a'nga or Bôjjha'nga, or Sa'tta Bojjha'ngâ, *p.*, meditation on the seven kinds of wisdom, which are:—energy, recollection, contemplation, investigation of scripture, joy, repose, and serenity.—82, 198.

Bôdhisa'ttva, *skt.*, Bôdhisa'tta, *p.*, he whose essence (*sattva*) is becoming enlightenment (*bôdhi*). The term denotes (1) one who is about to become a Buddha, but has not as yet attained Nirvâna; (2) a class of saints who have only once more to be born again to enter into Nirvâna; (3) in later Buddhism any preacher or religious teacher.—17, 19, 21–23, 26–31, 68; appearance of, 19; Bôddhisattvas, 110.

Bôdhi-tree, a tree of the species *ficus religiosa.*—29.

Bra'hma, Anglicised form of *skt.* stem-form *Brahman* (nom. s. *Brahmâ*). The chief God of Brahmanism, the world-soul. See also *Sahampati.*—35, 36, 69, 120–121; Brahma, a union with, 120; Brahma, face to face, 118; Brahma's mind, 120.

Brahmada'tta, *skt.* and *p.*, (etym. given by Brahma,) name of a mythical king of Kâshî, *skt.*, or Kâsî, *p.*—90, 91–94, 170, 178.

Bra'hman, the priestly caste of the Indians. Anglicised form of *Brâhmana* (*skt.* and *p.*). Priests were selected from the Brahman caste, but Brahmans were not necessarily priests; they were farmers, merchants, and often high officials in the service of kings. Brahmans, the two—117, 122.

Buddha, *skt.* and *p.*, the Awakened One, the Enlightened One.—Buddha is also called Shâkyamuni (the Shâkya sage), Shâkyasimha (the Shâkya Lion), Sugata (the Happy One), Satthar, nom. Satthâ, *p.*; Shâstar, *skt.*, (the Teacher), Jina (the Conqueror), Bhagavat (the Blessed One), Loka-nâtha (the Lord of the World), Sarvajña (the Omniscient One), Dharma-râja (the King of Truth), Tathâgata, etc. [See Rh. Davids's B. p. 28.] B., faith in the, 200; B., I am not the first, 217; B. not Gautama, 140; B., refuge in the, 46, 47, 52, 56, 104, 146, 182, 183, 224, 230; B. remains, Gautama is gone, 220; B. replies to the dêva, 146; B., the sower, 173; B., the teacher, 111; B., the three personalities of, 225; B., the truth, 2, 217, 227; B., truly thou art, 123, 129; B. will arise, another, 218; B.'s birth, 7; B.'s death, 218; B.'s farewell address, 204; consolidation of B.'s religion, 75; Buddhas, the praise of all the, 232; Buddhas, the religion of all the, 56; Buddhas, the words of immutable, 15, 18.

Cha'nna, *skt.* and *p.*, prince Siddhârtha's driver.—12, 18, 19.

Chu'nda, *skt.* and *p.*, the smith of Pâvâ.—211, 214, 215.

Dâgô'ba, modernised form of *skt.* Dhâtu-ga'rbha, "relic shrine," (also called Stûpa in Northern Buddhism) a mausoleum, tower containing relics, a kenotaph.—224, 225.

Dâ'namati, *skt.* and *p.*, name of a village. The word means "having a mind to give."—131.

Dê'va, *skt.* and *p.*, any celestial spirit, a god especially of intermediate rank, angel.—Dêva, questions of the, 146; Buddha replies to the dêva, 146; Dêvas, 22, 40, 43, 57.

Dêvada'tta (etym. god-given) brother of Yashôdharâ and Buddha's brother-in-law. He tried to found a sect of his own with severer rules than those prescribed by Buddha. He is described undoubtedly with great injustice in the Buddhist canon and treated as a traitor. [About his sect see Rh. Davids's B. p. 181–182.]—69–70, 95–97, 191.

Dêvapu'tra, *skt.*, Dêvapu'tta, *p.*, (etym. Son of a God) one of Buddha's disciples.—223.

Dha'rma, *skt.*, Dha'mma, *p.*, originally the natural condition of things or beings, the law of their existence, truth, then religious truth, the law, the ethical code of righteousness, the whole body of religious doctrines as a system, religion.—31, 33, 35, 48, 49, 52, 56, 62, 67, 146, 148, 149, 158; let a man take pleasure in the dharma, 149; the goodness of the dharma, 114.

Dharmakâ'ya, *skt.*, the body of the law.—227.

Dharmapa'da, *skt.*, Dhammapa'da, *p.*—111.

Dharmarâ'ja, *skt.*, Dhammarâ'ja, *p.*, the king of truth.—72, 110.

Dhyâ'na, *skt.*, Jhâ'na, *p.*, intuition, beatic vision, ecstasy, rapture, the result of samâdhi. Buddha did not recommend trances as means of religious devotion, urging that deliverance can be obtained only by the recognition of the four noble truths and walking on the noble eightfold path, but he did not disturb those who took delight in ecstasies and beatific visions. Buddha's interpretation of the Dhyâna is not losing consciousness but a self-possessed and purposive eradication of egotism. There are four Dhyânas, the first being a state of joy and gladness born of seclusion full of investigation and reflexion; the second one, born of deep tranquillity without reflexion or investigation, the third one brings the destruction of passion, while the fourth one consists in pure equanimity, making an end of sorrow. [See Rhys Davids's B. pp. 175-176.] In the Fo-Sho-hing-tsan-king, the Dhyâna is mentioned twice only: first, III, 12, vv. 960-978, where Ârâda sets forth the doctrine of the four Dhyânas which is not approved of by Buddha, and secondly, at Buddha's death; when losing consciousness, his mind is said to have passed through all the Dhyânas.—155.

Dîrghâ'yu, *skt.*, Dîghâ'vu, *p.*, the etymology of the word is "live-long." Name of a mythical prince, son of king Dîrghêti.—90-94.

Dîrghê'ti, *skt.*, Dîghî'ti, *p.*, literally "suffer-long." Name of a mythical king, father of prince Dîghâ'vu.—90, 91, 93.

Ga'yâ Kâshyapa, brother of the great Kâshyapa of Uruvilvâ.—52.

Ganges, the well known river of India.—11, 196.

Gau'tama, *skt.*, Go'tama, *p.*, Buddha's family name.—7, 38, 227; Gautama denies the existence of the soul, 130; Gautama is gone, Buddha remains, 220; Buddha not Gautama, 149; Gautama the shramana, 219; Gautama Siddhârtha, 95, 217, 225.

Gau'tamî, name of any woman belonging to the Gautama family. Krishâ Gautamî, 14, 186, 187.

Gavâ'mpati, *skt.*, Gava'mpati, *p.*, literally "lord of cows," a friend of Yashas.—48.

Hînayâ'na, the small vehicle, viz., of salvation. A name invented by Northern Buddhists, in contradistinction to Mahâyâna, to designate the spirit of Southern Buddhism. The term is not used among Southern Buddhists.—Pp. ix-x.

Hir'anyavatî, *skt.*, Hira'ññavatî, *p.*, a river.—215.

Ikshvâ'ku, *skt.*, Okkâ'ka, *p.*, the name of a mythological family from which the chiefs of the Shâkyas claim descent.—7.

Indra, one of the principal Brahman gods.—120, 177.

Indriyâ'ni or pancha-indriyâni, the five organs of the spiritual sense. (See Balâni.)

Î'shvara, *skt.*, Î'ssara, *p.*, (lit. independent existence) Lord, Creator, personal God, a title given to Shiva and other great deities. In Buddhistic scriptures the *skt.* Îshvara (not the *p.* Îssara) means always a transcendent or extramundane God, a personal God, a deity distinct from, and independent of nature, who is supposed to have created the world out of nothing.—60, 61.

Jain, modernised form of *skt.* Jaina; an adherent of the Jain-sect which reveres Vardhamâna (Jñâtaputra) as Buddha. (See *Jainism.*)—37.

Jainism, a sect, founded by Vardhamâna, older than Buddhism and still extant in India. It is in many respects similar to Buddhism. Buddha's main objection to the Jains was the habit of their ascetics of going naked. The Jains lay great stress upon ascetic exercises and self-mortification which the Buddhists declare to be injurious.

Ja'mbu, *skt.* and *p.*, a tree.—14, 28.

Jâmbû'nada, *skt.*, Jambû'nada, *p.*, a town of unknown site. (Also the name of a mountain and of a lake.)—180.

Ja'tila, *p.*, "wearing matted hair." The Jatilas were Brahman ascetics. Buddha converted a tribe of them, and Kâshyapa, their chief, became one of his most prominent disciples.—49, 53.

Ji'na, the Conqueror, an honorary title of Buddha. The Jains use the term with preference as an appellative of Vardhamâna whom they revere as their Buddha.—38.

Jî'vaka, *skt.* and *p.*, physician to king Bimbisâra. According to tradition he was the son of king Bimbisâra and the courtesan Sâlavatî. We read in Mahâvagga VIII that after his birth he was exposed but saved; then he became a most famous physician and cured Buddha of a troublesome disease contracted by wearing cast off rags. He was an ardent disciple of Buddha and prevailed upon him to allow the bhikshus to wear lay robes.—75, 76.

Jê'ta, the heir apparent to the kingdom of Shrâvastî.—70, 71.

Jê'tavana, a vihâra.—70–72, 146, 169, 174, 185.

Jñâtapu'tra, *skt.*, Nâtapu'tta, *Jain Prakrit*, the son of Jñâta. Patronym of Vardhamâna, the founder of Jainism.—124.

Jyô'tishka, *skt.*, name of a householder, son of Subhadra.—99, 100.

Kâlâ'ma, *skt.*, and *p.*, (see Ârâda).

Ka'nthaka, prince Siddhârtha's horse.—18, 19.

Kapilava'stu, *skt.*, Kapilava'tthu, *p.*, the capital of the Shâkyas, the birthplace of Buddha.—7, 10, 64, 69, 71.

Ka'rma, anglicised form of *skt.* stem-form *ka'rman* (nom. s. *karma*), the *p.* of which is *ka'mmam.* Action, work, the law of action, retribution, results of deeds previously done and the destiny resulting therefrom. Eitel defines karma as "that moral kernel [of any being] which alone survives death and continues in transmigration." Karma is a well-defined and scientifically exact term. Professor Huxley says, "In the theory of evolution, the tendency of a germ to develop according to a certain specific type, e. g., of the kidney bean seed to grow into a plant having all the characters of *Phaseolus vulgaris* is its 'karma.' It is 'the last inheritor and the last result' of all the conditions that have affected a line of ancestry which goes back for many millions of years to the time when life first appeared on earth." We read in the Anguttara Nikâya, Pancaka Nipâta: "My action (karma) is my possession, my action is my inheritance, my action is the womb which bears me, my action is the race to which I am akin [as the kidney-bean to its species], my action is my refuge." [See the article "Karma and Nirvâna" in *The Monist*, Vol. IV, No. 3, pp. 417-439.]—22, 25, 26, 68, 72, 96, 98, 132, 137, 151, 199, 215.

Kâ'shyapa, *skt.*, Ka'ssapa, *p.* (the etymology "He who swallowed fire," is now rejected), a name of three brothers, chiefs of the Jatilas, called after their residences, Uruvilvâ, Nadî, and Gayâ. The name Kâshyapa applies mainly to Kâshyapa of Uruvilvâ, who is also called Mahâ-Kâshyapa, for he was one of the great pillars of the Buddhistic brotherhood. He took at once, after his conversion, a most prominent rank among Buddha's disciples. After Buddha's death, it is said, he convened the first synod and acted as chairman. He is mentioned as the first compiler of the canon and called the first patriarch.—49-53, 100, 141-142, 227.

Kâ'shî, *skt.*, Kâ'sî, *p.*, the old and holy name of Benares.—90 et seq., 170.

Kaundi'nya, *skt.*, Kônd'añña, *p.*, name of Buddha's first disciple, afterwards called Âjñâ'ta Kaundi'nya in *skt.* and Aññâ'ta Kônda'ñña in *p.*—42, 44.

Kaushâ'mbî, *skt.*, Kôsa'mbî, *p.*, a city.—85, 88, 89, 165.

Klê'sha, *skt.*, Kilê'sa, *p.*, error.

Kô'lî, a little kingdom in the neighborhood of Kapilavastu, the home of Yashôdharâ.—11.

Kô'sala, *skt.* and *p.*, name of a country.—63, 64, 91, 117.

Kri'shâ Gau'tamî, *skt.*, Ki'sâ Gô'tamî, *p.*, the slim or thin Gautamî. Name (1) of a cousin of Buddha, mentioned in Chap. VI, p. 14;

(2) of the heroine in the parable of the mustard seed.—14, 186, 187.

Krishna, one of the most prominent Brahman gods.—49.

Kushina'gara, *skt.*, Kusinâ'ra, *p.*, name of a town.—212, 213, 215, 222, 223.

Kûtada'nta, a Brahman chief in the village Dânamati; is mentioned in Sp. Hardy's *M. B.*, p. 289, and in *S. B. E.*, Vol. XIX, p. 242 [Fo, v. 1682]; also called Khânumat.—131, 140.

Lu'mbinî, *skt.*, a grove named after a princess, its owner.—7.

Li'cchavi, *skt.* and *p.*, the name of a princely family.—202, 203.

Ma'gadha, *skt.* and *p.*, name of a country.—53, 58, 59, 76, 97, 194, 196.

Mâ'rga, *skt.* ma'gga *p.*, path; especially used in the Pâli phrase "Ariyo atthangiko maggo," the noble eightfold path, which consists of: right views, high aims, right speech, upright conduct, a harmless livelihood, perseverance in well-doing, intellectual activity, and earnest thought. [See *S. B. E.*, Vol. XI, pp. 63 and 147.]

Mahârâ'ja, the great king.—73.

Mahâsê'tu, the great bridge. A name invented by the author of the present book to designate the importance of Christianity compared to the Hinayâna and Mahâyâna of Buddhism.—ix, x.

Mahâyâ'na, the great vehicle, viz., of salvation. Name of the Northern conception of Buddhism, comparing religion to a great ship in which men can cross the river of Samsâra to reach the shore of Nirvâna.—ix, x.

Maitrê'ya, *skt.*, Mêttê'ya, *p.*, etymology, "full of kindness"; the name of the Buddha to come.—215, 218.

Ma'lla, *skt.* and *p.*, name of a tribe.—213, 215, 218, 222–224.

Manasâ'krita, *skt.*, Manasâ'kata, *p.*, a village in Kôsala.—117, 118, 120, 121.

Mandâ'ra, *skt.* and *p.*, a flower of great beauty.—8.

Mâ'talî, *skt.* and *p.*, name of a demon in the retinue of Yama.—177.

Mâ'ra, *skt.* and *p.*, the Evil One, the tempter, the destroyer, the god of lust, sin, and death.—8, 29, 30, 35, 74, 110, 111, 116, 152, 182, 207, 208, 209.

Mâta'nga, *skt.* and *p.*, literally, of low birth; the Mâtanga caste comprises mongrels of the lowest with higher castes.—174.

Ma'thurâ, *skt.* and *p.*, name of a place.—179.

Maudgalyâ'yana, *skt.*, Môgallâ'na, *p.*, one of the most prominent disciples of Buddha, a friend of Shâriputra.—58, 67.

Mâ'yâ, *skt.* and *p.*, delusion, magic, enchantment. The veil of Mâyâ is the illusion of self which lies upon the eyes of the worldling who thus is unable to see things as they really are and misunderstands his relation to his fellow-creatures.—6, 178.

Mâ'yâ, Buddha's mother. (See Mâyâ-dêvî.)—7, 77.

Mâyâ-dê'vî, also called Mahâ-Mâyâ, or simply Mâyâ, *skt.* and *p.*, the wife of Shuddhôdana and mother of Buddha. She died in childbed, and Buddha ascends to heaven to preach to her the good law and the gospel of salvation.—7, 77.

Mu'ni, *skt.* and *p.*, a thinker, a sage; especially a religious thinker. Shâkyamu'ni, the sage of the Shâkyas, is Buddha.—148, 150.

Nadî' Kâ'shyapa, *skt.*, Nadî' Ka'ssapa, *p.*, brother of the great Kâshyapa of Uruvilvâ.—52.

Nâ'dika, *skt.* and *p.*, name of a village.—199.

Nâ'ga, *skt.* and *p.*, literally serpent. The serpent being regarded as a superior being, the word denotes a special kind of spiritual beings; a sage, a man of spiritual insight; any superior personality. Nâga kings, 8.

Naira'ñjana, *skt.*, Nera'ñjarâ, *p.*, name of a river whose modern name is either Nilajan or Phalgu.—207-208.

Nâla'ndâ, *skt.* and *p.*, a village near Râjagriha.—194-197.

Na'ndâ, the daughter of a chief of shepherds.—28, 29.

Nidâ'na, *skt.* and *p.*, cause. The twelve nidânas, forming the chain of causation which brings about the misery in the world. [See Oldenberg, *Buddha*, Engl. tr., pp. 224-252].—31.

Nirgra'ntha, *skt.*, Nigga'ntha, *p.*, literally "liberated from bonds"; a name adopted by the adherents of the Jaina sect.—124, 129; Nirgranthas, give also to the, 130.

Nirmâ'na Kâ'ya, *skt.*, the body of transformation.—227.

Nirvâ'na, *skt.*, Nibbâ'na, *p.*, extinction, viz., the extinction of self; according to the Hinayâna it is defined as "extinction of illusion," according to the Mayâyâna as "attainment of truth." Nirvâna means, according to the latter, enlightenment, the state of mind in which upâdâna, klêsha, and trishnâ are extinct, the happy condition of enlightenment, peace of mind, bliss, the glory of righteousness in this life and beyond, the eternal rest of Buddha after death. Buddha himself has refused to decide the problem whether or not Nirvâna is a final extinction of personality. When questioned, he indicated by his silence that the solution is not one of those subjects a knowledge of which is indispensable for salvation.—2, 6, 14, 16, 32, 33, 35, 38, 40, 52, 53, 55, 58, 61, 64, 65, 77, 82, 99, 102, 104, 122, 132, 133, 142, 143, 166, 197, 199, 211, 215, 224; where is Nirvâna? 133; Nirvâna not a locality, 134; the city of Nirvâna, 110; the harvest, Nirvâna, 173; the one aim, Nirvâna, 142: Samsâra and Nirvâna, 2, 6, 197.

Nyagrô'dha, *skt.*, Nigrô'dha, *p.*, a tree, *ficus indica* well known for its air roots.—208.

Pâramitâ', *skt.* and *p.*, perfection, or virtue. The six pâramitâs are: almsgiving, morality, patience, zeal or energy, meditation, and wisdom.

Parivrâ'jaka, *skt.*, Paribbâ'jaka, p., a sect belonging to the Tîrthika school.—83.

Pâtalipu'tra, *skt.*, Pâtalipu'tta, *p.*, also called Pâtaligâma, a city on the Ganges north of Râjagriha and belonging to the kingdom of Magadha, the frontier station against the Vriji (Vajji), the present Patna. Buddha is reported to have predicted the future greatness of the place, which is an important passage for determining the time in which the account of Buddha's sojourn in Pâtaliputra was written. It is still uncertain, however, when Patna became the important centre which it is now. It was the capital of the country when Meyasthenes, the ambassador of Selencus Nicator, at the end of the third century B. C., visited India. He gave in his book a detailed description of the city.—194, 195, 196; Pâtaliputra, three dangers hang over, 196.

Paushkarasâ'di, *skt.*, Pôkkharasâ'di, *p.*, a Brahman philosopher.—118.

Pâ'vâ, *skt.* and *p.*, a village where Buddha took his last meal consisting of boar's meat and rice.—211.

Prajâ'patî or Mahâ-Prajâ'patî, *skt.*, Pajâ'patî, *p.*, the sister of Mâyâ-dêvî, second wife of Shuddhôdana, aunt and foster-mother of Buddha. She is also called by her husband's family name Gautamî (feminine form of Gautama).—10, 69, 78, 89.

Pra'kriti, *skt.*, name of a girl of low caste.—174, 175.

Pradyô'ta, *skt.*, Pajjô'ta, *p.*, name of a king of Ujjayinî.—76.

Pratimô'ksha, *skt.*, Pâtimô'kkha, *p.*, (usually spelt Prâtimôksha in Buddhistic Sanskrit,) literally, "disburdenment." It is the Buddhist confession. Rhys Davids says "that it almost certainly dates from the fifth century B. C. Since that time—during a period that is of nearly two thousand and three hundred years—it has been regularly repeated, twice in each month, in formal meetings of the stricter members of the Order. It occupies, therefore, a unique position in the literary history of the world; and no rules for moral conduct have been for so long a time as these in constant practical use, except only those laid down in the Old Testament and in the works of Confucius" (p. 163).—83–85.

Prasê'najit, *skt.*, Pasê'nadi, *p.*, (also called Pasenit) king of Kôsala, residing at Shrâvastî.—72.

Pravra'jyâ, *skt.*, pabba'jjâ, *p.*, the act of leaving the world for receiving admittance to the Order. The first step of the Buddhist ordination. (See Upasa'mpadâ.)

Pu'kkasha or Pu'kkasa, *skt.*, Pu'kkusa, *p.*, name of a low caste.—213–214.

Pu'nyajit, *skt.*, Pu'nnaji, *p.*, a friend of Yashas.—48.

Pûrvârâ'ma, *skt.*, Pubbârâ'ma, *p.*, the Eastern garden.—79.

Râ'hula, *skt.* and *p.*, the son of Buddha, was admitted to the fraternity while still a boy. Buddha gave him a lesson in truthfulness [see Chap. XLVI]. He is always named among the prominent disciples of Buddha and is revered as the patron saint of novices.—11, 67, 69, 70, 143, 144, 145.

Rainy season (see Varsha).—49, 204.

Râ'jan, *skt.* and *p.*, nominative form of the stem râjan, a king (in composition râja).

Râjagri'ha, *skt.*, Râjaga'ha, *p.*, the capital of Magadha and residence of king Bimbisâra.—19, 53, 57, 59, 64, 77, 83, 95, 99, 122, 193.

Ra'tna, *skt.*, ra'tana, *p.*, "jewel."

Ri'ddhi, *skt.*, I'ddhi, *p.*, defined by Eitel as "the dominion of spirit over matter." It is the adjusting power to one's purpose and the adaptation to conditions. In popular belief it implies exemption from the law of gravitation and the power of assuming any shape at will. (See Riddhipâda.)

Riddhipâ'da, *skt.*, Iddhipâ'da, *p.*, the mode of attaining the power of mind over matter, four steps being needed: (1) the will to acquire it, (2) the necessary exertion, (3) the indispensable preparation of the heart, and (4) a diligent investigation of the truth.—154, 156.

Ri'shi, *skt.*, i'si, *p.*, a prophet or seer, an inspired poet, a hermit having acquired wisdom in saintly retirement, a recluse or anchorite.

Saha'mpati, occurs only in the phrase "Brahmâ Sahampati," a name frequently used in Buddhist scriptures the meaning of which is obscure. Burnouf renders it *Seigneur des êtres patients*; Eitel, Lord of the inhabitable parts of all universes; H. Kern [in *S. B.*, XXI, p. 5] maintains that it is synonymous with Sikhin, which is a common term for Agni.

Sai'nya, *skt.*, Sê'niya, *p.*, military, warlike, an honorary title given to Bimbisâra the king of Magadha.—53, 57, 83.

Samâ'dhi, *skt.* and *p.*, trance, abstraction, self-control. Rhys Davids says (*B.* p. 177): "Buddhism has not been able to escape from the natural results of the wonder with which abnormal nervous states have always been regarded during the infancy of science. . . . But it must be added, to its credit, that the most ancient Buddhism despises dreams and visions; and that the doctrine of Samâdhi is of small practical importance compared with the doctrine of the noble eightfold Path." Eitel says (*Handbook*, p. 140): "The term Samâdhi is sometimes used ethically, when it designates moral self-deliverance from passion and vice."

Sambhô'ga Kâ'ya, *skt.*, the body of Bliss.—227.

Samyakpradhâ'na, *skt.*, Sammappadhâ'na, *p.*, right effort, exertion, struggle. There are four great efforts to overcome sin, which are: (1) Mastery over the passions so as to prevent bad qualities from rising; (2) suppression of sinful thoughts to put away bad qualities which have arisen; (3) meditation on the seven kinds of wisdom (Bôdhi-anga) in order to produce goodness not previously existing, and (4) fixed attention or the exertion of preventing the mind from wandering, so as to increase the goodness which exists. [See the Mahâ-padhâna Sutta in the *Dîgha Nikâya*. Compare *B. B. St.*, p. 89, and Rh. Davids's *Buddhism*, pp. 172–173.]

Samsâ'ra, *skt.* and *p.*, the ocean of birth and death, transiency, worldliness, the restlessness of a worldly life, the agitation of selfishness, the vanity fair of life.—2, 6, 33, 197.

Samskâ'ra, *skt.*, sankhâ'ra, *p.*, confection, conformation, disposition. It is the formative element in the karma as it has taken shape in bodily existence.—134, 137, 138.

Sa'ngha, *skt.* and *p.*, the brotherhood of Buddha's disciples, the Buddhist church. An assembly of at least four has the power to hear confession, to grant absolution, to admit persons to the priesthood, etc. The sangha forms the third constituent of the Triratna or three jewels in which refuge is taken (the *S. B. of the E.* spell Sa*m*gha).—43, 48, 52, 56, 69, 77, 81, 84–90, 146; sangha may be expected to prosper, 194.

Sa'njaya, *skt.* and *p.*, a wandering ascetic and chief of that sect to which Shâriputra and Maudgalyâyana belonged before their conversion.—58.

Sha'kra, *skt.*, Sa'kka, *p.*, Lord; a cognomen of Indra.—57.

Shâ'kya, *skt.*, Sâ'kya, *p.*, the name of a small tribe in the northern frontiers of Magadha.—11, 20.

Shâkyamu'ni, *skt.*, Sâkyamu'ni, *p.*, the Shâkya sage; a cognomen of Buddha.—20, 22, 26, 27, 29, 50, 51, 53, 59, 78, 100, 101, 120.

Shâ'la, *skt.*, Sâ'la, *p.*, a tree, *vatica robusta*; shâla-grove, 215, 218; shâla-trees, 216.

Shâripu'tra, *skt.*, Sâripu'tta, *p.*, one of the principal disciples of Buddha; the Buddhistic St. Peter.—58, 59, 64, 67, 70, 71, 89, 100, 189, 197, 198; Shâriputra's faith, 197.

Shra'mana, *skt.*, Sa'mana, *p.*, an ascetic; one who lives under the the vow, 30, 34, 50, 69, 78; the Shramana Gautama, 219; the vision of a shramana, 15.

Shrâ'vaka, *skt.*, Sâ'vaka, *p.*, he who has heard the voice (viz. of Buddha), a pupil, a beginner. The name is used to designate (1) all personal disciples of Buddha, the foremost among whom are called Mahâ-shrâvakas, and (2) an elementary degree of saintship. A shrâvaka is he who is superficial yet in practice and comprehension, being compared to a hare crossing the stream of Samsâra by swimming on the surface. [See Eitel *Handbook*, p. 157.]—151, 152.

Shrâva'stî, *skt.*, Sâva'tthi, *p.*, capital of Northern Kôsala. It has been identified by General Cunningham with the ruins of Sâhet-Mâhet in Oudh and was situated on the river Rapti, northwest of Magadha.—63, 71, 79, 82, 88, 89, 166, 174, 189.

Shuddhô'dana, *skt.*, Suddhô'dana, *p.*, Buddha's father. Tradition made of Shuddhôdana the king of the Shâkyas, but we have to add that this does not appear in the oldest records. Oldenberg (in his *Buddha*, English version, p. 99, giving his arguments on pp. 416–417) speaks of him as "a great and wealthy land-owner."—7, 11, 12, 19, 64, 65, 68, 77.

Si'mha, *skt.*, Sî'ha, *p.*, literally, "lion." Name of a general, an adherent of the Nirgrantha sect, converted by Buddha, 124–

126, 128–130; Simha, a soldier, 126; Simha's question concerning annihilation, 124.

Siddhâ'rtha, *skt.*, Siddha'ttha, *p.*, Buddha's proper name. Etymology "He who has reached his goal."—9–19, 29, 64–70, 140.

Ska'ndha, *skt.*, Kha'ndha, *p.*, elements; attributes of being, which are form, sensation, perception, discrimination, and consciousness.—24.

Smrityupasthâ'na, *skt.*, Sati-patthâ'na, *p.*, meditation; explained as "fixing the attention." The four objects of earnest meditation are: (1) the impurity of the body, (2) the evils arising from sensation, (3) ideas or the impermanence of existence, and (4) reason and character, or the permanency of the dharma. (Rh. D. B., p. 172.) The term is different from "bhâvana," although translated by the same English word. (*S. B. of the E.* XI, p. 62.—211.)

Sô'ma, *skt.* and *p.*, derived from the root *su*, to press in a wine-press; not as, according to Eitel, Chinese scholars propose from "exhilarate (*su*) and mind (*mana*)." Name of a plant and of its juice, which is intoxicating and is used at Brahmanical festivals; the Sôma drink is identified with the moon and personified as a deity.—120.

Srigâ'la, *skt.*, Sigâ'la. *p.*, literally, "jackal"; name of a Brahman converted by Buddha.—122, 123.

Subâ'hu, *skt.* and *p.*, a friend of Yashas.—48.

Subha'dra, *skt.*, Subha'dda, *p.*, name of a shramana. Subha'dra, Buddha's last convert, must not be confounded with another man of the same name who caused dissension soon after Buddha's death.—99, 218–220.

Su'mana, *skt.* and *p.*, name of a householder.—167.

Sû'tra, *skt.*, Su'tta, *p.*, literally "thread," any essay, or guide of a religious character.

Tapu'ssa, *skt.* and *p.*, a merchant.—34, 35.

Târu'kshya, *skt.*, Târu'ccha, *p.*, name of a Brahman philosopher.

Tathâ'gata, *skt.* and *p.*, generally explained as "the Perfect One." The highest attribute of Buddha, 17, 38, 39, 43–45, 51, 53, 56–59, 62, 64, 67, 69, 70, 74, 78, 80, 82, 83, 96, 97, 100, 101, 107–111, 116, 159; robe of the Tathâgata, 107; soldiers of the Tathâgata, 110; the law the body of the Tathâgata, 225; Tathâgatas are only preachers, 111.

Tî'rthika, *skt.*, Ti'tthiya, *p.*, a religious school of India in Buddha's time.—83.

Trikâ'ya, the three bodies of personalities of Buddha, the Dharmakâya, the Sambhôga-kâya, and the Nirmâna-kâya.—227.

Trira'tna, the three jewels or the holy trinity of the Buddha, the Dharma, and the Sangha, a doctrine peculiar to Northern Buddhism. (See Trikâya.)

Tri'shnâ, *skt.*, ta'nhâ, *p.*, thirst, the egotistical desire of existence, selfishness.—30, 116.

U'draka, *skt.*, a Brahman philosopher.—22, 25.

Ujja'yinî, *skt.*, Ujjê'nî, *p.*, name of a city.—76.

Upâdâ'na, *skt.* and *p.*, desire, a grasping state of mind. One of the nidânas.

Upagu'pta, *skt.*, name of a Buddhist monk.—179.

Upâ'li, a prominent disciple of Buddha. Before his conversion he was, according to the Buddhistic tradition, court-barber to the king of the Shâkyas.—69, 89, 225.

Upasa'mpadâ, *skt.* and *p.*, admittance to the Buddhist brotherhood, ordination. (See Pravrajya.)

Upava'rtana, *skt.*, Upava'ttana, *p.*, a grove in Kushinagara. The word means a rambling-place, a gymnasium.—215, 218.

U'paka, *skt.* and *p.*, name of a man, a Jain, who met Buddha but was not converted by him —37, 38

Upava'satha, *skt.*, Upô'satha, *p.*, the Buddhist sabbath. Rhys Davids says (pp. 140-141): "The Upôsatha days are the four days in the lunar month when the moon is full, or new, or half way between the two. It is the fourteenth day from the new moon (in short months) and the fifteenth day from the full moon (in the long months), and the eighth day from each of these. The corresponding Sanskrit word is Upavasatha, the fast-day previous to the offering of the intoxicating sôma, connected with the worship of the moon. Instead of worshipping the moon, the Buddhists were to keep the fast-day by special observance of the moral precepts; one of many instances in which Gautama spiritualised existing words and customs."—83, 84, 87; observe the Upavasatha or Sabbath, 105.

Uruvi'lvâ, *skt.*, Uruvê'lâ, *p.*, a place south of Patna on the banks of the Neranjarâ river, now Buddha Gayâ. The residence of Kâshyapa, the chief of the Jatilas.—27, 49, 50, 52, 182.

Vaishâ'lî, *skt.*, Vêsâ'lî, *p.*, a great city of India, north of Patna.—193, 201–204, 210.

Va'rana, *skt.* and *p.*, a tree; *Crataeva Roxburghii.*—162, 163.

Vardhamâ'na, *skt.*, Vaddhamâ'na, *Jaina Prakrit*, proper name;

the founder of Jainism. Also called Jñâtapu'tra in *skt.* and Nâtapu'tta in *Jaina Prakrit.*

Va'rsha, *skt.*, Va'ssa, *p.*, rain, rainy season. During the rainy season of Northern India, which falls in the months from June to October, the shramanas could not wander about, but had to stay in one place. It was the time in which the disciples gathered round their master, listening to his instructions. Thus it became the festive time of the year. In Ceylon, where these same months are the fairest season of the year, Buddhists come together and live in temporary huts, holding religious meetings in the open air, reading the Pitakas and enjoying the jâtakas, legends, and parables of Buddhism. [See Rhys Davids's *B.*, p. 57.]

Varshakâ'ra, *skt.*, Vassakâra, *p.*, lit. "rain-maker." Name of a Brahman, the prime minister of the king of Magadha.—192, 193.

Va'runa, *skt.* and *p.*, a Brahman deity, the god of heaven and regent of the sea; one of the guardians of the world.—120.

Vâsavada'ttâ, *skt.* and *p.*, a courtesan of Mathurâ.—179, 180.

Vâsi'shtha, *skt.*, Vâse'ttha, *p.*, name of a Brahman.—117, 120.

Vê'das, 39, 118, 119; I know all the Vêdas, 139.

Vêṇuva'na, *skt.*, Vêluva'na, *p.*, a bamboo-grove at Râjagriha, 58, 204; Vêṇuvana vihâra, 95.

Vihâ'ra, *skt.* and *p.*, residence of Buddhist monks or priests; a Buddhist convent or monastery; a Buddhist temple.—63, 64, 80, 95, 100, 102, 190, 216.

Vi'mala, *skt.* and *p.* (etym., the spotless), name of a friend of Yashas.—48.

Vi'naya, 49.

Vishâ'khâ, *skt.*, Visâ'khâ, *p*, a wealthy matron of Shrâvastî, one of Buddha's most distinguished woman lay-disciples. Says Oldenberg, *Buddha*, English translation, p. 167: "Every one invites Visâkhâ to sacrificial ceremonies and banquets, and has the dishes offered to her first; a guest like her brings luck to the house."—79, 80, 82, 83; eight boons of Vishâkhâ, 80; gladness of Vishâkhâ, 82, 83.

Vri'ji, *skt.*, Va'jji, *p.*, name of a people living in the neighborhood of Magadha, 100, 192, 193; assemblies of the Vriji, 192.

Ya'ma, *skt.* and *p.*, also called Yama-râ'ja, death, the god of death —183, 184.

Ya'shas, *skt.*, Ya'sa, *p.*, the noble youth of Benares, son of a wealthy man and one of Buddha's earliest converts.—45, 48.

Yashô'dharâ, *skt.* Yasô'dharâ, *p.*, wife of Prince Gautama Siddhârtha before he became Buddha. She became one of the first of Buddhist nuns. [See Jâtaka, 87–90; Commentary on Dhammapada, vv 168, 169: Bigandet, 156–168; Spence Hardy's *Manual*, 198–204; Beal, pp. 360–364: *B. Birth Stories*, 127.]—11, 66–69, 77, 78, 95.

PRONUNCIATION.

Pronounce:

a as the Italian and German short *a*.	u as *oo* in g*oo*d.
â as *a* in f*a*ther.	û as *u* in r*u*mor.
e as *e* in t*e*nt.	ai as in *eye*.
ê as *e* in *e*ight.	au as *ow* in h*ow*.
i as *i* in h*i*t.	ñ as *ny*.
î as *i* in mach*i*ne.	jñ as *dny*.
o as *o* in l*o*t.	ññ as *n-ny*.
ô as *o* in h*o*me.	ch as *ch* in *ch*ur*ch*.
	cch as *ch-ch* in ri*ch* *ch*ance

s, j, y, and other letters, as usual in English words.

Double consonants are pronounced as two distinct sounds, e. g., *ka'm-ma*, not *kă'ma*.

The h after *p*, *b*, *k*, *g*, *t*, *d* is audible as in du*b h*im, be*g h*er, bric*k h*ouse, an*t h*ill. Pronounce Tat-hâgata, not Ta-thâgata.

To the average European it is difficult to catch, let alone to imitate, the difference of sound between dotted and non-dotted letters. All those who are desirous for information on this point must consult Sanskrit and Pâli grammars.

Lest the reader be unnecessarily bewildered with foreign-looking dots and signs, which after all are no help to him, all dotted ṭ, ḍ, ṃ, ṇ, and italicised *t*, *d*, *m*, *n* have been replaced in the text of the book by t, d, m, n, ñ, ññ, dotted ṛ and italicised *s* have been transcribed by ny, nny, rî, and sh, while the Glossary preserves the more exact transcription.

We did not follow the spelling of the *Sacred Books of the East*, where it must be misleading to the uninitiated, especially when they write italicised *K* to denote spelling of the English sound ch, and italicised *g* to denote j Thus we write "râjâ," not "râ*g*â," and "Chunda," not "*K*unda."

INDEX.

Abstain from impurity, 106.
Abstinence, 39.
Abode in me, truth has taken its, 140.
Abodes of truth, 63.
Abolish all the lesser, 220.
Abolished, omens, 151.
About to pass away, 216.
Absolution, 84.
Abuse, the sermon on, 145.
According to their deeds, 188.
Address, Buddha's farewell, 204.
Adoration be to thee, 150.
Aim, one, one essence, one law, 141.
Aim, the one, Nirvâna, 142.
Aim, the preacher's sole, 108.
All creatures received the message in their own language, 41.
Alone, let a man walk, 88 (see also *Solitary*).
Altercations, 86.
Always in danger of death, 188.
Ambrosia, lake of, 98.
Angels rejoice, 8.
Anger, by love overcome, 115.
Annihilation, 124, 125.
Annihilation of egotism, 126.
Annihilation, Simha's question concerning, 124.
Another Buddha will arise, 218.
Anxious to learn, must be, 207.
Anxious to learn the truth, be, 106.
Apoplexy, struck by, 169.
Appearance of Bôdhisattva, 19.
Appearance, the glory of his, 189.
Appeared, the saviour, 229.
Appeased not by hatred, hatred, 87.
Are all paths saving paths? 118.
Artisans, the chief of the, 179.
Asceticism, 196.
Ascetics, naked, 75.
Assemblies of the Vriji, 192.
Assemblies, various kinds of, 156.
Assured of final salvation, 221.
Astrology and forecasting by signs forbidden, 210.
Atman and the *I*, 26.
Atone for your evil deeds, you will have to, 178.
Atonement by blood, 132.
Audience, like unto the color of my, 156.
Avoid dying, not any means to, 187.

Bad deeds easy to do, 112.
Bamboo grove, 122.
Bathing in the Ganges, 11.
Battle is better, death in, 208.
Battle of life, 128.
Battle, the elephant no longer fit for, 145.
Battles, fight your, 129.
Be married unto the truth, 181.
Be ye lamps unto yourselves, 206.
Beauty, to restore to you a nobler, 180.
Becoming, gradual, 138.
Bee collects nectar, the, 115.
Being, the purpose of, 228.
Beings, preach to all, 109.
Beneath, water gurgling, 172.
Best, truth is, 42.
Better bore out both eyes, 79.
Blessed One, has to suffer, the, 205; Blessed One, refuge in the, 129, 130, 140, 220; Blessed One swooned, the, 28; Blessed One walked unshod,

the, 94, Blessed One, wearisome to the, 199.
Blind man, 21.
Blind men, 119.
Blind received sight, 7.
Blind, the man born, 159.
Blind, truth is hidden to the, 226.
Blind, your eyes are, 166.
Bliss be diffused, let the, 168.
Bliss, the communication of, 167.
Bliss where suffering is, 16.
Blood, atonement by, 132.
Blood has no cleansing power, 132.
Blood, shedding of, 26.
Blow, give the rock a good, 172.
Blow off the impurities, 115.
Body of flesh? Why preserve this, 217.
Body of the law, 140; the body of the law will endure, 217.
Body, the worldling nourishes his, 167.
Bonds that tie all souls together, 232.
Boons of Vishâhkâ. eight, 80.
Brahma, 69, 118.
Brahman, 58, 117, 118, 119, 120, 131, 132, 133. 136, 137, 146, 164, 165, 166, 168, 173, 174, 175, 183, 184, 185, 192, 193, 195.
Brahman lore, the substance of, 119.
Bridler of men's hearts, 200.
Bright, the sun is, 117.
Bright, thinkers are, 117; warriors are bright, 117.
Bubble, 31.
Buddhahood, omens of, 8, 9; signs of Buddhahood, 8.
Burning, everything is, 52.
Burning mansion, the, 158.
Butterfly, like the, 211.
By deeds one becomes an outcast, 174.

Calamities, ten great, 191.
Carp not, 106, 107.
Cart, as a worn out, 206.
Cast-off rags, 75, 77.
Caste, I ask not for, 174.
Cause of further migrations, 99.
Cause of selfhood, the. Found! 33.
Cease by hatred, hatred does not, 115.
Ceremony, 123, 196.
Chance, 61.
Change, grief at, 14; self is change, 138.
Charcoal, 185.
Charity, rich in returns, 20; the sermon on, 63.
Charms are treacherous, 180.
Chastity, 106.
Che, 101, 103.
Cherish no hatred, 106.
Chickens should break the egg-shell, 122.
Chief of the artisans, the, 179.
Children, I am your father, ye are, 140.
Children of truth, clay can be changed into, 131.
City of Nirvâna, the, 110.
Clay can be changed into the children of truth, 131.
Cleanses from sin, the truth, 223.
Cleansing power, blood has no, 132.
Cleaving to self, 137.
Cloth of gold, robes of, 213.
Cloud, like a, 142.
Cloud of good qualities, 110.
Cloud of error, 217.
Coil, the, 31.
Color of my audience, like unto the, 156.
Combination, individuality a, 25; combination subject to separation, 25.
Come forth into the light, 122.
Come into the world to befriend, 190.
Come to teach life, 133.
Commandments, the ten, 105.
Communication of bliss, the, 167.
Complete surrender of self, 127.
Compounds will be dissolved, 217.
Comprehension of things, truth the correct, 34.
Concord, two ways of re-establishing, 89; meeting in concord, 193; re-establishment of concord, 88.
Conditions of welfare, eight, 192, 193, 194.
Conduct, upright, 194.
Confer the ordination, 49.
Confession of trespasses, 84.
Conquerors, the greatest of, 111.
Conquest of self, 128.

Consolidation of Buddha's religion, 75.
Contact of the object and senses, 54.
Contemplation, earnest, 194.
Continuity, sameness and, 137.
Coop, the fowl in the, 103.
Correct comprehension of things, truth the, 34.
Correlatives, 16.
Courtesan, 81, 179, 201-204.
Covet not, 106.
Crane, the wild, 103; the cruel crane, 162.
Creatures, all, received the message in their own language, 41.
Criminal, punishment of the, 126.
Criminal's act, punishment the fruit of the, 127.
Crossed the river, 196.
Crossed the stream, he had, 189.
Cultivate good-will, 55.
Culture of the mind, 70.

Danger of death, always in, 188.
Dangers hang over Pâtaliputra, three, 196.
Dark, do not call the world, 166.
Dart of lust, the, 161.
Dead are many, the, 187.
Dead not saved by lamentation, 188.
Deaf and dumb speak, the, 8.
Death, always in danger of, 188; Buddha's death, 218; fate after death, 188, 189; death is near, 208; no escape from, 13; death in battle is better, 208; in the domain of death, 103; self is death, 133, 138, 140; thoughtlessness, the path of death, 112.
Deeds, according to their, 188; bad deeds easy to do, 112; by deeds one becomes an outcast, 174; passed away according to his deeds, 172.
Deeper, dig, 109.
Delusion and truth, 31.
Delusions, 39.
Denies the existence of the soul, Gautama, 130.
Desert, a waterless, 120; rescue in the desert, 169; a sandy desert, 170.
Desire, the extinction of sinful, 116.
Desolation, a hopeless, 120.
Despot, the, 178.
Destiny of warriors, 128.
Destroyed, hell is, 199.
Dêvadatta, sect of, 95.
Die until, etc., I shall not, 208; truth cannot die, 217.
Died in the faith, he, 184.
Diffused, let the bliss be, 168.
Dig deeper, 109.
Disciple, the first woman lay-, 48.
Disciple, a, flagged, 169.
Dissatisfied, the people, 59.
Dissolution, necessity of, 222.
Dissolved, compounds will be, 217.
Distinction, without, 142.
Doctrine, preach the, glorious in the beginning, the middle, and end, 49; my doctrine is like the great ocean, 156; doctrine like unto fire, 157; doctrine like unto water, 157.
Doffed their robes, the bhikshus, 80.
Dog, the hungry, 176.
Domain of death, in the, 103.
Do not call the world dark, 166.
Do not rely on external help, 206.
Do not scold, 89.
Door of immortality, 36.
Draught-ox, exertion is a, 173.
Drink, the refreshing, perception of truth, 98.
Drinking? Is the water not fit for, 143.
Dumb, the deaf and, speak, 8.
Dust, like one who flings, 146.
Dust of worldliness, 36.
Dwelling-place, wisdom has no, 133.
Dying, not any means to avoid, 187.

Each day one hemp-grain, 27.
Earnest contemplation, 194.
Earnestness is the goad, 173; earnestness is the path of immortality, 112.
Earth, peace on, 8.
Earthquake, 222.
East, face towards the, 194.
Eating of flesh, the, 39.
Ecstasy, the song of, 197, 198.
Eddies of transmigration, 144.
Efficacy, rituals have no, 27.
Egg-shell, chickens should break the,

122; I have first broken the egg-shell, 221.
Eggs, hen brooding over, 122.
Ego, the, 24; ego, an illusion, 26; the instability of the ego, 41.
Egotism, the annihilation of, 126.
Eight boons of Vishâkhâ, 80.
Eight conditions of welfare, 192, 193, 194.
Eight wonderful qualities, 156, 157.
Eightfold path, the, 33, 122, 211.
Eightfold, the best way is the, 116.
Eldest, I am the, 221.
Elephant, powerful, 144; the elephant no longer fit for battle, 145.
Elevate the mind, 74.
Emaciated from fasts, 207.
Embrace of truth, the, 181.
Empire, the wheel of, 207.
Emptiness and immaterial life, 23.
Enabled me to do so, faith, 190.
Endure, thoughts will, 112.
Enemy, his greatest, 115.
Enlightened Teacher, refuge in the, 123.
Entities, souls not separate and self-existent, 132.
Envy not, 106.
Epidemic, 101.
Eradication of self, 126.
Error, self an, 55; error be thou my guide, 231.
Errors, 107.
Escape from death, no, 13.
Essence of life, truth is the, 231; one in essence, 232; one essence, one law, one aim, 141.
Eternal, truth the image of the, 3.
Everlasting life, 128, 182.
Evil actions, thou canst not escape the fruit of, 139.
Everything is burning, 52.
Evil by good, overcome, 115; evil deeds, you will have to atone for your, 178; ignorance the root of evil, 31; pain is the outcome of evil, 113; evil powers no surrender, 127.
Evolution, 138; in the course of evolution, 228.
Exertion is a draught-ox, 173.
Existence is spiritual, all, 130; thirst for existence and selfhood, 30.
Expulsion, sentence of, 85, 86.
External help, do not rely on, 206.
Extinction of self, the, salvation, 4; the extinction of sinful desire, 116; the extinction of thirst, 116.
Eye, the, âtman and, 26; eye of truth, 45; mental eye, 186; spiritual eye, 227.
Eyes, better bore out both, 79.

Face to face, Brahma, 118; the universe face to face, 121; face to face with him, 220.
Face towards the east, 194.
Facing towards the west, 195.
Faith alone can save, 190; faith enabled me to do so, 190; great is thy faith, 198; lineage of the faith, 198; hast thou faith, 209; he died in the faith, 184; faith is the seed, 173; faith in the Buddha, 200; Sharipu-tra's faith, 197; such faith have I, 197.
Falter not, wise people, 112.
Famine, 100.
Farewell address, Buddha's, 204.
Fashion themselves, wise people, 112
Fashioned, truth cannot be, 231.
Fasts, emaciated from, 207.
Fate after death, 188, 199.
Father, 158, 159; father and son, 184; I reverence my father, 123; ye are my children, I am your father, 140.
Fault, found no 208.
Faults of others, the, 114, 115.
Fell upon him, sickness, 204, 211, 212.
Fetch me some water, 212.
Fever, self is a, 42.
Few, the living are, 187.
Fight your battles, 129.
Fire, doctrine like unto, 157.
Fire, sermon on, 52.
First broken the egg-shell, I have, 221.
First Buddha, I am not the, 217.
First lay-member, the, 47.
First women lay-disciples, the, 48.
Fish, the giddy. 161.
Fit for battle, the elephant no longer, 145.

Fit for drinking? Is the water now, 143.
Fit to live, more, 128.
Five meditations, 153.
Five roots of mind, the, 23.
Five wishes of Bimbisâra, 56.
Fivefold gain, 195; fivefold loss, 195.
Flagged, a disciple, 169.
Flagging, religious zeal, 29.
Flame, sameness of the, 135.
Flesh, the eating of, 39; thorn in the, 116; let the flesh waste away, 208; why preserve this body of flesh? 217.
Flings dust, like one who, 146.
Flowers out of season, 216; lotus flowers, 30; mandara flowers, 8.
Following the Master over the stream, 189.
Fool, 113; the listless fool, 168.
Foolish, pleasures destroy the, 114; foolish talk, 119.
Forbidden, miracles, 99–101.
Forecasting by signs forbidden, astrology and, 210.
Found no fault, 208; found! the cause of selfhood, 33; found the truth, 43.
Foundation of the Kingdom of Righteousness, 37.
Four kinds of offering, 165; four kinds of merit, 164; four simples, 160; the four quarters, 121; the four noble truths, 32, 160; the four signs, 12; where four roads cross, 118.
Fowl in the coop, the, 103.
Fragrant like the lotus, 180.
Free your mind of ignorance, 106.
Fruit of evil actions, thou canst not escape the, 139; the fruit of immortality, 173; the fruit of the criminal's act punishment, 127.
Fruits, ripe, 188.

Gain, fivefold, 195.
Ganges, bathing in the, 11.
Gautama Gate, 196.
Giddy fish, the, 161.
Gift of religion, the, 116.
Gift, the king's, 57.
Give also to the Nigranthas, 130; give, if thou art asked, 115; give the rock a good blow, 172.
Gives away, he who, etc., 215.
Giving away, 63.
Glad tidings, 1.
Gladness of Vishâkha, 82, 83.
Glorious in the beginning, middle, and end, preach the doctrine, 49; the truth is glorious, 46, 47, 56.
Glory of his appearance, the, 189; the truth in all its glory, 229.
Goad, earnestness is the, 173.
Goal, the, 99, 117.
Gods and men, teacher of, 200.
Goes out to wage war, 110.
Gold, robes of cloth of, 213.
Gone into the yoke, 116.
Good qualities, cloud of, 110; happiness is the outcome of good, 113; overcome evil by good, 115; good tidings, 16; cultivate good-will, 55; good works are rain, 173.
Governs all things, karma, 101.
Grace, the time of, 161, 170.
Gradual becoming, 138.
Grant me my life, 164.
Great is thy faith, 198.
Great understanding, muni of, 148.
Greatest enemy, his, 114; the greatest of conquerors, 111.
Greedy tailor, the, 162.
Grief at change, 14; overcome grief, 206; selfish in my grief, 187.
Grounded, that it be well, 198.
Grove, bamboo, 122.
Guide, error be thou my, 231.
Guiding-rein, mind is the, 173.

Happily, let us live, 119.
Happiness is the outcome of good, 113; vanity of worldly happiness, 2.
Happy, he is altogether, 122; make thyself happy, 209.
Hard times teach a lesson, 103.
Harvest Nirvâna, the, 173; thou wilt reap the harvest sown in the past, 138.
Hast thou faith? 209.
Hatred appeased not by hatred, 87; cherish no hatred, 106; hatred ceases by love, 115; hatred does not cease by hatred, 115.
He promoted him higher, 160.

He who gives away, etc., 215.
He who walks righteously is ever near me, 218.
Hearts, bridler of men's, 200.
Heaven, hope of, a mirage, 102; like one who spits at heaven, 146; pleasures of self in heaven, 133.
Heavenly songs, 216.
Hell is destroyed, 199.
Helmet of right thought, 79.
Help, do not rely on external, 206; now my lot to help, 191.
Hemp-grain, each day one, 27.
Hen brooding over eggs, 122.
Hereafter, the, 139.
Heresies, 61.
Hermit, layman and, 46.
Higher, he promoted him, 160.
Hold fast to the truth, 206.
Holiness better than sovereignty, 21.
Homage, worthiest, 216.
Honor, so great an, 202.
Honored be his name, 57.
Hope of heaven a mirage, 102.
Hopeless desolation, a, 120.
Householder, 158.
Hungry dog, parable of the, 176.

I am not the first Buddha, 217; I am the eldest, 221; I am the truth, 141; I am thirsty, 212; I ask not for caste, 174; I have first broken the egg-shell, 221; no room for the I, 54; I reverence my father, 123; I shall not die until, etc., 208; such faith have I, 197; the I perishable, 54; the I, the soul, 23; the thought of I, 24; the transmission of the soul and the I, 25.
Idea of self, the, 217.
Identity, 135; identity and non-identity, 131, 135; identity of self, 137; where is the identity of my self? 134.
Idle talk, invocations are, 139.
If thou art asked, give, 115.
Ignorance, free your mind of, 106; ignorance the root of evil, 31.
Illimitable light, 232.
Illusion, self an, 34, 128; the ego an illusion, 26.
Illustration by a lamp, 135; illustration by a letter, 134.
Image of the eternal, truth the, 3.
Immaterial life, emptiness and, 23.
Immeasurable light, 98.
Immolation, 132.
Immortal, life, 99; the immortal path, 64.
Immortality, 60, 66, 187; door of immortality, 36; earnestness is the path of immortality, 112; immortality in transiency, 3; immortality in truth, 133, 140; the fruit of immortality, 173; the water of immortality, 128; truth and immortality, 6.
Immutable, the words of Buddha, 15.
Impure is nakedness, 80, 82.
Impurity, abstain from, 106; purity and impurity belong to oneself, 111
Impurities, blow off the, 115.
In the course of evolution, 228.
Incantations, 122; incantations have no saving power, 27.
Incarnation of the truth, 225.
Individuality a combination, 25; the wheel of individuality, 53.
Inexhaustible life, 152.
Instability of the ego, the, 41.
Instruction, words of, 148.
Instrumentalities, 52.
Invocations, 120; invocations are idle talk, 139.
Is it wrong to go to war? 126.

Jewel, a, 225; precious crown jewel, 110.
Jewels and worldliness, 46.
Jungle, a pathless, 120.

Karma governs all things, 101.
Keep my hold on life, 204.
Kill not, 106.
King Bimbisâra, 19, 20, 54, 76, 97.
King of kings, 224; king of truth, 110, 141; powerful king, 110.
Kingdom of Righteousness, Foundation of the, 37, 43.
Kingdom of truth, 38, 217.
King's gift, the, 57.
Kings, Naga, 8.

King's seal, stamp of a, 184.
Knew me not, they, 157.
Knowledge remains, 134.
Kusa-grass, 172.

Lake of Ambrosia, 98.
Lake, still, like a, 113.
Lame walk, the, 8.
Lamentation, dead not saved by, 188.
Lamp, illustration by a, 135.
Lamps unto yourselves, be ye, 206.
Land, pure, 152, 153.
Language, all creatures received the message in their own, 41.
Last word, 222.
Law, body of the, 140; one aim, one essence, one law, 141; the law the body of the Tathagata, 225; the body of the law will endure, 217.
Laws are temporary, many, 226.
Laws of righteousness, obedience to the, 132.
Lay disciples, the first women, 48.
Lay member, the first, 47.
Lay robes, 77.
Layman and hermit, 46.
Layman, priest and, alike, 74.
Leaning against the lintel, 216.
Learn, must be anxious to, 207.
Learning, availeth not, 139.
Lesser, abolish all the, 220.
Lesson given to Râhula, 143.
Lesson, hard times teach a, 103.
Let a man walk alone, 88.
Let the bliss be diffused, 168.
Let the flesh waste away, 208.
Let us go into the world, 223.
Let us live happily, 117.
Let us obey the truth, 226.
Let your light shine forth, 95.
Letter, illustration by a, 134.
Letter, in the, 89.
Lie not, 106.
Life, battle of, 128; come to teach, 133; life everlasting, 128, 182; grant me my life, 164; keep my hold on life, 204; life immortal, 99; inexhaustible life, 152; reason in the struggle for life, 228; seek thou the life that is of the mind, 133; truth is life, 133; life yearns for the truth, 231; what is life in this world? 208.
Light, come forth into the, 122; illimitable light, 232; immeasurable light, 98; let your light shine forth, 95.
Like a still lake, 113.
Like unto the color of my audience, 156.
Lily, the, on a heap of rubbish, 117.
Lineage of the faith, 198.
Lintel, leaning against the, 216.
Listen to both parties, 89.
Listless fool, the, 168.
Little by little, 161.
Live happily, let us, 117.
Live, more fit to, 128.
Lives of men, 176.
Living are few, the, 187.
Living, luxurious, 166.
Living in paradise, 184.
Lobster, 163.
Locality? is wisdom a, 133.
Locality, Nirvâna not a, 134.
Logic holds universally, 136.
Lord, glorious, 129, 219.
Lord, pass away, 209.
Loss, fivefold, 195.
Lost, a treasure that can never be, 150.
Lost son, the, 160.
Lot to help, now my, 191.
Lotus-flower in water, the, 40, 62, 99.
Lotus-flowers, 30, 78.
Lotus, fragrant like the, 180.
Love, hatred ceases by, 115; love of truth, 128; overcome anger by love, 115; the world filled with love, 121.
Lust, the dart of 161.
Luxurious living, 156.

Macarisms, 34, 35, 42, 149.
Made up of thoughts, 111.
Magic power, 100.
Main, rivers reach the, 199.
Make thyself happy, 209.
Maker, Îshvara, the, 60, 61.
Maker, the, self, 60.
Man, a blind, 21.
Man born blind, the, 159.
Man, who is the strong? 105.

Mango-grove, 117, 197, 211.
Mansion, the burning, 158.
Many, the dead are, 187.
Married unto the truth, be, 181.
Master, out of reverence for the, 221.
Master over the stream, following the, 189.
May be expected to prosper, Sangha, 194.
Me, this is done by, 112.
Meats remained undiminished, 181.
Medicines, 75, 186, 218.
Meditation (see bhâvana and satipatthâna in the Glossary), 30, 153, 211.
Meeting in concord, 193.
Men, blind, 119; teacher of gods and men, 200; the lives of men, 176.
Men's hearts, bridler of, 200.
Mental eye, 186.
Merit, four kinds of, 164.
Merit, the order (sangha) the sowing-ground of, 200.
Message in their own language, all creatures received the, 41.
Migrations, cause of further, 99.
Mind, Brahma's, 120; culture of the, 70; elevate the mind, 74; mind is the guiding rein, 173; seek thou the life that is the mind, 133; the five roots of mind, 23; there is mind, 130.
Miracle-mongers, 152.
Miracles, 151.
Miracles forbidden, 99-101.
Mirage, hope of heaven a, 102.
Mirage, the cause of self a, 42.
Mirror of truth, the, 199, 200.
Mission, the preachers, 107.
Moon, the, shines by night, 117.
Moral powers, 82.
Moral sense, 82.
More fit to live, 128.
More, sin no, 161.
Mortification not the right path, 28.
Mortification profitless, 39.
Mortification vain, 40.
Mother, a, 55, 99.
Muni of great understanding, 148, 150.
Mustard seed, the, 185, 187.

Naked ascetics, 75.
Nakedness, impure is, 80, 82.
Name, honored be his, 57.
Nature of religion consists in worship and sacrifice, the, 131.
Nature of the rope, the, 55.
Nature of self, the, 54.
Near, death is, 208.
Near me, he who walks righteously is ever, 218.
Necessity of dissolution, 222.
Nectar, the bee collects, 115.
Needed, the one thing that is, 132, 217.
Noble, eightfold path, the, 211, 231.
Noble truths, the four, 32.
Non-action, 124, 125.
Non-existence of the soul, 132.
Non-identity, identity and, 131, 135.
Not any means to avoid dying, 187.
Not worthy of yellow robes, 88.
Nothing remains, 140.
Nothing will remain, 199.
Nothingness stares me in the face, 132,
Nourishes his soul, the wise man, 167.
Novices, precepts for the, 104.
Now is the time to seek religion, 16.
Now my lot to help, 191.

Obedience to the laws of righteousness, 132.
Obey the truth, let us, 226.
Object and senses, contact of, 54.
Observe the Upavasatha or Sabbath, 105.
Ocean, 199; rivers in the ocean, 190; my doctrine is like the great ocean, 156.
Offering, four kinds of, 165.
Omens abolished, 151.
Omens of Buddhahood, 9.
One hemp-grain each day, 27.
One in essence, 232.
One, the truth is but, 116, 142, 231.
One thing that is needed, the, 132, 217.
Oneself, purity and impurity belong to, 111.
Order, rules for the, 105.

Order, the, (sangha) the sowing-ground of merit, 200.
Ordination, 46, 48, 49 [see also Pravrajya and Upasampadâ in the Glossary].
Others art thou thyself, 139.
Others, the faults of, 114, 115.
Our water is all gone, 171.
Outcast, the, 174; by deeds one becomes an outcast, 174; who is an outcast? 174.
Outcome of evil, pain is the, 113.
Outcome of good, happiness is the, 113.
Outwitted, 164.
Overcome anger by love, 115.
Overcome evil by good, 115.
Overcome grief, 206.
Ox led to slaughter, 188.

Pain is the outcome of evil, 113.
Parable, 144, 158, 168.
Parable of the hungry dog, 176.
Paradise in the West, the, 152; living in paradise, 184; the paradise of the pure land, 153.
Parties, listen to both, 89.
Party in search of a thief, a, 182.
Pass away, about to, 216; pass away Lord, 209; pass away now, 208; people pass away, 188; the truth will never pass away, 131.
Passed away according to his deeds, 172.
Passion, rain and, 112.
Past, thou wilt reap the harvest sown in the, 138.
Path of transmigration, weary, 211; sign of the right, 121; the eightfold, 33; the immortal path, 64; the noble eightfold path, 122, 211, 231; mortification not the path, 28; walk in the noble path, 139; a pathless jungle, 120; are all paths saving? 118. [See also Maggo in the Glossary.]
Peace on earth, 8.
Peacemaker, the, 175.
Peak, Vulture's, 194.
People dissatisfied, the, 59; people pass away, 188; wise people falter not, 112; wise people fashion them selves, 112.
Perception of truth, the refreshing drink, 98.
Perishable, the *I*, 54.
Personalities of Buddha, the three, 225.
Pestilence, 102.
Physician, 16, 160, 186; the best physician, 147; without beholding the physician, 218.
Pit, treasure laid up in a deep, 149.
Pity me not, 21.
Plantain-tree, 31.
Playthings, 159.
Pleasure, he who lives for, 113; let a man take pleasure in the dharma, 149.
Pleasures destroy the foolish, 114 pleasures of self in heaven, 133; why do we give up the pleasures of the world, 151; religious wisdom lifts above pleasures, 185.
Potter, 141; potter, vessels made by the, 188.
Power, incantations have no, 27; magic power, 100.
Powerful elephant, 144.
Powerful king, 110.
Powers, moral, 82.
Practise the truth, 139.
Praise of all the Buddhas, the, 232.
Prayers, 120; prayers vain repetitions, 27.
Preach the doctrine, glorious in the beginning, middle, and end, 49; preach to all beings, 109.
Preacher's mission, the, 107; the preacher's sole aim, 108.
Preachers, Tathâgatas are only, 111.
Precepts, 220; precepts for the novices, 104; ten precepts, 104; walk according to the precepts, 216.
Precious crown jewel, 110.
Precious jewel, a, 225.
Priceless, the lives of men are, 176.
Priest and layman alike, 74.
Prince, test of the, 10.
Problem of the soul, the, 23.
Profitless, mortification, 39.
Prohibitions, 101.

Promoted him higher, he, 160.
Propound the truth, 107.
Prosper, sangha may be expected to, 194.
Prospered, bhikshus, 100.
Punishment of the criminal, 126.
Punishment, the fruit of the criminal's act, 127.
Puppets on a string, 103.
Pure land, the paradise of the, 152, 153.
Purity and impurity belong to oneself, 111.
Purpose of being, the, 228.
Purpose, speak to the, 106.

Qualities, cloud of good, 110; eight wonderful qualities, 156, 157.
Quality, the thing and its, 24.
Quarrels, 86.
Quarters, the four, 121; the six quarters, 122.
Question concerning annihilation, 124.
Questioned, the sages, 11.
Questions of the dêva, 146.

Rabbit rescued from the serpent, 21.
Rags, cast-off, 75, 77.
Râhula, lessons given to, 143.
Rain and passion, 112.
Rain fell, 80.
Rain, good works are, 173.
Rare in the world, 201.
Real, truth makes things, 5.
Reap the harvest sown in the past, thou wilt, 138.
Reap what we sow, we, 132, 178.
Reason, as the helpmate of self, 229.
Reason in the struggle for life, 228.
Reason, no truth is attainable without, 230.
Reasoning ceases, 134.
Rebirth without transmigration of self, 26.
Rebuked, the bhikshus, 94.
Received the message in their own language, all creatures, 41.
Re-establishing concord, two ways of, 89.
Re-establishment of concord, 88.
Reform to-day, 103.
Refreshing drink, the, perception of truth, 98.
Refuge in the Blessed One, 129, 130, 140, 220.
Refuge in the Buddha, 46, 47, 52, 56, 104, 146, 182, 183, 224, 230.
Refuge in the Enlightened Teacher, 123.
Refuge is his name, 190.
Rejoice, angels, 8.
Religion, Buddha's, consolidation of, 75; now is the time to seek religion, 16; seeing the highest religion, 116; the gift of all religion, 116; the religion of all Buddhas, 56; worship and sacrifice the nature of religion, 131; thou tearest down religion, 131.
Religious man, the, and truth, 105; religious wisdom lifts above pleasures, 185; religious zeal flagging, 29.
Rely on yourselves, 206.
Remain in thy station, 62; nothing will remain, 199; the truth will remain, 217, 221.
Repetitions, prayers vain, 27.
Rescue in the desert, 169.
Restore to you a nobler beauty, to, 180.
Revere the traditions, 227.
Reverence for the Master, out of, 221
Reverence my father, I, 123.
Rice-milk, 81.
Rich in returns, charity, 20.
Righteous cause, war in a, 127.
Righteousness, foundation of the kingdom of, 37; source of all righteousness, 98; the kingdom of righteousness, 43; the throne of truth is righteousness, 230.
Right path, mortification not the, 28.
Right path, sign of the, 121.
Right thought, helmet of, 79.
Ripe fruits, 188.
Rituals have no efficacy, 27.
River, crossed the, 196.
Rivers in the ocean, 190.
Rivers reach the main, 199.

Roads cross, where four, 118.
Robe of the Tathâgata, 107.
Robes, lay, 77; robes of cloth of gold, 213; the bkikshus doffed their robes, 80.
Rock a good blow, give the, 172.
Room for the *I*, no, 54.
Root of evil, ignorance the, 31.
Roots of mind, the five, 23.
Rope, the nature of the, 55.
Rubbish, the lily on a heap of, 117.
Rules for the order, 105.

Sabbath, 84; observe the Upavasatha or Sabbath, 105.
Sacrifice, 27; sacrifice of self, 132; the nature of religion, worship and sacrifice, 131.
Sacrifices, 26; sacrifices cannot save, 139.
Sages questioned, the, 1.
Saint, a sinner can become a, 151.
Salvation alone in the truth, 206, 207; assured of final, 221; salvation the extinction of self, 4; work out your salvation, 211, 221.
Sameness and continuity, 137.
Sandy desert, a, 170.
Save, faith alone can, 190.
Saving paths? Are all paths, 118.
Saving power, incantations have no, 27.
Saviour of others, a, 141.
Saviour appeared, the, 229.
Saviour, truth the, 5, 42.
Scepticism, 106, 107.
Schism, the, 85.
Scold, do not, 89.
Search of a thief, a party in, 182.
Season, flowers out of, 216.
Season, rainy, 49, 204.
Sect of Dêvadatta, 95.
Seed, faith is the, 173.
Seeing the highest religion, 116.
Seek thou the life that is of the mind, 133.
Self, 60; self an error, 55; self an illusion, 34; self and the cause of troubles, 42; self and truth, 3, 33, 127; self begets selfishness, 5; cleaving to self, 137; complete surrender of self, 127; eradication of self, 126; self-extinction, 132; identity of self, 137; illusion of self, 123; pleasures of self in heaven, 133; self is a fever, 42; self is change, 138; self is death, 133, 138, 140; self-mortification, 75; my self has become the truth, 141; reason as the helpmate of self, 229; rebirth without the transmigration of self, 26; sacrifice of self, 132; the cause of self a mirage, 42; the conquest of self, 128; the extinction of self, salvation, 4; the idea of self, 217; self, the maker, 60; the nature of self, 54; self, the veil of Mâyâ, 6; truth and self, 133; truth guards him who guards his self, 111; thou clingest to self, 102; where is the identity of my self, 134; which is the true self? 138.
Selfhood, the cause of, found, 33.
Selfhood, thirst for existence and, 30.
Selfish is my grief, 187.
Selfishness, self begets, 5.
Selfishness, surrender, 55.
Sense, moral, 82.
Senses and object, contact of, 54.
Sentence of expulsion, 85, 86.
Sentiency, truth vibrated through, 228.
Separation, combination subject to, 25.
Sermon on abuse, the, 145; the sermon on charity, 63; sermon on fire, 52.
Serpent, rabbit rescued from the, 21.
Seven kinds of wisdom, 82.
Sevenfold higher wisdom, 198.
Shaveling, 174.
Shedding of blood, 26.
Shine forth, let your light, 95.
Shines by night, the moon, 117.
Sick bhikshu, the, 190, 191.
Sickness fell upon him, 204, 211, 212.
Sight, blind received, 7.
Sign of the right path, 121.
Signs forbidden, astrology and forecasting by, 210; signs of Buddhahood, 8; the four signs, 12.
Sin appears sweet, 113.
Sin no more, 161.

Sin, struggle against, 211.
Sin, the truth cleanses from, 223.
Sinner can become a saint, a, 151.
Six quarters, the, 122.
Slaughter, 27.
Slaughter, ox led to, 188.
Smith, Chunda, the, 211, 214, 215.
Snake, a wet rope no, 41.
So great an honor, 202.
Soldier, a, Simha, 126.
Soldier of truth, a, 129.
Soldiers of the Tathâgata, 110.
Solitary, 116.
Son, the lost, 160.
Son, father and, 184.
Song of ecstasy, 197, 198.
Songs, heavenly, 216.
Sorcerers, 152.
Sorrow compared with a sword, 14.
Soul, Gautama denies the existence of the, 130; non-existence of the soul, 132; the *I* the soul, 23; the problem of the soul, 23; the sum of the soul, 166.
Souls not separate and self-existent entities, 132.
Soup, a spoon tastes not the flavor of the, 169.
Source of all righteousness, 98.
Sovereign, make you, 207.
Sovereignty, holiness better than, 21.
Sow that you will reap, what you, 178.
Sow, we reap what we, 132.
Sower, Buddha the, 173.
Sowest, others will reap what thou, 139.
Sowing-ground of merit, the order (sangha) the, 200.
Speak, the deaf and dumb, 8.
Speak to the purpose, 106.
Speaking untruths, 144.
Speculations, 116.
Spells forbidden, 101.
Spirit, in the, 89.
Spiritual, all existence is, 130.
Spiritual eye, 227.
Spits at heaven, like one who, 146.
Spoon, a, tastes not the flavor of the soup, 169.
Spread the truth, 43.
Staircase, a, 118.
Stamp of a king's seal, 184.
Stares me in the face, nothingness, 132.
Station, remain in thy, 62.
Steal not, 106.
Stream, following the Master over 189.
Stream, he had crossed the, 189.
String, puppets on a, 103.
Strong man, who is the? 105.
Struck by apoplexy, 169.
Struggle against sin, 211.
Struggle for life, reason in the, 228.
Struggle must be, 127.
Subject to separation, combination, 25.
Substance, the, of Brahman lore, 119.
Such a one will wander rightly in the world, 148, 149.
Such faith have I, 197.
Suffer, the Blessed One had to, 205.
Suffering. bliss where there is, 16.
Sun is bright, the, 117.
Sun of the soul, the, 166.
Superstition, 122.
Supplications forbidden, 101.
Supplications have no effect, 151.
Suprabuddha, 95.
Surrender, 127.
Surrender selfishness, 55.
Surrender to evil powers, no, 127.
Swear not, 106.
Sweet, sin appears, 113.
Swooned, the Blessed One, 28.
Sword, sorrow compared with, 14.

Tailor, the greedy, 162.
Talents. [See Abhijñâ in the Glossary.]
Talk, foolish, 119.
Tastes not the flavor of the soup, a spoon, 169.
Teach the same truth, 232.
Teacher, Buddha the, 111; teacher of gods and men, 200; the teacher unknown, 156; we have no teacher more, 220.
Temporary, many laws are, 226.
Ten commandments, the, 105.
Ten great calamities, 191.
Ten precepts, 104.

Terms of the world, such are the, 188.
Test of the prince, 10.
That it be well grounded, 198.
There is mind, 130.
They know me not, 157.
Thief, a party in search of a, 182.
Thinkers are bright, 117.
Thing and its quality, the, 24.
Things as they are, 55.
Thirst for existence and selfhood, 30.
Thirst, the extinction of, 116.
Thirsty, I am, 212; water for the thirsty, 1.
This is done by me, 112.
Thorn in the flesh, 116.
Thou art the Buddha, 129; thou canst not escape the fruit of evil actions, 139; thou clingest to self, 102; thou tearest down religion, 131; thou wilt reap what thou sowest, 139.
Thought, helmet of right, 79; the thought of *I*, 24; we the result of thought, 111.
Thoughtlessness the path of death, 112.
Thoughts continue, 134; made up of thoughts, 111, thoughts of love, 121; thoughts will endure, 112.
Three dangers hang over Pâtaliputra, 196.
Three personalities of Buddha, the, 225.
Three vows, 44.
Three woes, the, 11.
Thyself, others art thou, 139.
Tidings, glad, 1; good tidings, 16.
Tie all souls together, bonds that, 232.
Time of grace, the, 161, 170.
Time to seek religion, now is the, 16.
Times, hard, teach a lesson, 103,
To-day, reform, 103.
Together, bonds that tie all souls, 232.
Toys, 159.
Traditions, revere the, 227.
Transiency, immortality in, 3.
Transmigration, eddies of, 144; rebirth without the transmigration of self, 26; weary path of transmigration, 211.
Transmission of the soul and the *I*, 25.
Treacherous, charms are, 180.
Treasure laid up in a deep pit, 149.
Treasure that can never be lost, a, 150.
Trespasses, confession of, 84.
Troubles, the cause of, and self, 42.
Truly thou art Buddha, 123.
Trumpeter, 121.
Trust in truth, 2.
Truth, a soldier of, 129; abodes of truth, 63; be anxious to learn the truth, 106; be married unto the truth, 181; Buddha the truth, 2, 217, 227; clay can be changed into children of truth, 131; delusion and truth, 31; eye of truth, 43; glorious is the truth, 46, 47, 56; hold fast to the truth, 206; I am the truth, 141; immortality of truth, 133, 140, 182; incarnation of the truth, 225; kingdom of truth, 38, 217; let us obey the truth, 226; life yearns for the truth, 231; love of truth, 128; my self has become the truth, 141; no truth is attainable without reason, 230; perception of truth, the refreshing drink, 98; practise the truth, 139; propound the truth, 107; salvation alone in the truth, 206, 207; spread the truth, 43; teach the same truth, 232; the embrace of truth, 181; the king of truth, 110, 141; the mirror of truth, 199, 200; the throne of truth is righteousness, 230; the religious man and truth, 105; the truth cleanses from sin, 223; the truth found, 43; the truth has been made known to me, 220; the truth will never pass away, 131; the truth will remain, 217, 221; the world is built for truth, 230; there is but one truth, 116, 142; trust in truth, 2; truth and immortality, 6; truth and self, 3, 4, 33, 127, 133; truth cannot be fashioned, 231; truth cannot die, 217; truth dawns upon me, 139; truth guards him who guards his self, 111; truth has taken its abode in me, 140; truth in all its glory, 29; truth is best, 42; truth is hidden to the blind, 226; truth is

life, 133; truth is one, 231; truth is the essence of life, 231; truth makes things real, 5; truth the correct comprehension of all things, 34; truth the image of the eternal, 3; truth the saviour, 5, 42; truth vibrated through sentiency, 228.
Truthful, be, 106.
Truths, the four noble, 32, 160.
Twelve nidânas, the, 31.
Two ways of re-establishing concord, 89.
Tyrant, 177.

Unclean, the vessel has become, 144.
Undiminished, meats remained, 181.
Unguents, 75.
Union of what we know not, 119.
Union with Brahma, 120.
Universally, logic holds, 136.
Universe, face to face, 121.
Unknown teacher, the, 156.
Unshod, the Blessed One walked, 94.
Untruths, speaking, 144.
Upright conduct, 194.

Vain, mortification, 40.
Vain repetitions, prayers, 27.
Vanities, 42.
Vanity, 24, 102, 112, 114, 151; vanity of worldliness, 101; vanity of worldly happiness, 2.
Various kinds of assemblies, 156.
Veil of Mâyâ, the, 178.
Vessel has become unclean, the, 44.
Vessels, 141; vessels made by the potter, 188.
Vibrated through sentiency, truth, 228.
Victor, the greater, 128.
Vision a shramana, the, 15.
Vows, three, 44.
Vulture's Peak, 194.

Walk according to the precepts, 216; let a man walk alone, 88; the lame walk, 8; walk in the right path, 139.
Wander rightly in the world, such a one will, 148, 149.
War, goes out to wage, 110; is it wrong to go to war? 126; war in a righteous cause, 127.
Warriors are bright, 117.
Warriors, destiny of, 128.
Water, doctrine like unto, 157; fetch me some water, 212; is the water now fit for drinking? 143; our water is all goue, 171! the lotus-flower in water, 40, 62, 99; water gurgling beneath, 172; water for the thirsty, 1; the water of immortality, 128.
Waterless desert, a, 120.
Ways, the best of, is eightfold, 116.
We have no teacher more, 220; we the result of thought, 111.
Wearisome to the Blessed One, 199.
Weary path of transmigration, 211.
Welfare, eight conditions of, 192, 193, 194.
Well, the woman at the, 174.
West, facing towards the, 195; the paradise in the West, 152.
Wet rope, a, no snake, 41.
What we know not, a union of, 119; what is life in this world? 208; what you sow that you will reap, 178.
Wheel, the, 41; the wheel of empire, 207; the wheel of individuality, 53.
Where does the wind dwell? 133; where four roads cross, 118; where is Nirvâna? 133; where is the identity of my self? 134.
Which is the true self? 138.
Who is an outcast? 174; who is the strong man? 105.
Why do we give up the pleasures of the world? 151.
Why preserve this body of flesh? 217.
Wild crane, the, 103.
Wind, as a great, 134.
Wind dwell? where does the, 133.
Wisdom has no dwelling-place, 133; is wisdom a locality? 133; religious wisdom lifts above pleasure, 185; seven kinds of wisdom, 82; sevenfold higher wisdom, 198.
Wise man nourishes his soul, the, 167; wise people falter not, 112; wise people fashion themselves, 112.
Wishes, five, of Bimbisâra, 56.
Without beholding the physician, 218.
Woes, the three, 11.
Woman, a worldly, 203; if you see a

woman, 78; the woman at the well, 174.
Women as a rule are, etc., 201; the first women lay-disciples, 48.
Word, last, 222; word of the Buddhas, 18.
Words of Buddhas immutable, the, 15.
Work out your salvation, 211, 221.
World dark, do not call the, 166; world filled with love, 121; let us go into the world, 223; rare in the world, 201; such a one will wander rightly in the world, 148, 149; such are the terms of the world, 188; the world is built for truth, 230; come into the world to befriend, 190; what is life in this world? 208; why do we give up the pleasures of the world? 151.
Worldliness, dust of, 36; jewels and worldliness, 46; vanity of worldliness, 101.
Worldling nourishes his body, the, 167.
Worldly happiness, vanity of, 2; a worldly woman, 203.
Worn-out cart, as a, 206.
Worship, 27.
Worship and sacrifice, the nature of religion, 131.
Worthiest homage, 216.
Worthy of yellow robes, not, 88.

Yashas, 45, 46, 47, 48, 121.
Yellow robes, not worthy of, 88.
Yoke, gone into the, 116.
Your eyes are blind, 166.
Yourselves, be ye lamps unto, 206; rely on yourselves, 206: yourselves have known, 221.

Zeal flagging, religious, 29.

[Names and terms must be looked up in the Glossary, where references to pages of the present book are separated by a dash from the explanation.]